Irena

John Saltburn

ISBN: 9798619384000

This book is dedicated to memory of Irena (1910 - 1983)

CONTENTS

1 PROLOGUE

Sound of running water was soothing like a single longing low frequency note gently played by an invisible musician. She reached with her left hand and checked the temperature under the spout. It was warm and pleasant so she began undressing. Without haste she removed her gray cardigan, folded it and placed neatly on a small table in the corner. She then removed her stockings and underwear and dropped them into a wicker laundry basket next to the table. Finally she undid her bra, folded it and placed next to the cardigan. She then stood motionless for a moment looking at her image in the mirror.
Despite advanced age her body had a look of a woman perhaps even half of her age, in mid thirties or so. With not much fat in typical places and hips pleasantly curved below the waistline her figure resembled an hour glass. Many much younger women would do anything to have such proportions and shape. No tissue breakdown anywhere.

She melancholically smiled.

As she was gazing at her own image in the mirror it began changing as if a clever photographer had placed a diffusing filter on his lens. All edges of her reflection softened and were now less defined. She looked even prettier than a moment ago. Slowly, the reflection began to morph. The hair darkened and the few silver streaks disappeared. Her skin tone was pink now and fresher, while the wrinkles on her face one by one faded away and dissolved until they were all gone. The girl in the mirror was perhaps no more than twenty two years old.

She reached for a silk white nightgown hanging on a brass hanger on the door behind her and put it on. From the book she brought in with her she took a dried leaf of a chestnut tree. Turning it around while looking at its intricate structure, she then glanced into the mirror one more time, stepped into the bathtub and without removing her nightgown sat in it.

The warm water embraced her body and for some reason made her think of May when flowers and trees are racing to bloom and birds are singing everywhere with energy and passion.

Looking at the leaf, she thought about her beloved city which she had lost forever years ago leveled by the war and about the single chestnut tree from which the leaf came that miraculously survived and was still standing at the Krucza Street number nine. She traveled there every Thursday to touch it and to cry for the past thirty years. That tree was the only living thing in the entire world that understood her and heard all of her secrets, sorrows and thoughts.

2 THE ROMANCE

May in Warsaw is always beautiful, even when it rains. Flowers are blooming everywhere and the green hue of grass and leaves is just about to reach its peak. The early morning air is as fresh as it can be – especially clean in parks and less so on busy streets. As the day begins, delivery vans and horse carts make their rounds around the city bringing breads and pastries baked overnight in countless bakeries big and small, cafes open up for business one by one emanating fragrance of the freshly ground coffee. Newspaper boys carrying stacks of newest editions position themselves at the corners of streets and begin shouting either names of their respective newspapers they sell or the most dramatic headlines of the day. People hurry to work to their offices, shops and stores. Some ride in horse drawn carriages, some in cars or taxis and some in trams which make their way through the traffic with a distinctive sound and familiar bells. Varsovians like their trams and are proud of the fact they are always on time. Some say you could set your clock by them.

In the first carriage of one such tram serving line number three a young woman was standing holding on to a handle by the door getting ready to disembark at the nearest stop. Unlike most of women more or less her age she had a straight, slim figure suggesting she was possibly pursuing some physical activity, some kind of sport perhaps. She had green eyes and was neither tall nor short. Her brown shoulder length wavy hair was parted off center of her head on the right side. Below the partition her hair was combed straight down while the other side was combed and arranged so that it covered nearly half of her forehead and if it was any lower it would cover her left eye completely. Something of a vamp – at least a little bit. She was wearing a simple beige dress and dark blue jacket. Fashionable shoes and a matching small purse held under her arm completed her elegant outfit.

The tram rang its bell to warn passengers waiting for it to keep their distance, slowed down and came to a halt. As the young woman was reaching the pavement, a young man who had left the tram via the door at the other end bumped into her, knocking her purse out of her hand.

"Oh, I am terribly sorry, miss!" he said bending down to pick up the purse and handing it to her.

"You could be more careful you know!" she snapped, upset at the accident.

"I haven't done it on purpose, I'm really sorry and hope you're all right. I am already late to work as is."

"All right then, I'm fine. Thank you."

But the young man was staring at her face and did not move an inch.

"Haven't you said you were in a hurry?" she asked somewhat surprised and annoyed he had not walked away.

By now the tram and all passengers were gone and they were the only two people left on the tram stop.

"My name is Stan. Stan Szumski. I'm truly sorry I nearly knocked you down."

"We've done this, haven't we?" she asked with some amusement in her voice.

"You are the most beautiful girl I've ever seen!"

Hearing the compliment she recomposed herself and looked at him. He was smartly dressed in a white shirt and a dark red tie, dark brown jacket and matching trousers. His hair was combed up and back as many young men were wearing these days. His face was thin and his eyes were blue. They seemed to be unusually intense and for a moment she felt as if she was standing there naked with him looking at her. Just such extraordinary idea made her heart beat a bit faster.

"Thank you," she said trying to hide her smile and getting ready to leave, "I have to go."

"I know it's presumptuous but can I see you again, please? What is your name?"

"Irena."

Her response was automatic and she immediately regretted giving it away as he was not really her type and besides, she was seeing somebody anyway and did not fancy a change. But those eyes of his made her loose some of her usual self control. She recovered though.

"Sorry, no. You can't. I need to go and so do you, I gather. You must be really late by now, aren't you?"

She started walking in her intended direction.

He remained where he was for a moment just watching her walking away, then turned to go his way but suddenly changed his mind, spun around and caught up with her.

"I'm sorry - I can't take no for an answer and just let you go. I know how you must feel and think, but - please believe me I am not…"

"You are not what?"

"I'm not… I'm not …" he was searching for something sensible to say.

"I'm not a pick-up artist! I work at the accounting agency around the corner over there," he pointed towards some buildings in a distance.

"Look," she said, "I'm glad to hear you are not a pick-up artist although your persistence seems to suggest otherwise and I'm not interested where you work!"

"Where do you work, then?"

"What makes you think I work?"

"At this time of the day everybody rushes to work so I've just assumed you must be like everybody else, on your way to some office."

They made several steps in silence.

She abruptly stopped.

"The way I see it you will get fired for being late and I have to go. I'd like to go alone and I don't want company, okay?"

She resumed walking.

"Please, Irena. I'll do anything, I will meet you anytime, anywhere, just please let me see you."

"No."

By this time they were in front of a car dealership selling Polski Fiat cars and she reached for the door leading to the showroom.

"You work here?" he asked with a smile, "at Fiat's?"

"Good bye!" she opened the door and walked inside with a slight smile on her face.
Stan was standing on the street looking as she disappeared from view inside the dealership. He then glanced at his watch.

"Oh, shit!" he exclaimed and took off like a sprinter towards the bookkeeping agency located about a kilometer away.

*

"Szumski!" mister Zalewski, owner of the bookkeeping agency "Two plus One" shouted across the hallway through the open door of his office.

Stan walked towards him.

"Good Morning, sir," he said.

"No, Szumski, it is more of a good afternoon," he replied.

"Sir?" Stan knew he was late and it was no good.

"This is the second time within eight weeks and I'm getting fed up," said Mr.Zalewski.

"You have a good mind but your discipline leaves a *lot* to be desired. What was it this time, may I ask?"

"Er…" hesitated Stan.

He rather liked his boss and did not want to lie but the real reason was not good enough for the serious and upset at the moment owner of a serious agency.

"Well…?"

Stan decided to stick to the truth because he detested liars and certainly did not want to be one of them.

"I've met the most beautiful girl I've ever seen, sir. I'm really very sorry and I know it is a ridiculous excuse but I couldn't let her go. I tried to talk to her."

What the hell — Mr. Zalewski thought — *it's May. Young people fall in love*

— it would be sad if they didn't. But his face remained stern.

"I will not tolerate this, Szumski. If it happens again you are out — do you understand?!"

"Yes, sir" sheepishly acknowledged Stan.

"Go back to you desk now and you work extra half an hour today, got it?"

"Yes, sir. I'll be happy to stay full hour if it helps."

"Don't press you luck. Now go."

"Right, thank you sir," Stan turned around.

"One more thing..."

"Sir?" he turned around again to face his boss.

"Good luck with the girl. Hope she is worth it."

Stan was his best accountant with a flawless record, was easy to work with and had a knack at working with figures. But his sense of discipline was below acceptable standards.

"Yes! - thank you sir," Stan smiled back and rushed to his desk.

When the large office clock finished its chime at seven in the evening, Stan placed his pencil in a recess in the base of his desk lamp and closed the large ledger book he was working on. He then walked to the shelf by the door and signed off for the day, entering the time right after his name. It was an honorary system which meant that nobody was monitoring the entries. It was just assumed that everybody entered true and accurate time when coming or going. Since he was the last one to leave as all personnel left at six, he made sure the spring latch was engaged and shut the door. He then said good-bye to the porter at the main gate and walked towards the tram stop. When he was closer he saw the approaching tram and realized unless he runs he would not catch it. There were some people at the stop and they were getting in while he was still few steps away. In the end he managed to hop on the step of the last door of the second carriage as it was already moving. It was a quite common sport among young men in Warsaw to hop on the tram as it was moving away or hop off before it came to a full stop. This practice was hated by the drivers, conductors, passengers and police but the culprits were not easy to catch and the practice itself was not a crime. Rather, it was a frequently dangerous nuisance with unpleasant and sometimes even deadly accidents.

Stan, having lots of practice, executed his jump perfectly and was on his way home. But when he casually glanced towards the first carriage he could not help but notice Irena in there. She was in a company of a young well dressed fellow. They were sitting together, chatting. Stan instantly forgot about everything else and began watching them intensely. Soon it was time for him to get off as the tram was approaching his stop. Irena and her companion were still talking and he decided to stay aboard and see where they were going. Following them like this was a bit absurd and under normal circumstances Stan would condemn such behavior as childish. But he had been thinking of Irena all day and had hard time concentrating on his work so his reasoning was somewhat impaired. He wanted to know more about her and fate had so obviously presented him with an opportunity to do so. Of course, they could be going out to a restaurant, theater, to see a film or to a party so this could end at nothing. But Stan just wanted to follow her and see where she was heading.

At some point while the tram was still in motion, the pair suddenly got up, getting ready to disembark. Stan moved towards the door as well. Irena and her companion left the carriage engaged in their conversation and Stan followed them casually at a distance of several steps, hiding behind pedestrians. After ten minutes or so they turned into a side street. Stan approached the corner and carefully looked, only to see them entering the nearest gate. He waited few minutes and, once he was convinced that they were not coming out, he approached the gate himself. There was a rectangular sign on the wall: School of Dance, Lidia Jastrzębska. As he was standing there contemplating the sign, somewhere above him somebody opened the street side window on the second or third floor and Stan could hear someone playing piano. But it was not some intricate melody or exercises. The melody being played was rather slow with a sort of repetitive rhythm. He could hear a woman's voice explaining something and then counting along with the piano: "...and one, and two, and three, and four, and one and two and three and four! Smile, Anna, always smile!"

Stan moved a few steps back but could not see anything. He looked around and noticed a large tree across the street. It was rather full with lots of branches. Stan crossed the quiet street and looked around. There were no pedestrians at all at the moment so he reached for the lowest branch and with ease lifted himself up until his feet caught it. He then reached for a higher one and was now standing on the lowest branch but it was too low to see anything in the window. He climbed higher until he could see what was going on inside.

The dance studio was size of a large living room which was probably its original function before somebody or Madame Jastrzębska converted it for other purpose. In the corner there was an upright piano with a bespectacled young man sitting and playing it. The were large mirrors on the walls. In the middle of the room there were six young women in kind of loose outfits Stan had never seen. They were busy practicing what Stan guessed were ballet routines under the watchful eye of Madame Jastrzębska herself, or so Stan assumed. The door suddenly opened and another woman entered the room. It was Irena. She was wearing an outfit similar to those being worn by other girls. She quickly lined up with them and followed the orders of the teacher. Stan was watching the group intensely but he was focused on Irena. She seemed to have more grace in every movement she made. While not an expert, Stan figured she was the best in the group, which she really was, but he was not in a position to fully appreciate it.

Shape of a man appeared at the gate of the building where the dance school was. He leaned against the wall, pulled out a cigarette and lit it. Stan swore in his thoughts as he recognized the man as the one who walked Irena there and who was obviously waiting for her. As long as he was smoking Stan could not climb down as there was no doubt he would be seen. So he continued watching the ballet class, hoping it would be over in some reasonable time. He was hungry as the last meal he had that day was breakfast. He planned to stop at the small and not exactly elegant restaurant close to his flat to have a pork chop with potatoes with a simple cucumber salad and perhaps a small glass of vodka. But that plan was on hold now and Stan was so hungry he would eat anything at all if he could get to it immediately. But the bespectacled piano player continued his monotonous melody, Madame Jastrzębska kept going "...and one, and two, and three and four" and the girls kept repeating their routines.

Now that he knew what she was doing his interest receded, and Stan concluded that while he was very much interested in Irena, the ballet and dancing in general was not his thing. He did like music but of a different kind – he was a fan of Jan Kiepura, an actor turned singer or vice versa, Stan was not sure. Music was one thing but Stan did not like dancing at all. He tried it few times and was forced to dance at his school long time ago. He knew it was not his thing. "Leading" the partner was beyond his grasp and while he thought he did have some sense of rhythm, his legs were not exactly in agreement with their owner. Also - holding a partner was rather problematic because if the partner was not very attractive it was somewhat easier but if a partner was attractive Stan sometimes felt a strange itching and some excitement which he could not control. He did not like not being able to control his senses. His friends, when carefully asked about such things seemed to have completely different attitudes. Not only did they loved those odd sensations related to holding a partner, they in fact were looking forward to them and dancing seemed to be a vehicle to those experiences for them. While generally speaking Stan understood all of this, he was aware he was somewhat different and not completely sure which was better or correct. For the time being he figured not being a dancer was a handicap of sorts but it was not end of the world either.

The fellow in the gate finished his cigarette and went back to wherever he was before, while the activity in the studio continued.

How long can a dancing class take? - Stan wondered.

He was bored and not very comfortable standing on the tree. Taking advantage of the street being empty, he climbed down and jumped to the ground. What a relief for his feet!

He considered his options - he could go home as it was getting late, or he could stay and wait for them to come out. But what then? They could still go somewhere for supper, the guy could bring her home or – which only now occurred to Stan – they could just go home together for a simple reason. They could be married. He was trying to recall whether or not she was wearing a wedding band but he could not remember, in fact he thought she was wearing thin elegant gloves.

A slight breeze of cool air worked like a splash of cold water on his face. While still infatuated, he decided it was ridiculous and following them further did not make much sense. He had managed to gather enough new information as it was – he knew where she worked, he knew where she practiced her hobby, he knew she arrived on line number three tramway and he knew at which tram stop she disembarked. That was quite a lot for one day and with that he started back to the tram stop. He had to wait about fifteen minutes, then finally hopped into second carriage for a couple of stops, disembarked and walked the rest of the way. The restaurant he was thinking of earlier was of course open as it was not very late, it had more customers now. Some of them already managed to get drunk. He found a table, ordered his meal and the drink. He took a shot of vodka and relived the day in his mind.

Irena made such an unusual and strong impression on him and he could not stop thinking about her. For all he cared she was the most beautiful girl in the world and he desperately wanted to get to know her. Being an accountant and a book keeper Stan was organized and logical and he quickly decided he needed some basic plan. He would hunt for an opportunity to meet her either on the tram or the dancing school where – he figured – she may be sometimes going to by herself.

He finished the last bite of his pork chop, took the last sip of vodka and called for waiter to pay the bill.

The doorbell to Zofia Sokołowska flat gave a short ring. Zofia was in the kitchen reviewing her supplies and thinking of what to make for dinner. She wiped her hands with a towel and went to the hall. When she opened the door there was a delivery boy with a bouquet of flowers.

"Good afternoon, Madam. I have delivery for Miss Irena Sokołowska."

"I'm her mother" Zofia said, "Irena is not here. I will accept it on her behalf."

"Thank you, Madam. Good afternoon!"

He handed the bouquet to her and left.

Zofia took the bouquet and noticed there was a card in a small envelope attached to it. She resisted the temptation to peek inside and took the flowers to the kitchen, found a proper vase, filled it with water and then took it to Irena's room, setting it on the table there. She had to wait for Irena to return from her office to find out who the flowers were from. The last time Irena received such a delivery was some time ago and Zofia figured it must have been somewhat special.

The world was changing and sometimes she worried that good old manners were fading away fast. She was not at ease with the lifestyles of young women of the present day. They were working, they were going out on their own to cafes meeting friends and sometimes they were making casual acquaintances with men. And not even by proper introductions, but by striking casual conversations in public places. Zofia understood the natural progression of things in life but struggled with the diminishing forms of behavior younger generations were displaying. And the new fashions were only fueling it all. Girls were so proud wearing rather tight dresses or blouses and skirts showing their figures for the whole world to see! Some people called it vulgar. Zofia would not use that particular word perhaps, but she just did not like that fashion. Along with it came changes in how the young people were carrying themselves when they were out in public. One could see on the streets or in parks how loudly they were talking and laughing – both men and women. Zofia's standards were so different. In her younger days, young people met only at formal occasions and were properly introduced. There was no casual going out without parents not knowing where their youngsters were going. Only people of dubious origin were possibly doing things like that. But now her own daughter was dressing in those tight outfits, wearing a provocative hairdo and working at some office and, as she claimed, this was how things were now. "The world had moved forward, mum" she'd say, "we, the new generation are changing it for the better!"

Zofia tried very hard to find ways to understand and accept this modernity but deep down she was hoping for her daughters to find a proper "old fashioned" candidates for their hands.
The bouquet of flowers she had just accepted was more along the values she was hoping for.

Irena was late from work and she walked through the door at nearly six o'clock.

"My gosh Isia, where were you? I thought something ad happened to you."

"I met Janka for a coffee and pastries after work. I keep asking you not to worry about things like that. If something really happened you'd know."

"Don't say things like that!"

"Mum I keep asking you not to assume the worst. I can't live under pressure like this. I mean knowing you worry about me like this. If you assume I should be back at five and I'm not, this is not my doing. It's you."

"But it makes me nervous."

"Then think about something else. Sometimes it is not possible to tell you ahead of time and you know it. When I do something spontaneously, it's not planned."

Zofia seeing she was going to nowhere with this changed the subject.

"There was a delivery for you" she said.

"A delivery?" Irena raised her eyebrows, "I am not expecting anything. What is it?"

"In your room."

Irena went to investigate immediately and returned smiling with the envelope in her hand.

"From a secret admirer!"

"A... secret admirer?"

"It's somebody I actually met but I don't know how he knew where I live."

"What's his name?"

"Stan. Stan Szumski."

"Who is he?"

"He's an accountant in some firm not far away from where I work."

"How did you meet him?"

"At a tram stop," said Iren with a smirk knowing well what reaction this will produce.

"Good God!" exclaimed Zofia. This was almost exactly what she was afraid of.

"It's not a big deal, mum" explained Irena, "People do meet like this,

I told you many times."

"But you don't know who they are."

"Yes but it's not like I am letting him into my life or going into his. He seems all right, by the way."

"There are bad people out there, you know."
Zofia was always protective.

"They can lead you astray and take an advantage of you."

"I'm not stupid, mum, and I'm not a little naive kid."

"Had he asked you to go out with him?"

"I've only met him recently but yes he did."

"And?"

"I refused."

"Good. But it was nice of him to send you flowers. It seems sincere."

Irena laughed.

"You could be so naïve, mum. If one's intentions are sinister, a bouquet of flowers is a small price to cover it up."

"I don't like such jokes, Isia. It's not funny."

Irena kept teasing her mother for few more minutes until she was bored with it. After dinner she went into her room, sat down and looked at the beautiful bouquet. She opened the card once again and read it.

"You are the most beautiful girl in the whole world and my heart and soul are yours. There is no future without You. Stan."

*

Irena, her friend Janina and Irena's sister Barbara were sitting in the open air amphitheater in the Park Łazienkowski.

"I don't know if I ever get married" said Irena, "as I look at our family, it just seems so predictable and somewhat locked-in."

"I know what you mean," interjected Barbara, "I want more from life than being a housewife and run the household. It's so boring."

"But it's against nature," Janina disagreed.

"Aren't we free to decide how we live?" asked Irena, "we as people and as a nation are finally free. To me it implies self determination. Historically speaking there were always women who wanted to have their own lives and careers rather than getting married, having children and being stuck at home."

"You can always get married, even later in life if you change your mind."

"That would be hard – to find a husband being in your thirties or so."

"Unless you know some good tricks," smiled Barbara.

"What tricks?" Irena made a face not understanding what she meant.

"Bedroom tricks," explained Barbara.

"Don't be disgusting, Barbara."

Sometimes she was saying things that made Irena uneasy.

"It's life."

"For loose women no doubt."

Barbara smirked.

"We're all humans and we have our likes and dislikes, attractions and revulsions. Each one of us is different. You never know unless you try it," she added.

"You mean you tried?"

"I'm not going into details. You look at one person and you like him or her while you don't like another. You can say you don't like men or you are not interested in them but some day you will meet somebody and you'll know it's different. You'll feel it and then you change your views."

"I'm glad I don't have such problems," said Janina, "I have my Johnny and he'd just asked me to marry him."

Irena jumped as if jolted by lightning and grabbed Janina in a strong hug.

"Jani, I'm so happy to hear it! When is the big day?"

"We haven't decided on any specific date as yet but it will be some time next spring."

"Fantastic!"

"Congratulations, Janina!" Barbara hugged Janina too, albeit with less enthusiasm, but then again Janina was Irena's friend, not hers. They were more like acquaintances by default and did not know each other that well.

"We have to celebrate it!" decided Irena. "Let's go for a glass of champagne in the Palace café!"

*

"There's a phone call for you, Miss Sokołowska," the receptionist announced, "it is Mister Szumski. Should I put it through?"

Irena was surprised but then again he knew where she worked from the day they met.

"Yes, please do," she said.

There was a click in the receiver and there was Stan's voice:

"Hallo? Irena? This is Stan."

"Yes, I know. Hello Stan."

"I... I just wanted to know how you were."

"I'm fine, thank you. Thank you for the lovely flowers."

"I'm glad you like them."

"What do you want, Stan?" asked Irena dryly.

She felt neither bubbly nor chatty.

"I'd like to know you better. May I ask you to have a coffee with me?"

"No."

"Why not?"

"I don't really know you."

"I don't know you too but I'd like to. It's a way to get to know each other."

Irena hesitated. She was not really attached anymore, she had a couple of male friends but none of them was serious. She thought there was something intriguing about Stan's persistence.

"Irena?"

"I'm here."

"So how about it? Let's meet in the middle of the day – say this Sunday at Krakowskie Przedmiescie Street in "Daisy.""

"I don't know..." she was hesitating.

"Please?"

"All right," she had made up her mind, "What time?"

"What would be good for you?" his voice sounded excited and cheerful.

"Noon."

"Wonderful, I will see you then. I'm sorry but I have to go now. Thank you so much and good-bye!"

"Bye!"

Irena replaced the receiver. Going to have a coffee with him in the middle of the day was very safe. In her mind it was not even a date.

Stan was ecstatic. She agreed to meet with him! It was one little victory and he was pleased. After work he decided to go to "Daisy" to check it out. He did not want to have any unpleasant surprises. He had been there before a couple of times, but the last time was a rather long time ago so he figured it was prudent to check the place out just to make sure. To his joy, the cafe was just like he remembered it, somewhat better in fact, as it seemed that the interior was refurbished. Walls had different colors now and the entire decor was modernized. Leaving nothing to chance he reserved a table by the window for Sunday. It was going to be a perfect date. He knew his colleagues and friends would probably laugh at him for this but he did not care. As far as he was concerned a girl like Irena was a once in a lifetime opportunity and she deserved the best. Along the same lines, upon returning home he reviewed his wardrobe. He decided he'd wear the gray three-piece suit with a white shirt and a dark navy color tie with same color handkerchief in the buttonhole. Depending on the weather he would take a gray hat or go without it – this he'd decide just before leaving. He then checked his shirts and selected one for Sunday. Even though it was freshly cleaned he decided to give it to the cleaners to be pressed. He checked the time and seeing it was not too late he ventured out to the cleaners around the corner.

"Good evening, Mister Szumski!" the lady who owned the place greeted him. She knew her regular customers by their names.

"Good evening," he replied, "I need this shirt to be like new please."

She took the shirt and gave it a quick glance. It looked clean and fresh.

"Forgive me for saying so," she said, "but this shirt looks unused after the last cleaning. We've only returned it to you the other day. Have we done something wrong?"

"No, of course not but, you see - it was just hanging in the closet and it got... wrinkled."

He knew it was somewhat silly reasoning, but she smiled.

"A special occasion coming up?"

"Yes," he nodded.

"Don't you worry Mister Szumski, it will be better than new! Would same time tomorrow be all right for you?"

"Brilliant!" he exclaimed, "thank you so much!"

He also decided he needed a haircut and a manicure which he was going to have done the following day. With that his preparations would be complete. While being so excited at the prospect of a date with Irena he was not a fool. He knew a date was just a date and at worst it all could end at that. But on the other hand, one date could lead to another and this would pave the way to a proper relationship. And then, maybe one day...

*

Stan was so impeccably dressed that he was attracting attention of nearly every woman, young and old. Indeed, he looked as if he was going for his own wedding or at least to be somebody's best man. The weather cooperated too. It was sunny from the early morning with scattered clouds and an ideal temperature so that in his three-piece suit he was neither too hot nor too cold. He left his flat early as he decided to walk. "Daisy" was within half an hour to forty minutes stroll. As usual for Sunday mid-morning, the streets of Warsaw were full of people. Varsovians were usually fashionably dressed in general but on Sundays particular care was taken. Countless cafés were opened with street side tables nearly full. Many people enjoyed just sipping freshly brewed coffee while watching the passers by. Midmorning was a perfect time for a cup of coffee or tea with some pastry or ice cream or whatever else one may desire. Warsaw had a lot to offer – as in any big and modern city there were museums, art galleries, playgrounds for children, there were beaches on the Vistula River, paddle steamers river cruises, parks and ever-popular among the youngsters Warsaw ZOO. There were also travelling carousels big and small along with other attractions in parks mushrooming here and there. On such a perfect day people were everywhere. It seemed everybody was out. As the day progressed there would be concerts, some of the open air, theatres and cinemas as well as nightclubs with or without dancing and one could have a superb dinner in many restaurants. Foreign visitors were sometimes calling Warsaw "the Paris of the East" and Varsovians were proud of it. The city was vibrant and cheerful and offered something for everyone.

He made his way to "Daisy" ahead of time and having nothing to do but wait he sat down on a park bench nearby. A few minutes past the hour he spotted Irena walking towards him on Krakowskie Przedmiescie. She looked stunning, wearing a simply-cut dress and jacket with a brooch in left lapel. Her high-heel shoes matched her blouse perfectly and so did her purse. Her hair was arranged in that "vamp" style again where one eye was almost obstructed by falling hairline. It looked so casual while being so elaborated. Stan observed a couple of men turning around to look at her.

He got up and quickly walked to her.

"Hello Irena, it is so good to see you. Thank you for coming and may I say how beautiful you are."

She smiled lightly.

"Good afternoon, Stan. Thank you, you don't look too shabby yourself."

"Shall we go in?" he asked directing her attention to the entrance of the café.

"Reservation for Szumski," he said to the busboy and they were lead to a small table for two by the window overlooking the street.

They ordered two coffees and two "Napoleons", which were French pastry layered with custard and formed into a rectangle.

Irena mixed her coffee with a silver spoon and gently lifted the cup to her mouth. Her upper lip moved slightly forward as she carefully took the first sip while her eyes were looking straight at Stan. Stan felt a tingling down his spine thinking how seductive she seemed sipping her coffee. He almost lost his chain of thoughts so he quickly improvised.

"Do you have any siblings?"

"Yes, I have an older sister and younger brother, you?"

"Oh, I have two brothers but my dad had seven so I have plenty of cousins. We are a close family so it feels as if I had millions of siblings. I get along with some better than with others but sometimes I feel like an ant in an anthill."

Irena laughed.

"It's funny. I thought I had a big family but my Mum has just one sister and a brother who is a bishop. It's nothing comparing to you."

"There are advantages and disadvantages. Family dos are a nightmare to organize. Nobody has a flat large enough to accommodate all. Somebody wisely promoted the idea that for major dos like

Christmas family will subdivide and things like birthdays are spread over two weekends or so. But in summer we have family picnics. We all agree on a date and we venture out of town. Then we can be all together at the same time."

"That's a good idea," said Irena.

"As long as we don't meet at the same time on a tram stop. It happened once or twice and both carriages were full of Szumskis."

"Now this is funny. Do you get a discount on tickets?"

"I suppose we should," laughed Stan.

"What do you do on such picnics?" Irena was curious.

"Well, as soon as we get to our destination we open picnic baskets and begin to eat. We play some games too, there are so many of us we can have volleyball teams or there are a couple of separate card games going on simultaneously. Or we run a tournament."

"That sound like fun."

"You can come with me next time we have it. Girlfriends, boyfriends and fiancés are welcome."

"I'm neither," remarked Irena.

„But I'd like you to be."

"We've just met. What's the hurry?"

"Sorry, I didn't mean to rush you in any way."

"I like dancing," she changed the subject because she did not want to go where she was afraid the conversation could be heading, "do you?"

"Er..." Stan hesitated, "I'm a miserable dancer I'm afraid. What do you dance?"

"I practice ballet for many years now."

"I know," Stan slipped but was quick to recover, "I mean I see."

"I also like dancing in general – parties, ballrooms, whatever. When I dance I feel liberated."

"How so?"

"When I dance I have no worries at all. It feels as if I'm in a different world. I feel as if I could fly."

"Ehm," Stan was not sure what to say. Even though he loved listening to the music he did not like dancing at all as it was a struggle for him.

"What do you do at the Fiat's?"

"I'm the secretary to Mr. Sokopp."

"Who is he?"

"He owns the dealership. I've never seen a man as obsessed with cars as he is. What about you? What do you do?"

"I'm an accountant. I work for the Two plus One agency."

"Is it a good job?" inquired Irena.

"Yes. I like working with numbers. It's rewarding in sense that in the end everything has to balance. It is a bit like solving a math problem. When you get final result you can easily check if it is good or bad. I also like working alone - that is I'm an employee but I'm given certain clients and I work on their books – nobody else does it with me. Once I'm done my boss reviews it and approves the final figures."

"I wasn't any good at math at school," said Irena with a disarming smile, "hated it actually."

"That's all right," Stan returned the smile, "not everybody needs heavy math. As long as you are managing your daily chores you are fine."

Seeing her "Napoleon" pastry finished and coffee nearly gone he asked, "shall we go for a walk?"

"Where to?"

"How about we continue towards the King's Castle?"

"I'd like that. I only need a minute in the ladies room."

While she was gone Stan paid the bill and waited by the door. She came back and smiled.

"I'm ready."

Stan opened the door for her and they walked outside.

"I love Warsaw," Irena said, "do you?"

"In a manner of speaking, yes of course."

„But I mean I truly love it. I couldn't live anywhere else. I love life in the city. I'm so proud of all the new things and I follow news about what is planned for the future. It's all very exciting and I hope to live long enough to see things like the subway and the new arteries I read about. Dancing and Warsaw are in my heart and in my blood I guess."
"I don't see why you shouldn't see it all happening. The plans you are talking about are to be made reality within the next ten to fifteen years so you are talking late forties or so."

"My gosh, I will be so much older by then!" worried Irena.

"But you will be just as beautiful as today," he assured her.

"How can you possibly say things like that, how can you know?"

"Because you are timeless. Extraordinary beauty does not get diminished with time. Look at Greek sculptures."

Irena looked at him with different curiosity. She liked what he said with so much conviction. When she first met him by accident, she though he was a typical self-confident young man. But she liked how he was talking and chatting with him was so pleasant and natural. He did not seem to pretend to be someone he was not and it was difficult not to appreciate his compliments which sounded so genuine. And there was something solid about him too. *I suppose I would want a solid personality from a candidate for my hand* – she thought and immediately shrugged this away. It was so odd to think in such categories.

A street vendor was selling pretty small bouquets of mixed flowers and Stan bought one for her.

Chatting and joking, they arrived at the plaza in front of the King's Castle. In the middle of the square there was a single tall column with a statue of King Sigismund III Vasa.

"Do you think he did the right thing?" asked Irena looking up at the king.

"Moving the capital from Krakow to Warsaw? He had his reasons back then. I think Warsaw is more appropriate being in the middle of Poland. It would be so odd if somebody deiced to undo it and move it back to Krakow. You'd hate such a concept – wouldn't you?" he joked.

"Oh, it's inconceivable. You are right, I would hate it. Thank God nobody of sound mind would propose this. I do like the Sigismund's column. It's a good meeting point. I meet with friends here."

They admired the King's Castle facade with the clock tower in the center and continued to the Old Town square. This was the oldest part of Warsaw filled with narrow colorful buildings.

"It's great these old buildings stand untouched for so many centuries" Irena said, "I often come here too. I mean I love Aleje Ujazdowskie and the park but the Old Town is one of my many favorite spots."

"You really do love Warsaw," remarked Stan.

"Sometimes people say I love this or that but what they really mean is they merely like it. I can see how much enthusiasm you have for the city. It's a rare quality. I don't believe there are many people like you. You should consider getting into politics at some level and work for the benefit of the city."

"That's not funny," she clearly thought he was teasing her.

"It's not a joke, Irena. I mean it. It's just that there are not too many women in politics. But there must be a way. Your enthusiasm and energy could be channeled for the good of Warsaw."

"Perhaps when I'm older I'll consider joining some organization. For now I want to be with people and I want to dance my best years," she said.

After they walked through the Old Town, Irena decided it was time to go home. Stan wanted to escort her back to her door but she insisted on returning alone. In the end she let him bring her to a tram stop and they said good-bye there.

"Can I see you again?" Stan asked as the tram was approaching.

"Maybe," she said, "thank you, Stan. I had a good time."

The tram stopped and she boarded the first coach, looked back at him, smiled and waved. The tram moved forward. Stan looked after it for a while, then turned around and walked home.
Late afternoon was just as full of pedestrians as late morning.

Warsaw's streets were bubbling with laughter, conversations and well-dressed people. Now there were more young adults out there and fewer families with children. Stan had recently read that the city was growing steadily and by now was approaching 1.3 million Varsovians.

He was contemplating Irena's philosophy for life – her love for Warsaw and passion for dancing. It made her different than any girl he ever talked to. Usually girls were less aloof and rather easier engaged in silly conversations. More often than not they were looking for long term relationship and marriage. Irena was different.

*

For quite a while now Irena had a secret problem on her mind which bothered her from time to time. It had all began a few years ago when she noticed that her face was turning red at a slightest hint of sexuality in conversations. She quickly realized it was beyond her control and therefore she hated it. It was even more pronounced if somebody told a spicy joke. She just could not help it and ended up convinced that as long as she was remaining a virgin this would continue. At least such seemed to be the opinion among her friends. Not that they discussed it in detail. Irena either guessed or assumed certain things. But no matter how she looked at it, the fact remained she was very uncomfortable at times and figured that once she would had it behind her she could move on and be like everybody else. It was also certain attraction to the great unknown which – as she gathered – could be an extraordinarily pleasant and nearly just as much hazardous experience.

Considering all of those things, Irena also decided she was not going to wait till the wedding night. She wanted to know and experience it ahead of time. She also figured it would probably be better not to be in love as it would possibly make things only more complicated. By carefully talking with her sister and her friends she found out her ideas were not uncommon, apparently there were women who shared her views and did what she was thinking of doing.

She had a few candidates on her mind. All were obviously men she knew, some better, some less so. All were trying to pursue her and she was more or less flirting with them. Stan was one of them and while enjoying his company she felt very little physical attraction to him and this – obviously without his knowledge – placed him on top of her list. She took time to consider her plan. She then placed it on the backburner for some time, returned to it for a day or two, put it aside again and returned to it one more time. Finally, she concluded that she had considered everything and was ready. With that Irena decided the next date with Stan would be the one.

When Stan called to ask for another date, she pretended to hesitate but agreed. They were going to meet in front of the National Museum, then go to see the exposition and have dinner after that. Irena took special care getting ready and arrived intentionally ten minutes late. Stan was of course waiting there, impeccably dressed as always.

"Hello, Irena," he smiled and wanted to give her a peck on the cheek, but she quickly moved away.

"We're just friends," she reminded him with a light smile.

"Well, of course we are."
He did not seem to mind.

"Shall we?" he offered her his arm.

Stan had already purchased tickets so they proceeded to the gallery. They both took extra time looking at the Battle of Grunwald painted by the Polish master Jan Matejko. The painting is a mural, a large battle scene showing Poles and Lithuanians fighting with the Teutonic Knights on the 15th of July 1410. The painter showed the moment when the Grand Master of the Teutonic Knights was just about to receive a mortal hit. He was depicted trying to defend himself with a sword against two soldiers, one with an ax and another with a spear and it was easy to imagine one of them would soon hit the Grand Master in the chest, sealing his fate. To the right, in the center of the picture was Vitautas the Great, the grand prince of Lithuania with both hands raised high in the air as if celebrating victory over the Teutonic Knights.

Irena and Stan were staring at the painting for quite a while discussing who was who on the picture.
It was at least two hours later when they found themselves exiting the gallery.

"My feet are killing me," Irena made a sound, "feels like we've been walking for ages."

"We did. But we are also close to a lovely restaurant. I reserved the table at the Ujazdowska Restaurant for dinner. I hope it's all right."

"Yes, of course," Irena was deep in thoughts.

"We could go to see a film after that. They are playing King Kong, you must have heard about it?" he suggested.

"Oh, I don't know, I don't feel like it."

She had different plans.
They walked short distance to the restaurant and Irena was happy to sit down.

"Finally!"
She looked at her feet, then moved them under the table and removed her shoes.

"You don't mind, do you?"

"What are you talking about?"

"I removed my shoes."

"Of course not."

The waiter arrived and they ordered their drinks.
Irena asked for a glass of champagne.

"I'm in a silly mood," she declared making an attempt at looking seductively into Stan's eyes.

"Sounds good to me," he clearly did not notice, "it's Saturday, no work tomorrow. We can be silly all right."

The waiter returned with their drinks and they ordered their meal, both enjoying a roasted duck.

It was about seven thirty when they left the restaurant.

"Would you care for coffee and a pastry on the Krakowskie Przedmieście Street?" asked Stan not wanting the evening to end so soon.

"No, thanks. I don't want any more walking either."

"How about… a drink at my place?" risked Stan.

"Why not?"

He immediately hailed a cab and gave the address to the driver. The ride was short as it was not really far, almost a walking distance.

When the cab left, Irena hesitated.

"What's the matter?" he asked her.

"I've never been to a bachelor's apartment," she teased him.

"Er…" he suddenly wasn't sure what to say "we know each other well enough – don't we?"

"Yes," she said, "I was joking."

"You mean you were?"
"Yes. I have all sorts of friends. Some are bachelors and some are…" she hesitated, "well – you know, some ballet dancers are…" she had not finished.

"Yes," he acknowledged but he actually did not understand what she meant.

They arrived at his door.

"Here we are," he turned the key and stepped aside to let her go first.

"Welcome to the lion's den" he smiled.

Irena crossed the threshold slowly and looked around. Stan's place was surprisingly tidy. Maybe it was because he was an accountant. Furnishings were simple and practical.

"Please go left to the sitting room and have a seat. What can I get you?"

"Have you got any Champagne?"

"Yes, of course but it will not be as cold as in the restaurant I'm afraid," he disappeared in the kitchen.

"That's okay," she needed a bit more for courage.

He returned with a bottle and two glasses, handed one to Irena. The cork popped out with a bang and bounced off the ceiling narrowly missing the chandelier.

Stan filled her glass first and then his own. He placed the bottle on the table, came closer to Irena and asked:

"What shall we drink to?"

She stood up.

"To the lovely evening!" she clinked her glass against his.

She felt confident now.

"Okay but the next sip is to you, Irena. You are the most intriguing and beautiful girl I've ever met!"

He did not have time to drink because she kissed him on the mouth. He removed the glass from her hand and placed both hers and his on the table. He then took her into his arms and kissed her back. Irena was taken aback by his intensity. She embraced him as well and held on tight. Stan took her by the hand and lead to his bedroom. Still kissing her he unbuttoned her blouse while she undid his shirt. He then sat down on the edge of the bed and pulled her by her hand. She sat on his knees and kissed him again.

Stan's hand caressed her back and wondered about until it arrived at the closure of her bra. He brought his other hand up and undid it, then slowly slipped it from her arms.
She placed her hand under one of her breasts and with her other hand gently brought Stan's head towards her so that his mouth was so close she could feel his warm breath. He opened his mouth and caressed her with his lips and tongue. Irena felt a pleasant sensation running down her spine. The urge was getting intense, taking possession of her mind and senses.

*

A Polish-built Fiat 508 pulled in to the curbside of the Krucza Street and a man dressed in a tuxedo jumped out. He looked up to the second floor window, gave a long high pitched whistle and shouted: "Hey, Stan!"

Stan appeared in the window.

"I'll be right there!" he shouted back and his head disappeared.

There was usual evening traffic on the street but here and there one could see well-dressed people in groups, pairs or singles on their way to the New Year's Eve parties. There were signs Happy New Year 1931 on the streets, and there were still Christmas decorations in many shop windows.

It was minus two degrees Celsius and it was snowing lightly which made the streets appear pretty and festive.

Stan appeared in the main door and when he approached the waiting car, he discovered his cousin Mike being one of the occupants.

"Hi guys!" he greeted them, "thanks for coming to get me."

"It's going to be a great celebration," said Mike, "you've ever been to Bristol?"

"Yes, of course I've been there but not on the event like this."

"You'll love it," said the driver, "you've never seen that many pretty girls, I guarantee."

Stan smiled.

"Well…"

"Well – what?"

"No, no nothing, it's just that I have that girl on my mind so it's hard to focus on others, that's all."

"C'mon Stan," smiled Mike, "it's not like you."

"It's different," Stan did not pick up the joke.

"Oh," mused John sitting behind the wheel "it's serious then, isn't it?"

"As I said," Stan did not feel like explaining too much, "it's different."

The Bristol Hotel was among the top hotels in Warsaw known for its elegance and superb kitchen serving two restaurants. Located at the elegant Nowy Świat Street in the city center, it's New Years Eve Balls were well known among Varsovians. They were always the hot topic before and after the event and to be there one had to make a reservation months ahead of time. The food was highly rated and the pastries were always from the famous Blikle Bakery and Pastry Shop.

Stan and his group of friends, altogether a company of sixteen or so men and women, had one table for themselves. They all knew each other for many years now and some were childhood friends. By the time Stan, John and Mike arrived, their table was already full and the party was warming up with master of ceremonies at full swing. The ballroom was splendidly decorated. This year, the dominant color was white but it certainly had not made it all look plain. The artists – usually students of The Art School - produced spectacular flowers large and small and some wild animals, and the ceiling was painted like a night sky with stars and planets. In the corner there was a small orchestra and the center was left empty to serve as the dance floor. Several pairs were swirling around to the hits known from the radio. Stan glanced at them without much enthusiasm as he wasn't keen on dancing. He was not much of a party animal but did enjoy company in festive circumstances. He liked music too but - of course - dancing was not exactly his forte.

"Hello Hermione!"

Stan greeted a slender short haired girl who was just exchanging embraces with his cousin Mike. They were walking together for quite a while now and were getting along very well and Stan liked them both. John, the boy who drove them was single just like Stan was and other friends were pairs more or less. They were all gathering at birthdays and sometimes in summer they would venture out of the city for picnics. There were several places for such events to choose from as a couple of tram lines had their end loops outside of the city and sometimes close to a beach on the Vistula River.

Waiter appeared and the new arrivals ordered their drinks. Women usually chose cocktails while men went for shots of vodka to give themselves a little buzz. The master of ceremonies was announcing some new dance and was calling for more pairs to get the party going. Stan sat down next to Hermione and Mike, chatting and waiting for his drink. He was subconsciously scanning the ballroom, checking out the guests. He always did it in a crowd as if hoping to spot somebody he would know. Meanwhile, the song had ended and master of ceremonies announced a tango. Guests were being shuffled as some were returning to their tables to have a break or a drink while others were making their way to the dance floor. The music began and suddenly Stan felt a jolt along his spine. Among the pairs, he spotted Irena dancing with a tall and handsome man. Stan was electrified. As far as he could tell they were both very good dancers. Other pairs drifted to side and some even stopped dancing altogether to watch Irena and her partner. She was like an exotic feather animated by music.

As if having no weight at all she seemed just floating in the air with every movement of her body. So was her partner for that matter, but Stan could not care less about him.
The music and movements of her body was caressing Stan's mind in oddly erotic way. He could not take his eyes of her.

"Stan…. Stan?... STAN?!"

He suddenly realized somebody was calling his name. It was Mike.

"Our drinks are here, to our health!" and he raised his glass.

"Sorry" Stan answered absentmindedly and mechanically raised his glass.

"To our lovely ladies!" he said and they shot their vodka in a single gulp.

"Who are you looking at so intensely?" inquired Mike.

"Ah…err…. nothing, I mean nobody. I just spotted somebody I once met."

"Come Hermione, let's go dancing!" Mike invited her as music was coming to the end.

Stan looked at them leaving the table on their way to the dance floor and then began scanning other tables searching for Irena. He found her on the other side of the ballroom sitting in a company of friends. He could see her chatting to another girl and bursting into a laughter every now and then. It seemed they were good friends as they both behaved very naturally together, at least as far as Stan could tell. As the evening was progressing, he eventually relaxed a bit and was making some small talk with his friends. But every now and then he kept looking for Irena. He kept pondering an idea of walking up to that table if only to say hello to her but he was not completely sure and, above all, he would not want to do something wrong. Some time after the meal was served he made up his mind and decided to go for it. It was now just a question of choosing the right moment. Irena danced quite a lot, sometimes two or three numbers one after another. She was just dancing with different partners from among her friends but also once or twice she was asked by some other men. She could have known them or perhaps not. Asking strangers for a dance was not uncommon. He figured he was going to go to her when she returned to her table to rest after series of dances. Such a moment arrived late in the evening when she was brought back to her seat by some man, sat down and reached for a drink. Stan got up from his table.

"Back in a while, guys," he said with a smile to his friends.

As he was getting closer, his legs were getting heavier. His self-confidence suddenly dropped. She was so beautiful and seemed to be the center of attention whether at her table or at the dance floor. But he knew he was immaculately dressed, and felt that he was not bad looking so it was not like he was out of place.

As he was not more than one step next to her and about to say hello, he heard master of ceremonies announcing a waltz. And the waltz was one of the very few dances he could manage. In a flash he changed his mind and instead of the intended "hello" he bowed to her and simply said:

"May I have the honor of this dance please?"

She was busy chatting with her female friend and only with a corner of her eye registered somebody asking her to dance so she stood up and without quite looking at him she answered:

"Yes, thank you, I love to waltz."

It was only now when he straightened up that she realized who had asked her and was surprised.

"Stan?!"

"I'm afraid so."
He smiled, took her arm and led her to the dance floor.
The music began and one-two-three, one-two-three, they followed it around the ballroom.

"What are you doing here?" she asked.

"Looking for you," he smiled again.

"I don't believe you."

"Okay, I am stalking you."

"I don't believe that either. You may be persistent but you don't seem to be a creep."

"I'm not a creep," he agreed, "I just can't stop thinking about you."

"Oh, stop it. You don't even know me."

"Sure I do."

"Well, yes – but we do not really know each other. And I told you before – I'm not your girlfriend."

Stan smiled.

"Don't smile at me like that, okay?" she was annoyed because she knew well what his smile meant.

"What do you want from me?"

"I told you. I'd like to know you better. I've fallen in love with you."

"No you haven't. You shouldn't be saying things like that."

"Forgive me but you can't possibly know what's inside my mind and my heart. May I see you again please?"

"I don't know. No. I dance with you, but this is it. Isn't it enough?"

"For somebody that just wants to dance maybe so. But I want more. I don't even like dancing. I don't really know how to do it well."

"You are doing all right."

"No."

Perhaps he was saying too much.

"Waltz is the only dance I can manage."

"Nonsense," she insisted, "if you know one dance, you can expand to others."

The waltz was coming to an end and they stopped.

"It doesn't work like that for me I'm afraid. Thank you for this dance, Irena."

"Thank you," she replied and he escorted her back to her table. Nobody invited him to stay there so he returned to his friends.

"Hey Stan," John had already one drink too many, "I thought you said you didn't dance."

"That's right, I don't"

"What was that, then?"

"Waltz is the only one I can get away with. Well, maybe I could get away with a Polonaise too."

"Hope they play one and hope she likes it too," John said with a wink of his eye.

"Who?" asked Stan.

"I am a bit drunk, my friend, but I'm not blind. You haven't taken your eyes off her all night."

Others at the table laughed merrily.

"Go for it, Stan" said Hermione.

It was midnight, the music stopped and the clock began chiming the hour. Champagne corks were popping everywhere and the last seconds were counted by all guests:

"Three, two, one! Happy 1931!"

"Ladies and gentlemen!" shouted the master of ceremonies, "it's time for the Polonaise!"

Stan jumped to his feet. He was pushing and shoving people aside and ran as fast as he could to Irena's table. He saw one of her friends trying to make his way towards her, no doubt to ask her to dance but Stan just elbowed him aside:
"Happy 1931 Irena! may I have this dance please?"

"Haven't you just said you only waltz?"

"I may be able to get away with this one too. Please, please Irena, may I? – it will mean a lot."

Her friends were staring at them.

"Of course."

She smiled to him. She was beginning to like his persistence. Once again he led her to the dance floor. The pairs lined up one after another and the music began.

*

Irena was seeing Stan irregularly. She was not entirely sure what to do, really. She used him and felt bad about it but she also enjoyed his presence and it was quite obvious to her. She was definitely not madly in love with him and it was all she could do at the moment. It was not a fully-fledged romantic affair but she was not bothered by it. Irena was not exactly a romantic type and, unlike her friends, she had no dreams of being swept off her feet. She did not even like romantic books and stories. Irena loved life but in more practical terms. From that angle Stan was fun to be with. They had been to see films and plays, went to picnics, sometimes they'd meet in midday at cafes or in the evening for dinners. Stan always chose places to go to with care. Reluctantly, she had agreed to meet each other's families and this was a success. Stan's mother, Alexandra was a plump, kind hearted person and her husband, Ignacy was short and fast-talking man with cheerful eyes. Irena liked them both at first sight while it seemed Stan got along with her mother quite well. Irena's father had died of a heart attack at a young age and Irena had only a faint memory of him. Irena's mother saw in Stan an old style perfect gentleman and she appreciated it very much.
Irena's hesitations or not, their relationship slowly developed into a proper courting as far as Stan was concerned. He was deeply in love and could not imagine life without her even though he sensed her hesitation. He figured that a girl needed to think and adjust to the concept of marriage and he would not like a woman that would just go for marriage blindly. He thought time was actually on his side and by now he also knew she had not had other contenders for her hand so he did not feel threatened. And finally, ever since he had met Irena's mother, he felt she approved of him. It seemed he had almost everything in place.

*

Zofia Sokołowska looked at her daughter from a distance across the hallway. Zofia was in the kitchen while Irena was sitting on a sofa in her room looking through the window. She seemed deep in thought and her face showed neither happiness nor sadness. She had been dating that boy Stan for quite a while now but did not seem to be very cheerful about it and Zofia was worried. Like any mother, she wanted the best for her daughter. She did like Stan who was always polite to her and Irena's siblings; he had a solid job and was of middle-class origin. Zofia even met his mother once by pure chance – she was in the city park and there was Stan with his mother Alexandra coming straight at her. He introduced them of course and Zofia made a small talk with her. Alexandra seemed very pleasant and calm and Zofia had a good feeling about her. Every girl wanted the proverbial prince charming for a husband but in reality a nice, polite boy with a good solid job from a good home was the reality every parent was happy to accept.

Zofia walked to Irena's room.

"Can I talk to you, Isia?"

"Is it about Stan again?" Irena asked with some apprehension in her voice.

"You know, I want the best for you. I don't want to force this upon you but you need to balance it all in your mind. A woman needs to marry and have her own home and some day raise her own family. This is how the life cycle goes, it is all natural. We all were young once and had to go through emotions and expectations. It is just that one must also consider reality and make plans for the future."

"I know."

"But your plans - what you want to do is not exactly practical in the typical meaning of the word."

Irena was silent.

"Ballet dancing is extremely competitive and I daresay a cutthroat sort of competitive at that. Very few make it to the top and I really think to do so they have to be rather ruthless along the way. You are very talented dancer but you are not ruthless. I wouldn't want you to be that."

"So you want me to drop my ambition, is this what it is?" snapped Irena.

"I want you to calmly consider it all – chances and possibilities and make a sensible decision."

"Sensibly marry Stan, is that right?" Irena had a spark in her eyes.

"He is a nice boy from a good family and he loves you. What more a woman can ask for?"

"I don't know. I haven't got experience and I dislike this rational thinking. I wanted love but I wanted to be deep in love too. And I'm not."

"Sometimes love grows slowly until it blooms but it may take a while."

"As it was in your case?"

Zofia fell silent. Her case was a bit odd indeed and Irena knew it.

*

Zofia had actually two candidates who wanted to marry her. They even knew each other but despite competing for Zofia's hand they were on good terms. She chose the one she loved and she agreed to marry him. Plans were made and all was going well until one day not far from the wedding date her fiancée, while talking to her father casually asked about her dowry. Zofia happened to hear this as she was passing by the open door. The question she heard was to her as if a lighting bolt hit her heart. She remembered the scene all too well, how she had stormed in...

"What was is that you've just said?"

"Nothing, I'm just chatting with your father."

Her fiancée clearly did not sense the approaching storm.

"Zosia…" her father, knowing how impulsive she could be, saw the situation deteriorating fast.

"You've just asked about my dowry," hissed Zofia.

"Your father and I were talking about financial planning for us. Yes, I asked the question…" he was oblivious to the imminent danger when she interrupted him.

"If you are interested in my dowry, then you are not interested in me!"

She pulled her engagement ring off her finger and threw it at him.

"The engagement is off!" she exclaimed "I wish you a good day, sir!" and she stormed out of the room followed by her father pleading with her to stop. But to no avail.

He finally caught up with her in the hall reaching for the phone.

"Go to the post office at once, Mary, and dispatch this telegram!" she handed her a piece of paper.

"What are you doing, Zosia?" inquired her father.

"Never mind that. Is he's gone? If not, please go and tell him to leave. I don't want to see him again and I will never, ever speak to him. I mean it!"

"But Zosia…"

"I mean it!" her eyes sparkled with anger.

Few hours later the doorbell rang and Mary announced Mister Frank Sokołowski. He was the other young man madly in love with Zofia.

"Bring him in please!" Zofia said to the maid and turned to her father.

"Please get mother. I want you both with me here."

"What are you up to, Zosia?" he inquired.

"Please trust me, Dad" she replied, "just get mum."

Frank walked in and turned to Zofia.

"Here I am Zosia. May I say how lovely you look today? Lovely as ever!" he greeted her as her parents walked into the room. "Good afternoon, mister and Mrs. Widlica!"

"Afternoon, Frank" they greeted him. They seemed calm given the circumstances

"Frank," Zosia turned to him, "I believe you wanted to marry me?"

"Oh, yes Zosiu," he eagerly responded "I asked you more than once, you know I love you more than anything."

She extended her hand to him.

"Here is my hand, then."

The room fell silent. Frank was clearly confused.

"But – you are engaged to John, you told me so yourself."

"Not anymore," she said with a slight irritation in her voice, "Are you going to keep me waiting? – I'll not ask again!"

Frank fell to his knees.

"Zosiu, I swear on my soul and your parents here and God are my witnesses that I love you more than anything and to marry you is the greatest honor I can think of!" he assured her.

"I accept," said Zofia and with a smirk added' "don't worry about the engagement ring, just sort it out next week or whenever it is convenient – I am well aware you are not prepared to give it to me now. Now get up and give me a kiss!"

Frank happily obeyed.

Her mother nudged her husband.

"Come, let's leave them alone for a while. They need to talk."

Irena knew this story well. Everybody in the family knew it.
She gave her mother a long look.

"Mum, I feel like I'm standing at a crossroads having two roads to choose from. The one I prefer is difficult and I know you don't like it. The other one you want me to take but I am not too keen. I'm just afraid it may some day suffocate, or maybe even kill me. The trouble is that this second road seems secure for the years to come. Unfortunately it is what so many romantic stories seem to be about. The eternal dilemma. Should I follow my head or my heart?"

"Oh, darling, you mustn't say things like that" Zofia put her hands together as to a prayer. "Perhaps you should talk to your uncle Stanislaw."

"Why would I discuss my life's choices with a bishop?"

"He has a wisdom you and I don't have. He might help you decide."

"No. I don't want to do that. I will choose myself!"

Irena grabbed her purse and coat, and hurriedly pulled on her shoes. She glanced at herself in the large mirror to make sure she looked well and opened the door.

"I'll be back in two hours or so, mum," she said.

"Where are you going?"

"Outside, for a walk. I need fresh air to clear my head. I need to see the city and be among people. I'm suffocating inside. That's what I'm afraid of."

She walked across the Three Crosses Plaza, glanced at the church standing in the middle of it and proceeded towards Aleje Ujazdowskie which was one of her favorite streets to walk. There were always people there, all elegant, well dressed – groups of friends, couples, parents and grandparents with children. All of them sooner or later ended up in the park Lazienkowski with its statue of Frederic Chopin at the main entrance and the King's Palace in the center. There were also a couple of cafes where one could have a coffee or tea with a piece of pastry. Poles were fond of pastries and every town big or small had a bakery or two. The pastries, at least some of them, came from Italy and France long ago and they ranged from a slice of a variety of torts to a simple things called "pipe with cream" which was a small hard pastry in form of a 15 centimeters long pipe with a cream inside or even more simple – a kind of apple fritter known as pączek.
Irena always stopped at the cafe closest to the King's Palace so she could sit at a small table outside with a view to the palace and the open air amphitheatre nearby. She loved the park. Somehow ever since she was little she cared less for toys but loved going out. It was so much fun to walk the streets and look at people passing by, admiring shop windows, watching tradesmen going about their business and families as they walked by. Being a young adult now, Irena was so fond of Warsaw. She eagerly followed the news about the city, what was going on what was being built and planned. She always knew what was being played in theaters and what expositions were opened and where and she attended as many as she could. Sometimes she did so alone if there was nobody available to go with her. She wanted Warsaw to be a pearl among cities of Europe and the city seemed to be on its way there. There was general feeling of freedom and enthusiasm in Poland and Warsaw in particular thanks

so its regained independence since the Great War end and on the streets of Warsaw you could see it like nowhere else. Businesses were booming, new beautiful buildings were built and there were plans for spectacular arteries to crisscross the city with new bridges to be built to connect the east and west districts of Warsaw.

In the plans for the future, there was also something that only few capitals of Europe had - a subway system. Varsovians, so proud of their city, were eagerly anticipating the project to begin and Irena was, of course, one of them.

Nearly equally exciting was the new Warsaw Central Station which was just about to be built and, according to the plans, it was going to be impressive building with large arrival and departure halls to be adorned with art. It was intended to be Warsaw's calling card welcoming travelers from other countries.

Now, perhaps more than ever, Irena needed the city. She was walking slowly as she was not in a hurry. She passed the Frederick Chopin statue and was making her way towards the King's Palace. She felt a bit edgy and she knew why. She'd snap into such a mood whenever she was cornered by circumstances and found herself being indecisive. Not that she needed to act immediately – she did not. But still - on one hand there was Stan pursuing her relentlessly, clearly in love with her and wanting very much to marry her. On the other, she loved her life as it was. She loved her freedom, going out and enjoying the city life, meeting friends and above all she loved her dancing. She was good at that and she felt it was a matter of time before she would land a part in a real ballet. That would be a dream come true. Yet as much as she wanted to pursue her dream, she could not escape thoughts of marriage, now that the option was so clear to her.

She always wondered why none of the men interested in her was serious enough to mention marriage, even remotely. Was it her personality? Surely it couldn't be the looks, because she was being told by everyone how pretty she was. There was one man who asked her to marry him but it was a while ago and she was not ready. Although she liked him, she had turned him down and he disappeared. A friend told her he was supposedly heartbroken and moved to Krakow, he wanted to break away completely and start

afresh. She had a few friends but it was just flirting at best. And then Stan had appeared in such an unusual way. She was not madly in love with him but by now she got used to him and liked his company. The general wisdom or cynicism was advising her it was better to marry being level-headed about it rather than being infatuated and having one's head in the clouds. Marrying Stan, she would know what to expect, or at least she thought she would. He was not going to sweep her off her feet and give her a thousand and one magical nights. It was going to be much more down to earth. But it would be comfortable. And Irena liked being comfortable. She picked up the nearest flower and began pulling its petals one by one, playing "marry him", "don't marry him." The final petal said "marry him." Irena threw what was left of the flower on the ground and kept walking. Upon returning home some two hours later she found a bouquet of white roses waiting for her. There was a card attached to it.
"Just say the word and the world is ours! Always yours - Stan."

*

Church at the Three Crosses Plaza was full of guests, the majority being from the Szumski family. Stan had three brothers and at least seven first cousins. Some of them were married and had spouses and children. They were a close family and an event like a wedding was not to be missed by anyone. The Sokołowski family was smaller but had considerable amount of close friends who compensated for family size. Precisely at eleven o'clock the organist began the wedding march and Irena's uncle walked her down the isle towards the altar where the bishop was waiting along with Stan. Irena was calm and very much in control - she was not going to allow emotions take her over and cause a mistake. Perhaps it was the iron discipline of ballet classes and exercises that afforded her such self control. From this point of view she was almost like a royalty – perfect in every respect and at the same time somewhat aloof. Her uncle, his role finished, returned to his pew next to her mother Zofia and her siblings, Barbara and Marian.

The music stopped and the bishop began:

"Dear family and friends, we have gathered here today to witness and celebrate the marriage of Stan and Irena. Marriage is the promise of hope between two people who love each other sincerely, who honor each other as individuals, and who wish to unite their lives and share their future together. In this ceremony, they dedicate themselves to the happiness and well-being of each other, in a union of mutual caring and responsibility. If anyone present here knows reasons why these two should not be married, speak now or forever hold your peace."

As he spoke the last words a single knock resounded over the hushed congregation. It was as if somebody had knocked on the massive door or perhaps kicked the foot rest of the pews. The guests looked around, trying to locate the source of this sound.
The bishop raised his eyes from the bible and looked at the congregation, waiting for a moment and said:

"Is there anyone that wants to say something?"

There was no answer, the church was silent. He calmly continued and the ceremony went on as planned.
When the newlyweds appeared outside, the day was at full swing. Sunday noontime and a beautiful day meant there were lots of people on the plaza on their way to or from the Aleje Ujazdowskie, all cafes were full and guests at the tables were looking from a distance at the newly married couple emerging from church. After few steps, they disappeared in the crowd of well wishers, family and friends. An elegant horse-drawn carriage was waiting to take them to the reception. It was a white horse pulling a white carriage with a driver and a footman both dressed appropriately for the occasion.

*

Stan effortlessly picked Irena up with one arm under her back and another across under her knees and turned towards the door.

"Go ahead Isia, open it, but close your eyes immediately."

Holding him around his neck with her right arm, Irena unlocked the door with the gold plated key Stan had given her earlier and pushed

the door until it was wide open.
Stan carried her across the threshold.

"You can open your eyes now."

She looked around and exclaimed: "Good God, Stan!"

The room was full of white roses. They were on window sills and on every piece of furniture, they were lying on the floor and they were meticulously arranged in vases. They were large and small. Some were dressed up with greenery and white ribbons and some were just as if they were freshly cut. There must have been hundreds of them.

"I love you, Isia," he said, "I fell in love with you the moment I bumped into you on that tram stop way back."

"I love you Stan" she responded quietly and tried to kiss him lightly but he didn't let her. He took her into his arms and holding her tight he kissed her open mouth gently. Passion took over instantly. She reached up to undo her veil but he stopped her.

"No, leave it."

He reached to her back and began undoing long row of buttons one by one, continuing kissing her while she kept her arms around his neck. When he was done she walked out of her dress which collapsed to the floor. She stood before him in her veil, bra, slip and stockings – all in white. As she reached to undo his tie he slowly lowered her slip until she could step out of it. With his tie loosely hanging around his neck he removed his jacket and let it drop to the floor. They were kissing again and now he lowered his hands to widen the elastic which held her underwear in place. As he was pushing them slowly down her heartbeat increased and she was breathing a little heavier. She stepped out of them and began unbuttoning his shirt while he unfastened her bra, she then slipped her arms out of it and undid his trousers which dropped to the floor following all other garments. She wanted to remove her veil but he stopped her again.
"Come," he said and took her by her hand. They walked to the bedroom and he led her towards the large mirror.

"Look how beautiful you are" he whispered and stepped aside so that she was in front of the mirror alone. He removed his underwear and was looking at her. There was a moment of silence. He knelt in front of her and kissed her just below her belly button at first but each following kiss was placed lower and lower. She placed her hands on his head and caressed his hair.

*

Irena was walking on the Krakowskie Przedmieście Street towards the King's Palace. She was deep in thoughts and paid no attention to pedestrians, she actually bumped into a few and had to apologize. Not that she regretted her marriage to Stan, she was just bothered by the recurring little doubts. She felt she perhaps cheated him by not really loving him fully. Every now and then there would be a voice telling her she should have done better. Sometimes she'd wake up in the middle of the night feeling trapped. Stan loved her madly and did not see the world beyond her. But she knew she was unable to reciprocate and therefore she felt some sense of guilt. Going for a walk alone was a little like opening a safety valve. But it had become a paradox. She used to love company and being with friends. Now, while missing that part of her life she preferred to be alone. *Perhaps it's normal to have doubts* - she thought. At least she was still going to the dance studio. When she danced she felt free. Nothing mattered and the daily chores did not exist, it was as if she could fly physically and mentally. Expressing drama and happiness with movement of her body was a feeling like no other and she had it ever since she tried it for the very first time when she was a little girl. And the shows she participated in were the absolute pinnacle of it all. Preparations - make up, putting on her costume, warming up and finally walking on stage was something out of this world. Irena smiled to herself thinking of her dancing. She was good at it and she knew it.

The phone rang.

"Hello?"

"Irena, good morning – this is Lidia Jastrzębska."

"Oh, good morning!"
Irena liked the mistress of her dance studio.

"I have some exciting news for you. Mister Piotr Zajlich was asking about you. Apparently he had seen you somewhere and he'd like to talk to you about being a Coryphée understudy. Could you be here tomorrow afternoon to meet with him?"

Irena was speechless for a moment. Piotr Zajlich was director of The Warsaw Ballet!

"Yes, of course I will be there," she finally stammered.

"See you at one then. Good bye."

Irena hung up the phone and made a pirouette in the middle of the living room. It was what she always hoped for and dreamed about. A chance for a professional career! Long years of hard work were finally paying off handsomely. She looked at her image in the mirror and laughed merrily. She felt weightless and was extraordinarily happy. Nothing was going to stop her now. Nothing.

3. DECISIONS AND CONSEQUENCES

She woke up feeling somewhat queasy. Stan has gone to work already, he had to leave early for some reason, so he got up and left without waking her up. The room felt stuffy so she opened the window to let fresh air in but the feeling hadn't changed. Suddenly she felt an urge to go to the bathroom but when she got there the urge was gone. She looked at herself in the mirror. Her face looked perfectly normal. She felt she was going to be sick so she bent over the toilet and threw up.
As she was coughing and rinsing the unpleasant taste in her mouth with water she glanced at the mirror again and suddenly it occurred to her.

"Good God, I'm pregnant. Why, oh why now?"

She began crying uncontrollably. Through her tears she looked at her belly in the mirror. It was perfectly flat as it always has been but somewhere deep inside a new life was beginning and she had no doubts about it.

A few days later, and without telling anyone, she had consulted her doctor who only confirmed what she already knew anyway. She was going to be a mother. Being married she had accepted that she would have a child some day but at the same time she intended to have it on her own terms and, above all, planned well ahead.

The Warsaw Ballet wanted her starting soon and it was obvious they would reject her the minute she told them she was expecting. The timing could have not been worse and Irena was in turmoil. Her dream of so many years and what she perceived as a once in a lifetime chance seemed to be slipping away from her hand and there was nothing she could do about it.

Unless...

She got dressed and went for a walk to the park. She would always do this to clear her head before making any important decisions. She wanted the ballet above all and to save it she had no other option but to go and do something unthinkable, something she never thought she would be facing, something people occasionally whispered about dubious women doing. Irena was walking around the park pondering this. She was leaning towards not telling Stan or anyone else at all - she would only later tell him it was a miscarriage. It seemed only this way she'd save her engagement with the Warsaw Ballet.

With her mind made up she started home but on the way decided to go into the church at the Three Crosses Plaza. Initially she thought she would go to confession but then she realized one was supposed to confess things that were done. Otherwise it would be like seeking advice and she knew what advice she would get. She then only sat in the pews, prayed and otherwise contemplated her life.

She knew of a doctor to contact. There was a controversial female doctor known of being actively involved in emancipation of women. The gossip was she was a lesbian but nobody really knew if it was true or not. Her practice was on the other side of the river in the Praga district.

Upon returning home she phoned the practice and made an appointment giving a false name and address. This gave her few more days to reconsider but she knew in her heart that she did not need to. She wanted the ballet more than anything ever since the first lesson she had ever had.

"You will be in discomfort for a few days, Anna" said the doctor.

"That's all right," Irena replied.

"Do you have somebody to take you home and stay with you for the first 24 hours?"

"Sort of."

"Can you be more specific?"

"I'm going home on my own but there will be somebody with me."

"How are you going to get home?"

"I have a taxi coming in two hours."

"And you understand and accept the risks involved which I already explained to you?"

"Yes."

Irena was nervous and uneasy but still her mind was made up.

"You also must understand this procedure cannot be done multiple times. I won't do it again. These are my rules."

"I understand," said Irena.

"Very well, then" said the doctor, "please get ready."

*

Upon returning home after work Stan found Irena asleep in bed. It was unusual for her and he figured she must have been not well so he was moving about quietly. He changed from his usual suit to something casual and went to the kitchen where he found dinner. He noticed that Irena hadn't eaten so he prepared two plates and went on to warm their meal while waiting for her to wake up. He assumed she was not going to sleep continuously till the next day. He also put

the radio on and set it on the lowest audible volume not to disturb her.
There was a news segment about a new warship launched in Germany named Deutschland, as well as a discussion of Germany's new air force. If all of this was true, Germany was in direct violation of the Treaty of Versailles.

Stan poured himself a glass of wine, lit a cigarette and sat down on a chair pondering the news. Would it all lead to another war? The Great War ended more or less a decade ago and everybody knew how terrible it was. Would Germans start another one? The League of Nations and the Treaty of Versailles were designed to prevent Germany from building up her military again. If the reports were even partially true then it meant Hitler was ignoring the restrictions. Something in Stan's opinion was not adding up properly in all of this. *At least we have our pact with the Soviets* he thought. It gave Poland a some assurance of peace with the eastern neighbor, that is if the communists could be trusted at all.

Irena made a sound from the bedroom and Stan walked over to her.

"Are you all right, Isia?" he asked.

"Yes" she feebly responded, "well not exactly actually."

"What's wrong?" Stan was concerned. "should I call a doctor?"

"Oh no," Irena protested. "It's... you know, a woman thing. Sometimes I get really uncomfortable."

"I don't recall seeing you in such shape."

"Like every woman I don't like this subject, I hide it. But this time for whatever reason it hit me harder."

Stan was not in a position to pursue the subject.

"You haven't eaten anything" he said. "I have dinner ready. Would you like to eat now?"

"I'll eat something I guess" she said and began moving to get up.

"Stay where you are," said Stan "I'll bring everything here and we'll have dinner together. Would you like a glass of wine?"

"Yes please," she said. "You are so good to me, Stan."

He smiled and went back to the kitchen to get things ready.
They spent the evening quietly talking about all sorts of things, but the Warsaw Ballet dominated the conversation.

In a matter of a day or two Irena was back on her feet, but her mood was occasionally volatile. Sometimes it would catch her off guard and make her sad for a moment. She would usually brush it away and get busy with something. Otherwise she continued her work at Fiat's Dealership and she attended the dance studio three times a week where she worked particularly hard preparing herself for the new engagement with the Warsaw Ballet.

*

"Adria" was a popular restaurant and cafe in Warsaw. It also had a small stage and decently sized dance hall which allowed its owners to present cabaret shows and organize balls. One such occasion was the Annual Midsummer Ball which always drew a considerable crowd. To be there one had to make reservation of at least half a year ahead of time. Irena had attended this event countless of times before she married Stan. Not being keen on dancing but knowing how much she loved it, Stan was always making reservations for the two of them and a couple of friends, typically his cousin Mike and his wife Hermione. They would always meet other friends there as well so they usually ended in a group and always had a marvelous time. But deep down, Stan could never disconnect the place from his dislike of dancing. Irena of course was well known to be a fantastic dancer and was being asked to dance by friends and sometimes complete strangers. Stan did his best to dance with her too but took to the floor as little as possible. He was however, quite content sitting at the table, chatting, having a drink and otherwise watching the crowd.

Irena loved parties and they attended several each year. But sometimes Stan thought he wanted to have a family – children, one or two, maybe three. Being from a large and traditional family he struggled to reconcile in his mind Irena's dancing with raising children. The more he thought about it the more convinced he was one excluded the other and their life as such needed to change. It was not going to be easy and he knew it.

If she became pregnant she'd have to make changes in her life thought Stan. This was perhaps better than trying to reason with her. After all, nature would most likely kick in.

The orchestra began playing a waltz and Irena rushed up to him and grabbed his hand.

"C'mon, Stan – I know you have no problem with this one!"

She was breathing faster than normal, probably somewhat tired after dancing so much. Her eyes were sparkling with excitement and she was clearly in her own element. Stan followed her and in a moment they were swirling around among other couples. But at some point Stan lost his step.

"What are you doing?" she asked as if annoyed.

"I lost my step" he said.

"So start all over again."

They had to stop, Stan caught the music in his ear and started again.

"You should be leading decisively," she remarked.

"I know what I should be doing but it doesn't come naturally to me."

He was upset as talking about it only made it worse for him.

"See – you are doing better now," she said.

"It would be helpful if you were not patronizing," he snapped.

"I'm only trying to help," she said.

"The way you do it only intimidates me and makes it worse."

"But it's the easiest dance there is!"

"I'm sure it is for you."

Stan managed to keep calm. He did not want to spoil her evening as he knew that such events were clearly very special to Irena. But the way she would react to the slightest mistake he made was as if she was ridiculing him; they had such conversations countless of times before. He figured Irena while obviously good at dancing had neither talent nor patience for teaching. Anything she tried in order to help was producing the adverse effect and he was almost hating dancing by now.

"I told you many times Isia, one has to know one's limitations. I don't have a knack at it and I know it, that's all. Doing it with you does not make it easier," he then whispered into her ear "I'd rather do other things with you."

She laughed as she liked being teased in such a way, it was all part of the game, the prize of which was waiting home.
The orchestra announced a break so they returned to their table.

"You are not too shabby waltzing, Stan," Mike complemented him.

"I can barely manage this one" replied Stan, „what are we drinking?"

"Champagne!" Mike reached for the iced bottle next to him.
"Give me your glass please," he asked.

Stan sat down and took a sip.

"What do you think of what's going on in Germany?" asked Mike.

"It sounds suspicious" answered Stan.

"On one hand," he continued, "some papers dismiss Hitler as some sort of megalomaniac who has hard time to be taken seriously, on the other they write he is building up his military ignoring all treaties. And on the "third" hand our leaders seem to be ready for anything. I find it all difficult to reconcile."

"It's politics, Stan. By being friendly with British and French we are annoying Hitler. At the same time England is afraid of communism so they look at him as a tool to be used against Russians and therefore they kind of prefer him over communists running Germany."

"Well, the trouble is we are between Hitler and the Soviets."

"Yes, this hasn't changed. We therefore should not annoy Herr Hitler whether he is a ridiculous figure or not. One should never underestimate one's enemy."

"Oh, I do agree with that. The only thing is we are sitting between two enemies and what's worse they seem to be interested in expanding in opposite directions. Can we be friendly with both?"

"Well, it is like Pilsudski said – we are standing a bit precariously with legs on two stools. It can't last forever."
"I don't fall for Pilsudski's rhetoric. What we have now is effectively a dictatorship and political opposition is locked up."

"He stepped in because we were slipping into chaos," said Stan, "the country is only recently reborn and those at the top are fighting their little battles for their egos instead of concentrating on working together to build up Poland's strength. Wouldn't you do the same?"

"Raise hand at the democratically elected government? – Never!" Mike nearly shouted.

"Sometimes I think we as a nation are so irresponsible. Facing mortal danger we unite and put all differences aside immediately. Once the danger is over we go after each other's throats. I really detest that. No wonder they call us hot tempered. And it's not a complement."

"But the law is the law. How dared he and who gave him the right to decide what's good and what's bad?!" Mike was agitated as usual after one drink too many.

"Well, perhaps he deserves a little credit for actually putting Poland back on the map of Europe after 150 years?"

"Does it mean every time he doesn't like something he has the right to intervene? Mind you – his intervention in May cost over nearly four hundred lives, from which about a hundred and fifty were civilians. And there was nearly a thousand wounded. Don't try to tell me this was okay."

The orchestra began playing again and Hermione grabbed Mike by the hand. They crossed to the dance floor while a friend of Irena's asked her for the dance. No doubt Hermione did it on purpose to stop them arguing as they would easily spiral out of control. Mike was Stan's favorite cousin, they had the same sense of humor and loved jokes but they could not discuss politics calmly.

Some acquaintance of Irena's appeared and asked her to dance. Stan was left alone at the table but he didn't mind.

*

Before she was going to begin rehearsals with the Warsaw Ballet ensemble, Irena was given certain number of routines to practice on her own. Accordingly and in agreement with the Lidia Jastrzębska School of Ballet and Dancing she had reserved blocks of time when she could be there by herself with only the pianist playing for her. She had not even had to pay for this arrangement as Madame Jastrzębska was quick to realize that having on her school's profile a pupil who advanced straight from there to a Coryphée in the most prominent ballet in Poland was worth more money from prospective new pupils than what she'd gain by charging Irena the usual fees. Thus the arrangement was mutually beneficial and both the school and Irena were happy. She was going there three times a week straight after work for four-hour long sessions. Sometimes Stan would come to meet her there and then they'd return home together or they'd go to a restaurant for a late dinner and go home later or they just go for drinks somewhere and had dinner at home. It made their week days busy and they were passing by quickly one by one.

*

The black swan was swirling in vicious pirouettes getting ever closer. It's eyes were glowing intense red. The wave of air propelled by the enormous wings was like a hurricane and Irena had hard time maintaining her posture. When it came face to face with Irena it hissed at her and she could see the wide open beak with row of sharp teeth laced with blood. She screamed in horror - and woke up.

The room was silent and dark and Stan was sleeping next to her. She wiped her forehead with her hand and noticed it was moist with sweat. Her heart was beating at a fast rate and she was breathing heavily as if after strenuous exercises.
She moved and Stan woke up.

"What's the matter Isia?" he asked.

"I had a bad dream," she said.

Stan turned on the small nightlight and looked at her.

"Are you all right? You seem pale and shaken."

"Yes, yes, I'm fine. It was just... irrational and scary."

Stan got out of bed.

"Where are you going?" she asked.

"I'll get you glass of milk. It'll do you good and help falling asleep."

He walked to the kitchen while Irena remained sitting on bed still thinking of the dream. She couldn't remember ever having such a vivid and unpleasant nightmare.

Two weeks later or so, she had that queasy feeling again. She dismissed it at first, thinking she must have eaten something the night before. Some food not exactly agreeing with her, or perhaps one drink too many no matter how good it was. Such things do happen. She was not going to have anything standing across her way towards the professional career. When it happened again she thought it was due to increased regime of physical exercises and ballet routines. It could possibly explain this, it did happen to her in the past. But after three or four consecutive days of feeling queasy in the mornings and throwing up on the fifth she had to face what her body was so clearly telling her. Once again she was staring at her image in the mirror trying to look deep into her own eyes.
"No, not that again" she whispered and in a sudden influx of rage she grabbed a bottle of perfume standing there and threw it at the mirror which almost exploded in hundreds of pieces that went flying around her. She looked down and in every larger piece she saw her reflection staring up at her. She felt sick one more time and once again threw up into the toilet. She then started to cry uncontrollably.

By now it was time for her to leave for work and she was not even close to be ready but she did not care. She was in pain but it was not physical and therefore it was far worse.
The phone rang and after the fifth ring she snapped back into reality. She walked to pick it up.

"Hallo?"

"Mrs. Szumska? This is Joann, the receptionist."

"Oh, good morning Joan.."

"We are concerned because you have not arrived and you have not called either..."

"I'm so sorry, Joan, I was violently sick. I will be there in an hour."

"Do you need any help or should I send a car for you?"

"No, thank you. I'm all right now."

"See you soon, then?"

"Yes. Good bye."

Irena hung up the phone.

She had not heard Stan walking in until he appeared in the bathroom door and found her finishing the clean up. She was brushing pieces of mirror onto a small shovel. He immediately noticed remains of the mirror frame still hanging above the sink.

"Are you all right, Isia?" he asked, "what happened?"

"I'm pregnant!" she began to cry.

He bent down and hugged her trying to lift her up but since she was not trying to get up he sat on the floor and just held her in her arms. It was what he wished for but he knew perfectly well what it meant for her dancing ambitions.

"I'm happy, Isia" he whispered and kissed her on her head while still holding her tight.

"It's a blessing but I know it may not be how you wanted it."
She was sobbing uncontrollably.

"It's not that I don't want family and children" she managed through the tears, "but I wanted at least just one season in the ballet. You have no idea how much I wanted it."

"It's God's will" he said.

They were both religious, perhaps she was even more than he was but she was also in a clear contradiction and violation of one of the commandments which he knew nothing about at all.

She was feeling guilty but had no intention of telling him anything so she just kept sobbing in his arms. Stan always thought a woman would be ecstatic upon finding herself pregnant but he knew Irena was not exactly a typical housewife.

He eventually got her out of the bathroom and convinced her to lay down on a sofa. He then called her office and explained she was not coming to work after all. He thought of giving her a shot of vodka but discarded the idea and took a shot himself to calm his nerves. He could not help but feel guilty. He was not keen on Irena's pursuing a career in the ballet. He did not believe that she could ever truly make it and he was afraid that could possibly spell a disappointment to her. Motherhood – he figured – would be a natural way of focusing her attention on something else. Every now and then he would poke his head into the living room and found Irena asleep on the sofa. She must have been exhausted. He did not quite understand how exactly the mirror broke but it was not that important after all. He would give the empty frame to a shop around the corner and a new mirror would be fit in a day or two.

Later that night they were lying in bed with Irena curled up around Stan. Her eyes were swollen from crying but she was reasonably calm.

Stan reached for his cigarette case.

"Please don't" Irena said. "This is bad for the baby."

"Sorry" he put it down. "You know, I will just quit. It will be better for all of us."

"How are you going to do that?"

"What do you mean? I just did it. I will not smoke anymore."

"They say it's hard."

"It's all in your mind, you know. I see no problem even if I have an urge for a while because I know it's going to be better for you and for us."

"If I only could do it with the ballet…" she shed a couple of tears again. "I don't know how I will bring myself to withdraw."

"Would you want me to do it for you?" asked Stan.

"I don't know… yes. Would you?"

"I shall do so tomorrow."

He almost added "with pleasure" but bit his lip in time as it would be a wrong thing to say.

*

Stan walked into the Lidia Jastrzębska Dance School. He ascended to the first floor and knocked on the door marked "Administration".

"Come in please!" a female voice responded and he opened the door.

A middle aged woman was sitting at the desk shuffling some papers.

"Can I help you?"

"Good morning, madam," he mustered his best smile and manners, "I came here to notify you that one of your students, Irena Sokołowska-Szumska is resigning as she is not going to continue dancing," he explained.

She could clearly not contain her surprise.

"But… why? She is our top dancer and has fantastic prospects for the future! Has something happened? Can we help in any way? And who are you anyway? Why couldn't she do it in person?"

"My name is Stan Szumski and I am her husband. I have full right to speak on her behalf."

"Ah… er…" she stumbled looking for words "yes, of course. But if I may ask why wouldn't she notify us herself?"

Stan was slightly upset as it was not really her business but he wanted to be pleasant so he smiled again:

"She is not well at the moment. We are expecting our baby and she does not feel up to it. Doing this in person would be too stressful for her. I am doing so on her behalf as her well-being is the most important to me."

"Of course, of course," she repeated.

"Congratulations to you and Irena. I wish we knew. Madame Lidia would do something for her I'm sure and send a note at least."

He did not want to continue the pleasantries so he simply asked:

"Do we owe you anything? Are there any outstanding bills due from Irena?"

"No, I don't think so," she answered, "please let me double check, it will only take a moment."

She shuffled pages of a thick book in front of her. In a minute or two she found what she was looking for, drove her finger across a long line of handwriting and turned to Stan.

"As I thought. All her bills are paid."

"That's it then," Stan was getting ready to leave.

"Thank you for your help, Good bye."

She stopped him:

"Mr. Szumski?"

"Yes?"

"Please do convey our congratulations to Irena. We had no idea. I wish Madame Lidia and I could do so in person. Also, please tell her she is always welcome back whenever she wants."

"Thank you. Good-bye."

He turned around, closed the door and walked away.

4. PARENTHOOD

Stan was nervously pacing the corridor of the maternity ward. He could hear Irena screaming in pain and muffled voices of nurses attending to her.
He pulled out a cigarette but a nurse who happened to be passing by scolded him:

"Not here, sir, you can smoke outside if you must."

"I can't move away from here," he said, "my wife is in there having our baby."

She smiled and walked away.

Irena, it seemed, stopped screaming and the door opened. A nurse stuck her head out and called his name.

"Mister Szumski!"

"Yes?" he answered eagerly.

"You can come in now."

As soon as he crossed the threshold he saw Irena holding their newborn baby. He nearly ran across the room.

"Isia!"

He gave her a kiss.

"Meet Gabriela!" she said.

"Can I touch her?"

"Yes, but be very gentle."

Ever so carefully Stand kissed the little girl on her head.

"She's so tiny!" he had never seen a newborn baby.

"How do you feel? It must have hurt a lot?"

"Yes, I never thought it would hurt quite so much."

"When can I take you home?"

"In a few days I guess."

A nurse came.

"I'm very sorry but your wife needs to rest now."

"Of course" Stan moved away, "when can I return?"

"Go home, Stan" said Irena.

"Nonsense!" he protested, "I want to be here with you both. My place is with you!"

The nurse smiled, she clearly liked what he said.

"I think your wife will sleep at least three hours."

"So see you then, Gabriela and Isia!"

"Go home and rest" insisted Irena but he only waved her away.

"After what? You need to rest, not me. I'll see you both later!"

He walked out of the room. There were three of them now.

Once on the street he looked around, uncertain what to do or where to go for three hours and he did not feel like going home. He spotted a sign at some distance which could possibly be a bar or a restaurant. When he came closer he read the sign and burst with laughter. The bar was named „Stork".

He ordered a plate with some cold cuts and a glass of vodka. When he swallowed the first sip he could feel how his nerves tight after listening to Irena's screams were pleasantly loosening up. He felt happy and proud. He was a father now. What a wonderful feeling! He couldn't wait to return to Irena and Gabriela.

*

Irena was a good and caring mother. She had everything organized well and she had established a daily routine which she followed without deviation. Little Gabriela was always fed on time, changed or at least checked every hour and her clothes and supplies were always at ready. It was all like a Swiss clock – precise and on time. Stan for his part could not have enough of his daughter and was always in a hurry from work to spend time with her and Irena. He loved going for a stroll with a pram and, weather permitting, they were often going to Aleje Ujazdowskie and Park Lazienkowski which they did on Saturdays and Sundays. He also – perhaps unlike other men – was involved and ever ready to do whatever was needed. He was changing diapers like a seasoned nanny, he washed them, he loved everything that had to do with his daughter but above all he loved carrying her around. He talked to her and sang to her even though so obviously she could not respond but he knew she probably appreciated it. He also happily stayed with Gabriela alone to give Irena a break so she could go out for a walk or to meet a friend. The only thing was that he passionately wanted Irena maybe even more than before. But Irena was tired to begin with as she was caring of the baby most of the day and she never had the passion to match that of her husband. More often than not once in bed she wanted to go to sleep and kept refusing Stan's advances. Many a night Stan was lying in bed next to her listening to her rhythmic breathing, pondering life and thinking of what the future would be like. He so desperately wanted to make love to her. One such night he could suppress it no longer. She said good night and turned away but without uttering a word he reached for her. His hand slithered under her cover and traveled far enough to reach her shoulders.

"Leave me alone Stan, I want to sleep," she whispered.

"Not this time," he whispered back while his hand was gently caressing her, "I love you, Isia and I want you. You've been keeping me waiting a long time."

"I… I… don't want to."

"You don't like it anymore?"

"A woman needs a break after giving birth."

"You had your break long enough. You've been to a doctor for a check-up and told me you were fine."

"Yes, but..."

His kiss stopped her from talking. She was responding now but Stan thought there was something different. He thought she was more habitual or mechanical. But as he entered her he could no longer think in logical and rational terms. His passion took him over as it always did until he brought her to the end some and then he finished inside her.

"It didn't hurt did it?"

"No."

"What is it then?" he asked sensing some tension in her.

"You mustn't do it like that."

"Like what?"

"I don't want more children."

"But, Isia..." he began but she interrupted him.

"It's going to ruin my figure. I see it changed as is."

"You are more beautiful than ever – what are you talking about?"

"I know what I'm talking about. The bones move each time and I will be wider and wider, I don't want that."

"But it is normal, that's how it is."

"Maybe so but it is my body and I want it slim and slender as I always was."

He was not quite prepared for such argument, but he was not also up to a serious conversation. It was late and he needed to get up in the morning and go to work.

"It's normal for people to have children and want them," he said, "don't you want family?"

"I have my family – you and Gabriela. But this is enough for me."

"Well, it's not enough for me. I always thought of having at least two children."

She sat on bed and looked at him.

"At least two?" she repeated, "I can't handle that so you will have to find somebody else."

"You are talking nonsense, Isia. I don't want to find someone else. My world is you."

"Go to sleep, Stan," she ignored what he said, "or you will be late tomorrow."

"I was on time tonight," he smirked.

"Don't even try," she knew the hint when she heard one. She laid down and turned away from him.

"Good night," she said.

„Night-night, doll."

"Don't call me that! I hate it."

When Matilda was born Stan was just as happy as with Gabriela. Matilda seemed to be so different from her sister. While Gabriela was rather slim, Matilda was rather chubby baby.

"Hope she grows out of it," remarked Stan.

"I'm sure she will" Irena seemed sure, "apparently, I was like her."

"I thought she'd look similar to Gabriela but no matter how hard I search for similarities I can't find any."

"I'm not similar to neither my brother nor sister. Runs in the family, I'd say."

"Hmm – I guess you are right," smiled Stan, "just want to make sure she's mine."

"What's that supposed to mean?" she asked with anger in her voice.

"Calm down, Isia" he burst with laughter, "just a joke, that's all."

"A stupid one too."

She was not entertained at all.

She fell silent for a moment and then added.
"Since we are at this sort of thing..."

"Yes, dear?"

"I want you to understand well – no more children, okay?"

"But.." he tried but she interrupted.

"No, Stan. This is it. I don't want to go through this again so you'd better get it into your head and get used to it."

Stan looked at her carefully and saw she meant it. *I guess we will have to be very careful* he thought. As if reading his thoughts she said:

"If need be we will sleep separately. I don't want to take the risk. Keep that in mind."

Stan loved both girls and spent as much time with them as he could. He took them for walks to parks, for rides in trolleys all over the city, took them to playgrounds and to cafes for pastries and bought them presents for any occasion he could think of. Some cousins remarked he was spoiling them but he did not care. He loved his daughters more than anything in the world and nobody would take his joy away. With time Irena was more preoccupied with running the household letting the girls go to the courtyard and play with other children. Every now and then she would stick her head out the window to check on them. They never ventured outside the courtyard even though Matilda was trying to convince her older sister to do so.

*

"C'mon Gabriela, let's just take a peak at the street."

"No," Gabriela never agreed, "there are dangers out there and mum would be upset if we do."

"What dangers?" Matilda was persistent.

"I don't know. Bad people. Somebody can grab you or me and we'd never see our parents again."

"I don't believe it – all people out there are nice."

"How do you know?"

"Because I was there."

"You little idiot," Gabriela was upset, "does mum know?"

"Of course not," smirked Matilda.

"You mustn't do such stupid things," said Gabriela and just to tease her added, "but then again, if somebody grabs you nobody is going to worry. I am the real daughter and I was first. Mum and dad just found you in a heap of trash somewhere."

"No they didn't!"

"Yes they did. Mum told me about all about it."

"It's not true!" Matilda's eyes were getting wet but she was holding the tears back as she did not want to show her sister how she felt.

"Yes it is. You are just a find. Why do you think we don't look alike?"

"No!" Matilda was not crying just yet but her eyes were overflowing with tears.

"That's why you want to go to the street because this is where you came from!"

"You are mean Gabriela and I haven't done anything to you."

"Just a find!"

"I'm going to tell Mum!" Matilda turned around and ran into the house.

"Go ahead," Gabriela shouted after her, "It won't change anything."

Gabriela, amused, followed her with her eyes.

"Sweet little idiot!" she muttered t herself.

Sometimes she did not like her younger sister at all. Everybody seemed to love the golden-haired Matilda. She was always bubbling and smiling to everyone and she seemed to get along with everyone – kids and adults alike.
The moody Gabriela had her likes and dislikes and she thought this was how things and the world around her should be. Being on friendly terms with everyone seemed almost foreign to her. Some children they played with in the courtyard were such plain idiots and had unpleasant parents. Gabriela would rather not have anything to do with them at all. If she did, it was only because there was no other way. As far as she could remember the best times were when there were only three of them – mum, dad and her. All attention was focused on her. But once Matilda arrived Gabriela felt pushed somewhat aside. All attention was given to that chubby little sister of hers.

Gabriela was convinced Matilda was playing into their parent's hands on purpose so sometimes when she for some reason had a not a very good day she'd let Matilda have it. Normally Matilda would not tell on her sister but this time she must have felt really hurt because it did not take long to hear their mother's voice calling her from the window:

"Gabrielaaaaa!"

"Yes?!" she responded.

"I need you here at once please!"

Gabriela had no doubts as to what was that about. The little brat told on her. Without hurry she climbed the stairs to the second floor and walked through the door. Irena appeared in the hallway.

"How could you be so mean?!" Irena was upset.

"I wasn't" denied Gabriela, but she knew it would not work.

"You teased your sister telling her she was found on a heap of rubbish!"

"If she does things to me it's okay but when I say a word..." Gabriela tried to defend herself.

"She doesn't. What had she ever done to you?"

Gabriela could see Matilda down the hallway looking at her.

"She... she..." Gabriela tried to come up with something.

"She doesn't," Irena was angry, "I will not have you act like this. You are sisters and you should love and support each other."

"Mum is right," said Matilda.

"Shut up!" barked Gabriela, "nobody is asking for your opinion!"

"No!" Irena raised her voice, "you don't speak like that. This is exactly what I'm talking about. I want you to apologize to Matilda and give her a hug."

Gabriela did not move an inch.

"Now!" said Irena.

Gabriela was fighting her anger. She hated being ordered to do anything and she felt humiliated.

"Do it!" Irena was getting upset.

Slowly as if with hesitation Gabriela walked towards Matilda, she then embraced her as little as it was possible and murmured something which could be understood as "I'm sorry" if one really hoped this is what it was. She then turned around and walked to her room, closed the door and stood by the window looking outside.

"It's all right now," Irena said to Matilda, "go out and play with your friends."

"You haven't found me in a trash, have you Mum?" asked Matilda.

"Of course not, sweetheart. Go now, you still have some time to play before dinner."

Gabriela saw Matilda emerge from the door and join children in the courtyard. They seemed to be happy to see her. Matilda was telling them something for a while and when she was done the girls exploded with laughter. One of them looked in direction of the window in which Gabriela was standing so she quickly moved away. She didn't want to be seen. *The little creep probably told them the whole thing and they're laughing at me!* Gabriela was upset.

After a while she got bored watching the children and she walked out of her room.

"Don't you want to go outside too?" asked Irena.

"No."

"You are older and you should be wiser," Irena said "and you should not tease her like that. You should not tease her at all, or anybody else for that matter."

"You and dad are always on her side!"

"We are on nobody's side. If either one of you does something that is wrong we deal with it fairly. I'm not saying your sister is better or worse than you, dad and I love you both equally."

Gabriela said nothing, she was just looking at the bookshelf in front of her.

"It's not the first time we have had such a talk. If you do not change, she will end up not liking you when you are adults. Would you want that?"

"I don't care" Gabriela hissed defiantly.

"Only crude people don't care" said Irena, "and you are not one of them. You don't want to be estranged from your sister. It would be very sad."

Gabriela rose up to her feet.

"I guess I will go out" she said.

"All right. Dinner will be as soon as dad comes from work."

Gabriela walked down the staircase and entered the courtyard. A group of children were playing in the far corner and they had not noticed her. She watched them for a moment and then turned left towards the gate leading to the street. She could see the traffic in the opening. Every now and then a pedestrian or two walked by. Sometimes a car would drive by.

"Hello Gabriela," the concierge emerged from the side door and Gabriela nearly jumped in surprised by her voice.

"Oh, hello Mrs. Majewska," she answered.

"Going anywhere special?" the concierge asked.

"No, not really. Just wanted to take a peak. I have nothing to do and don't want to play with that bunch of little kids."

"I see," Mrs. Majewska smiled. "But unless you told your mum, please don't go far."

"My dad will be coming home from work any time now. I thought I'd wait for him here."

"Good girl," Mrs. Majewska smiled again, "I'm sure he'll be happy to see you."

"There he is!" Gabriela spotted him near the gate on the street side and ran towards him.

"Hi daddy!"

He smiled, stopped and put his briefcase down so that he could open both arms and give her a hug.

„What are you doing on the street?" he asked.

„I was just waiting for you at the gate. I wasn't on the street."

"That's good. Let's go home. Mum is probably ready with dinner."

They entered the courtyard but before they ascended to the third floor Gabriela turned around.

"I will call Matilda, she's playing with those kids," she explained and turned towards the courtyard.

"Matilda! Dinner now!"

Matilda duly walked over to her.

"Dad is home and we are having dinner now," Gabriela said to her and as she walked by she added, "the find".

Matilda turned around and gave her angry look.

"All right, all right," smirked Gabriela, "just joking – okay?"

Matilda ran upstairs quickly and slammed the door when Gabriela was just about to enter so she narrowly avoided having her nose smashed.

"Idiot!" she exclaimed reaching for the door handle.

She pushed it open and entered the flat.

"C'mon Gabriela," Irena was walking from the kitchen to the dining room with dinner plates in her hands "we are at the table."

Later in the evening when Gabriela and Matilda were already asleep Irena and Stan were sitting in the kitchen sipping a cherry liquor.

"The situation with Germany is getting worse" said Stan.

"I take it you heard on the radio?"

"Yes," Irena replied.

"The trouble is," Stan explained, "our papers and radio are playing it down while playing our strength up. I don't like it."

"What does that mean?"

"The truth is somewhere in the middle. We are not as strong as they want us to believe and Germans are stronger than they say."

"Where does it lead to?"

"I worry it may end up with Hitler attacking us."

"But what about France and England?"

"These are just agreements, Isia. Just for the show. Look at the reality. Both are separated from us and Germany sits between us and them. Nobody will come here to fight with us and for us. Nobody ever did."

"But surely they could attack them from the other side?"

"It would help if they did and I would like to believe they would, but... I doubt it."

"Good God," Irena said.

"I could be wrong, Isia, but I'm trying to look at this realistically. I don't know politics but I know economy. The good economy is in

Germany. The rest of Europe is weak. France spent a lot of money building up their defenses and they have confidence in them. But mind you – this is just a defensive mechanism. As I understand the way it is built makes it impossible for their army to advance forward of it. As to England – they care first and foremost for their fleet, they always did. This is where their strength is. Their army is perhaps reasonable in size but their equipment may not be as modern as Hitler's. And being on an island it is doubtful they would launch an invasion on Germany in order to help us. At best they can send ships to fire at Germany, maybe sent airplanes to drop bombs. But they will not come here.

Hitler is armed to teeth. Since Germany was in shambles after the Great War he had to build everything from scratch and therefore everything they have is most modern and new."

"It's all so depressing, Stan. Why are you telling me this?"

"Because we must be prepared even if only mentally. Pilsudski was right when he said the war will come. At the time he was predicting it, he said he did not know if it will be war with Germans or Russians. But today it is rather obvious – it will be war with Hitler. Numbers of incidents are on a rise too. Germans who live in Poland are getting bold. Have you heard how a couple of Nazis in Gdansk threw a Polish fellow in front of a train?"

"How cruel! Was he killed?"

"He survived but he had his legs amputated. If this is the kind of thing they will be doing, this war could surpass the Great War in its brutality. I really hope I'm wrong on this one."

Irena was silent. She recalled when, as a little girl during the Great War, she saw bodies of a father and daughter killed by a bomb thrown from a Zeppelin. She was more horrified now than back then.

"What can we do?" she said eventually.

"You and me? – nothing. We can only be ready so that we don't panic when it happens. And panic may occur. It can be destructive so it is important that we keep our heads clear."

He raised his glass.

"I love you Isia, I always did and I always will and I will do all I can to protect you and the girls. Here's to you!"

She clinked her glass with his and they finished their drinks.

"It's getting late," she said, "it's time to go to sleep."

"Don't you mean to bed?" he asked with a smile.

"No. I mean to sleep. Especially after such a gloomy conversation."

5. WAR

Evening of the 31st of August 1939 was one of those days when the setting sun gives the world intensely orange hue and when it gets closer to the horizon, the sky turns red as if there was a great fire raging in the distance.
The air was completely still and the evening was pleasantly warm. But because of the mobilization announced the day before, the usual traffic was subdued and here and there people were standing in groups discussing what many feared an imminent war. The recent demand by Hitler called for Poland to grant Nazi Germany permission to construct extra territorial highway that would connect the city of Gdansk with the mainland Germany. The demand was designed to either humiliate Poland or to use the refusal as an excuse to go to war. It was no longer a secret that Nazi Germany was armed to the teeth and had a large army at the ready.

Poles were proud of their military but were not aware of disparity in technology. Hitler's propaganda machine was censoring heavily everything about their army and equipment. What was sometimes leaking from Germany sounded so fantastic that some deemed it unbelievable. Sometimes irresponsible journalists were playing down the danger by writing about German "cardboard" tanks.

One such group of concerned neighbors was standing at Krucza Street number nine beside a beautiful chestnut tree and Irena was one of them.

"Oh, England and France will come to our aid" somebody said with conviction, "we have treaties with them."

"I hope the nature of their aid will be different than the one given to the Czechs" another voice sarcastically said.

"I heard there are ships from England on way carrying military supplies for us," Irena added.

An old woman, silent till now, sighed and said:
"Germans are bastards. I've seen them in the Great War and it was horrible. But in the Great War our enemies were fighting each other - Prussia, Russia and Austria. Now they are after us with all their fury. God help us!"

"Oh, granny, don't be so pessimistic," a woman in her fifties said in response to her, "it was different then. We have our army now and England and France will come."

"Nonsense!" barked the old woman "the so-called treaties are not worth the paper on which they are written. If Hitler attacks us nobody will move a finger to help us. And Russians will probably help him. And all of those treaties we have are just fancy talk. We had treaties before the partitions too."

"We live in modern times. Hitler maybe mad but Germans are civilized people and nobody really wants to die. They wouldn't dare starting another war."

"Remember what Pilsudski was saying?" somebody interjected, "We live between our mortal enemies and another war is unavoidable. The key is to be ready and guess where and when it begins. When he said that he also estimated another war would come in seven to ten years."

The group went silent. They all knew Pilsudski said those words not long before his death about five years ago.

*

Irena was awakened by an odd sound, a low growl droning from a distance far away. She got up, looked through the window at the empty street and checked the time. It was 4.40 in the morning. She checked on her daughters but they were both asleep so she returned to bed. Stanley was asleep too. He did not wake up when she moved. She was laying in bed quietly listening to that sound which was slowly getting louder. What could it be? She has never heard anything like it. After a while she could hear sound of sirens – first one, then another.

"A fire somewhere in the city," she thought. The sirens were not nearby. They muffled the growling sound and she was drifting away to sleep.

Suddenly there was banging at their door. Somebody was banging and shouting:

"Irena, Stan, everybody! Wake up NOW! Alarm!"

As she was running to the door Stan and her daughters woke up.

"Mum, dad – what's going on?" Gabriela was calling them.

Irena opened the door to find the concierge in her nightgown standing at her threshold.

"Mrs. Szumska!" she said gasping for air, "there is an air raid alarm, I've just heard it on the radio. They say all must go to cellars immediately. It's war!"
"What?"

Stan appeared behind Irena.

"To the cellars, everybody, NOW!" shouted the concierge and went on to warn the other tenants.

Irena and Stan looked at each other with bewildered eyes.

"Get the girls and go," said Stan "I will check the radio."

Irena did as she was told. She heard Stan turning the radio on and in a moment she heard the announcement:

"This is the Radio Warsaw. This morning at 4.45 German Army crossed our borders while German battleship "the Schleswig-Holstein" began firing out our military base on Westerplatte in Gdansk. We announce and air raid warning for Warsaw! All citizens are requested to go to the bomb shelters or cellars and remain there until further notice. Attention, attention, - it's coming!"

The droning sound was near now and as Irena, Stan and their daughters were racing down the staircase to the cellar they could hear an odd whistling sound which was clearly audible.

Suddenly there was an enormous explosion. Instantly the air was full of dust and smell of cordite which was stinging their eyes. Gabriela began screaming uncontrollably but Irena just dragged her and Matilda the remaining few steps and they were in the cellar, which was already full of people.

"Was it a bomb?" somebody asked.

"Must've been" replied Stan.

"We've been hit? Our building is hit?"

"I doubt it, but it was close I think. If it had hit us we wouldn't be talking."

Next one was further away and the third even further. They were sitting in the cellar in silence. Some people were sobbing and somebody was reciting "Our Father".
The air was thick with dust but they were afraid to open the door.

"Mummy, can I have my doll please?" asked Matilda.

"Shut up you idiot!" screamed Gabriela, "you want to get us killed?!"

"Be quiet, girls" Stan's voice was calm, "try to get comfortable and sleep, it's still early."

"They will kill us all here!" Shrieked Gabriela

"Nobody will kill us," Stan said. "Be quiet. Other people want to sleep or pray."

Irena remained silent. She was imagining the destruction and people buried under demolished buildings. She had that faint memory from the Great War when a Zeppelin dropped a bomb on the bridge in Warsaw which killed the father and his daughter. She was taken there by her mother. There were many people who wanted to see what happened. The railing on the bridge was broken and twisted, but not much really. But next to it there was a body of a man and a child lying on the pavement both covered with a white sheet. There were red stains on the sheet where their heads were. It was the first time she had seen dead people and she had not been able to get this sight out of her mind for years. Eventually, she had forgotten about it but now it all came vividly right back to her. If that was some twenty years ago, it was only going to be worse now. No doubt the bombs were improved in those twenty years and they were bigger as well. Fear was creeping up upon her and threatening to paralyze her, but she fought it off. She had her family to take care of and no bomb would stop her. But her heart was bleeding as she knew each bomb was hitting her beloved Warsaw killing her fellow Varsovians and demolishing their homes and lives.
By seven or eight in the morning somebody decided to open the door. Some went to turn the radios on for news while others went to their flats to get dressed and then emerged onto the street. Their building was untouched but a block away half of the building was in ruin as if gigantic fist had pounded its roof so that the top floor had collapsed. On the street side there were piles of broken bricks and splintered tiles and wooden beams. Rescue crews and volunteers were working searching for victims buried under the rubble. Irena wanted to take her daughters out to take a closer look but Gabriela gave her wild glance and withdrew to her room.

"I don't want to go and don't want to see anything!" she said, "you can go with Matilda. I stay here."

Her face was stern and voice was defiant.
Irena said nothing to her, she took Matilda by the hand and approached the bombed building.

It looked much worse up close. The pile that used to be two floors was a mixture of bricks, pieces of wood and some household items. Here and there one could see what remained of a wall with a still visible paint or pieces of wall paper on it. Pieces of clothing were thrown here and there, children's toys and kitchen utensils all scattered around. One of the rescue men working on top of the pile called another, then bent down and picked something that looked like a ball and handed it to him. Irena was quick enough and close enough to see it was a human's head. She felt cramp in her throat.

"C'mon Matilda, let's go back home," she said and they walked away. Tears were running down Irena's cheeks.

News from the radio was gloomy.
Poland was attacked along her entire border with Germany. The trouble was that the borderline was oddly shaped, like a bulge with its belly towards Germany and so Poland's territory was exposed as if to a giant jaw and she was attacked from North, West and South. While there were reports of Polish Army actually advancing against the enemy these incidents were rather localized. Most of the frontline was being pushed by the relentless onslaught.

Early in the afternoon there was another air raid alarm and again they all went to the cellar, this time only Irena with her daughters as Stan went to work as usual and Irena was worrying about him. Nobody knew how the war would impact their daily routines and their very existence but generally the people were rather stoic. Through the last 170 years Poles were used to wars big and small but in the end they survived. For the moment it seemed like yet another war.

After initial shock people were trying to continue as before. Later on day there was yet another alarm and they could hear explosions in a distance and after that they could see smoke from burning buildings overhead. The radio was reporting on a number of civilians killed in the raids and every next report was bringing more bad news. But despite it all, the Varsovians seemed defiant and optimistic. People hoped that their army would manage to defeat the enemy and defend their country. Wounded and bleeding, the capital of Poland was standing firm.

When an announcement came about England and France declaring war on Germany, crowds of people gathered in front of British and French Embassies cheering them both in an influx of optimism. They felt Poland was no longer alone. The two allies would no doubt hit the aggressor hard from the other side and force him to retreat. But they waited and waited and no such attack came. Bombings however continued relentlessly every day.

The following days were bringing more air raids resulting in more fires and destruction. During the day people who were not hiding in cellars sometimes managed to get a glimpse of the enemy planes.

The absence of Polish Air force was depressing. Polish planes were supposedly seen on the outskirts of the city in small numbers trying in vain to prevent the formations of bombers from reaching Warsaw. This news spread from person to person and with time more and more news traveled that way, some true and some false.

There was a rumor that on the 17th of September Poland was attacked along her Eastern border by the Soviet Union. This turned out to be true as the radio confirmed it. So now Poland was completely surrounded and was fighting her mortal enemies on both sides along her entire borders. Hope and optimism were slipping away. Everybody knew the history. With the exception of Polish communists, the population was well aware what can be expected from Russians regardless on their current political system. Soviet Union or Tsarist Russia – it made no difference to the Poles. Practically the same applied to the Germans. It did not matter who was in charge or what political system it was. For centuries the Germans always wanted to expand east and the Russians always gravitated west to project their image and to display their sophistication and culture to Western Europe. In either case Poland was always in their respective ways. Countless wars were fought and immeasurable number of lives lost. It seemed that fate had placed Poland once again in the path of yet another onslaught by both of her mortal enemies and the memory of partitioned Poland was looming on the horizon once again.

Warsaw capitulated on the 28th of September and the Polish Radio made its final broadcast on the 30th. The last battle of Polish Army against Germans took place a few days later on the 5th of October. Ironically, on the very same day Adolf Hitler watched his troops in the victory parade in Warsaw which took place in the beautiful Aleje Ujazdowskie, Irena's favorite street for Sunday walks.

The Polish government went into exile and became known as the Immigration Government. Poland was effectively partitioned for the fourth time in her history, this time between Hitler's Germany and Stalin's Soviet Union, and once again disappeared from the map of Europe.
Both invaders proceeded to dismantle Polish nationality and culture but this time with unsurpassed brutality. In Russian parts once again millions of Poles were rounded up and sent to Siberia. Military personnel was arrested. Officers were separated from lower ranked soldiers and placed in several camps near villages of Katyn, Kozielsk and Ostaszkow. Population left alone was told they were now citizens and subjects of the Soviet Union.

The part of Poland overrun by Germany was subdivided. The westernmost part was annexed to the German Reich, while the rest, including Warsaw was kept separate and called General Governorate and the Nazis had a special plans for it. In short - Poles were to be used to complete exhaustion and consequently extermination and replaced by German settlers. The administration was German of course. Poles could be hunted, arrested, thrown to jail, sent to labor or concentration camps or killed on the spot for any reason or for no reason at all. Stage for a mortal struggle was set.

*

Irena was walking down the staircase with Matilda and Gabriela and was just about to emerge to the street when a German in uniform blocked her way.

"Halt!" he barked a command that by now was well known by Poles.

Irena stopped.

"Papiere!" he demanded.

She slowly reached to her small purse and produced her kennkarte, an identity document issued by German administration to all Poles.

He examined it, compared her photo with her face which was now much thinner, he then looked down at the two girls who were waiting quietly staring back at him.

"Alles in ordnung," he said and moved half a step out of her way, "Sie konnen weiter gehen."

"Danke," responded Irena.

"Sprechen Sie Deutsch?" he inquired.

"Nur ein bisschen."

"Woher?"

"Ich habe in der Schule gelernt."

To her surprise he smiled.

"Sehr gut," he said and reached into his shoulder bag. He produced a loaf of bread and extended his hand to her.

"Take it please" he said, this time in Polish.

Irena hesitated.

"You don't recognize me, do you?" he asked.

"I'm afraid not, sorry."

Irena would much prefer to go rather than be seen in conversation with a German soldier.

"I'm Frank Weiser," he said, "I was working in the Fiat dealership with you. I was in the stockroom where the spare parts were kept."

Irena looked at him and suddenly she remembered. She automatically smiled back at him.

"Oh, yes - Frank. I remember of course, but…"

He was still friendly but his tone hardened.

"I am with Wehrmacht now. I was drafted and I had to obey, you understand."

Irena nodded.

He lowered his voice.

"At least I'm not in the SS."

"I see."

She was not sure how to respond.

"A bit of advice if I may," he continued, "next time you don't have to acknowledge knowing me if there are people around. I know it would be uncomfortable for you. And one more thing – we know somebody that lives in this building is wanted by our authorities. Do you know anything about it?"

"No."

Her answer was quick and firm.

He smiled again.

"Of course - I understand. It would be better for that person to disappear. You should go now. We have been talking too long and somebody may notice."

"Thank you, Frank," she said and walked away holding her daughters by their hands.

"Who was that man, Mummy?" inquired Matilda.

"Somebody I knew long time ago," answered Irena.

"He was a German. He's going to come at night and kill us all!" said Gabriela.

"Be quiet, Gabriela. You shouldn't be saying things like that," Irena scolded her.

But in truth, she shared at least some of such fears. She kept wondering who in their building was the one they were interested in, but could not figure it out.
The only logical person would be the husband of the lady who lived on top floor as he was an officer in the Army. He went to fight in the war and so far has not returned and his wife had no word of his whereabouts. She feared the worst, but it was also possible he was taken as a prisoner of war.

Life in the occupied Warsaw was miserable to say the least. The Germans introduced a food rationing system which not only was allowing a person only a minute portion, it was frequently impossible to buy it anyway. Severe food shortages were a fact of life and the black market was booming. The population was becoming malnourished, which was leading to diseases and higher mortality rates. The occupants introduced severe punishments for black market activities and typically it was the same as for many other offences – death. Streets were patrolled by military units and secret police was terrorizing the population. They enlisted "volksdeutsches" to infiltrate Polish society and to spy on them. A "Volksdeutch" was a person who signed an affidavit stating he or she was of German origin or descent. Regretfully there were opportunists who did so as they indeed had some German ancestry in them. Germans were not recognizing them as pure Germans but merely as of Germanic origin which gave them better treatment. They would not be arrested for any reason but they were required to work for the occupant in variety of ways including spying on Poles in search of members of the growing underground resistance groups. Being native Polish speakers "volksdeutches" were extremely dangerous and when exposed they were usually killed by the resistance. While initially the war was being more or less run according to the Geneva conventions, life under the occupation after the war was something else. Occupant could do anything – arrest people for any reason, throw them in jails and mercilessly torture them. They could and did shoot people on the streets. They organized mass executions as a punishment for actions carried out by the resistance, especially so when resistance assassinated German officers or soldiers.

They placed contingents of farm products on farmers and collected due volumes with an iron fist. Any farmer that would be found cheating would be shot, sometimes along with his entire family. Fear and terror were rampant. Among many elements of terror in Warsaw possibly the most feared were "łapanki". They were actions by Germans who suddenly would deploy two trucks full of soldiers to seal off section of a street. Anyone caught between them was checked for documents and more often then not arrested. Sometimes, depending on what Germans were up to they would just not bother with documents but take all rounded up pedestrians for a mass execution. "Łapanki" were totally random and could take place any time at any street. But as much as the occupant tried to stamp Poles out, they responded with defiance and determination. The resistance was organized and did its best to protect citizens and took revenge when and where it could. Secret schools and universities were set up. Underground press was publishing bulletins and other publications based on what the editors managed to pick up from the scarce radios. Radios were confiscated by Germans and anyone caught with one would be send to concentration camp or shot. But despite it all Varsovians kept their sense of humor. And so, slogans appeared on city streets saying things like "We have Hitler deep in our ass" or "Poland will prevail". Boy scouts risk their lives by tearing

Nazi flags from lamp posts or buildings, or removing German street names signs and thus uncovering original Polish ones. But all in all as the time was going by the situation was only getting worse. As the occupant was getting more brutal and murderous, people of Warsaw were more determined than ever.

On personal level war wiped out passion from Irena's life. Her energy was focused on caring for her family. Love was taken for granted and daily worries occupied all her thoughts and pushed any notions of intimacy far away. Protecting and preserving one's family became for many Poles the core of their existence.

Lying in bed next to Stan in those days Irena was thinking of the next day and how to make sure they all will be all right going to sleep next day. It was similar for Stan although his passion for Irena was ever present war or not. Late at night knowing that both daughters were sound asleep he'd try to reach out to her but her response was not what he was looking for and he could see it was as if intimacy for her was just switched off.

Some time in 1940 Stan returned from work with worried look on his face.

"What's the matter, Stan?"

Irena was quick to spot he was not in his typical cheerful mood.

"The work is drying out. We still service some businesses like repair garages and some retail shops but we are loosing many customers as they are closing down. I'm good at what I do but the future does not look good. This morning they let John go. Not that he was not working hard or making mistakes. The work is drying out and he was the most recent addition so he was the first to go."

"Are you in jeopardy?"

"Not for now because I have seniority but I do not know how long this will last. On the other hand, or perhaps I should say another part of bad news is there is talk about our company to be taken over by

Germans."

"My, God!" exclaimed Irena.

"Well," Stan said calmly "this could go two ways. They could throw us all out and that would be it for me, or they could keep us as is. In such case we probably would have a not bad proof of employment in case I was ever stopped for document control anywhere or fell in łapanka. As is it just says employed by the company so and so. If it is to be owned by them the same document would be saying I work for the bloody Reich. Nothing to be proud of, of course but in practical sense for daily life and security it would be somewhat better."

"I could always pick up sewing you know," Irena was worried but not disturbed, "there is a considerable demand for repairs of all sorts. People have no means to buy new clothes even if they can be found. Everybody I know is fixing things rather than shopping for new ones."

"No, Isia. You take care of the house and the girls. But I will be carefully looking for another job or otherwise what else could I do. I used to do carpentry long time ago and this, possibly similar to sewing is in some demand because people need repairs for the same reasons."

"How long it will last?"

"The job?"

"No, I mean the war."

"Nobody knows, sweetheart. Some of the things people whisper about sound unbelievable. Western Europe as such is overrun by Hitler and England is in shambles after Dunkirk. What Germans were trumpeting about the great victory is not far from reality. Hitler will probably make his move on England now or maybe on his Russian friends. But whether he does one or the other or both we are still in the middle of it in his clutches and we can't expect help from anyone because there isn't anyone."

"I worry so much about the future..."

"You are not alone. We are sub-humans to those bastards and as far as I gather they intend to annihilate us, to wipe us from the face of the earth but they are not going just to kill us suddenly. They want to use us and whatever resources we have left and exploit us to extinction. What they do to us is nothing comparing to what they do to Jews. There are rumors circulating they send them to camps where they kill them and burn their bodies in specially designed furnaces. It seems they industrialized mass murder."

"Is it true?"

"I believe so, I wouldn't put it past them."

"God almighty, they are worse than animals."

"They are modern day barbarians."

"What we can do then?"

"Resist and fight."

"That's so dangerous."

"Yes but since they plan to get rid of us anyway, there isn't much difference really. We can wait for them to murder us or we can pick our fight and if death comes, so be it."
"I've never thought the world would come to this."

"Neither did I."

Irena sighed and began getting their evening meal ready. Matilda and Gabriela were playing in the other room.
After dinner Stan got up and said to Irena:

"I need to go and meet someone."

"Now?! What about the curfew?"

"I'll be back before that, don't worry," Stan put on his coat and hat and was gone.

Polish Home Army was an underground resistance organization which was a direct replacement to what was the Polish Army before the war. Those who avoided the POW camps at the end of September 1939 joined the Home Army to fight the enemy in every possible way. Even those who were not in military before the war could join and even make progress in ranks due to system of education and training. The Home Army had various branches and specialties and more personnel was always welcomed and needed.

Stan joined as soon as he found out about its existence and was a lower rank officer in administration. He was responsible for the city block around the place where he lived. Among his duties was to be acquainted with people who lived there, be on guard when somebody new would move in, be on a lookout for any German activity in the area and otherwise provide help and assistance to people in need. He was also responsible for the maintenance and state of the building. All of those things while seemingly not that important were part of a bigger plan. Some day the armed fight was going to begin and then it all was going to be very useful to carry out urban warfare.
Irena knew nothing of his involvement with the Home Army.

Stan arrived at the agreed address and knocked on the door. It opened just a bit and somebody glanced at him to ascertain if he was alone or not.

"Yes?"

"Eagle," said Stan.

"Osprey," was the answer and the door opened.

Stan walked in.

"Hello Cloud," the man in the hallway greeted him, "I'm Kazek."

Using aliases was a commonplace and elementary precaution. Only pre-war friends and acquaintances knew each other real names. The reason for this was very simple – not knowing real names one could not divulge them even under torture. Many lives were saved that way.

"Sit down, please," he motioned to the sofa and Stan sat down.

"What you reported about your wife talking to that German soldier is worrying because if it was true they may be onto you. I did all I could to check it out and our own intelligence is sure you were never compromised in any way. Normally, at the slightest possibility of danger we'd recommend that personnel moves out immediately but in this case I decided to leave it entirely up to you. You keep low profile as is, your papers are good and you have a proven job and its history. If you move it will take us a long time to work out replacement in your area. Obviously I'd prefer that you stay but the decision is yours."

Stan pulled out a cigarette case and offered it to Kazek.

There was a moment of silence when they lit their cigarettes and got them going. Then Stan said:

"I don't want to go anywhere. I reported this to you because it is my responsibility and I would obey orders but since you give me a free hand I choose to stay. It's my home and I think it was just a bluff on his part. And besides, he is real, meaning my wife does remember him. He was all right then."

"I don't believe in "good" Germans," Kazek was clearly skeptical, "but some people are not completely rotten and some didn't really embraced Nazism even if they were forced to military. They were probably told what was going to happen to them if they'd refuse."

"I can't be afraid of everything," Stan added, "If I do so I won't be sane anymore."

"All right, then," smiled Kazek, "this is settled now."

"Are there any new orders?" inquired Stan.

"Not for now."

"What about news?"

"Our pilots are heroes in England. Luftwaffe is carrying out mass bombings, they want to bomb the British to submission but all reports are saying the defenders are shooting them down in great numbers and our pilots play no small role. They certainly have their chance to get even after September 1939. Back then they had only the outdated PZL-11s to fight with, now in England they fly modern planes called Hurricanes and Spitfires. They are supposedly better than whatever Germans have."

"That's good. Let the bastards get their own medicine," Stan was pleased.

"You'd better go now Cloud, or you miss the curfew."

"Right. Thank you, Kazek. Till the next time."

"Best of luck."

The men exchanged handshake and Stan left. He had only half an hour left but he needed only fifteen minutes walk. The curfew was no empty threat. Germans frequently were shooting people at sight during the forbidden hours.

*

For quite a while now Irena was being torn apart by wanting to participate in the underground resistance. On one hand she wanted to sign up to the Home Army, on the other she had two very young daughters. By doing any work for the resistance she'd increase the risk of something happening to her and then what would happen to both girls if she was gone? But doing nothing made her almost constantly disturbed and angry. Her beloved city was being raped by the vicious occupant, its inhabitants were being hunted and murdered and Irena felt it was wrong just watching the deadly struggle from the sideline. She thought she doing something about it.

She was not alone with such thoughts. The Home Army had women soldiers too. They were assistants to high ranking officers, couriers transporting messages between underground cells, they were lookouts and sometimes, what was possibly the most risky, they transported new bulletins from underground printers to distribution points. Getting caught with such material would land the courier in the feared cellars of Gestapo in Aleja Szucha. Couriers were tortured to obtain information about locations of printers and distribution points. Many were sent to prison hospital to get better after beatings and returned to Gestapo for further interrogations and torture. Some died in the process, some ended up either executed or sent to concentration camps. Once the Gestapo thugs decided they got information they wanted or realized they were not going to get anything at all, the fate of prisoner was sealed. Very few people survived such ordeal and those who did had assistance from the outside in form of highly risky, prearranged escapes from the prison hospital or sometimes as a result of bribing some official. That was not easy to achieve as it was very difficult to find access to the right one.

Irena, like all Varsovians was well aware of it all. By now in the occupied Warsaw, as odd as it sounds, the population got used to cruelty and terror, because it became fact of life. It was no longer that shocking as when it first began, it was now looming above them day and night. In her considerations Irena sometimes thought that hers or Stan's family would take care of their daughters if something bad happened to both of them. That was natural and rational thinking and every parent would have such thoughts. But she was not sure about her right to intentionally increasing risks to herself as a mother. She even went to church to discuss this with a priest. She could consult her uncle who was a bishop but she preferred not to. She spoke to a vicar in the St. Alexander Church at the Thee Crosses Plaza. The conversation had not helped her much. The priest quite wisely did not give her straight answer. Thus Irena kept pondering whether one's obligation to the motherland was greater than to one's family and children or not.

Late in summer she made her mind up and with help of her childhood friend she signed up. Her job was going to be to listen to radio stations broadcasting from England and USA and prepare reports on news from the war and pass them onto editors of the underground press.

Level of danger was real as Germans confiscated radios and owning a radio set was illegal and like many other things punishable by death. It was however less risky to operate as she would have to do it deep at night so her exposure to street check points or random controls was none. She'd be in danger only if Germans would be specifically searching her flat. But to make it safer, Stan agreed to construct a hidden compartment in their closet. In the end he built a very clever contraption which when folded away made the radio completely disappear and only if somebody decided to dismantle the entire closet the radio would be found.

Her duties were to listen to BBC and Voice of American and write synopsis of the most current news. Such prepared material was going to be delivered to editors of the underground bulletins. It would be either picked up from Irena by a courier or she had an option of delivering it herself. From this point forward she immersed herself in her new duties and was happy leading a double life so to speak. She was a perfect and typical housewife during the day and the conspirator at night. The advantage was that her listening activities were not colliding with daytime at all. The hardest part was not to share the news with anyone at all. During training it was explained and stressed to her she was not allowed to say anything to anyone including her own family as it could pose a mortal danger to her.

The system worked well and she was particularly pleased when sometimes she heard people whispering about the news they've just read in some bulletin and she knew it was result of her work a night or two earlier.

One day in the Fall of 1943 Irena was coming home with her

daughters after visiting the nearby park when an odd poster caught her eye. The title said "Announcement" and went on saying that in case of any attack on German personnel certain number of hostages will be executed. The hostages were listed by name below the text. This was something new and horrifying. It seemed the occupant devised yet another instrument of terror. To find out how horrifying it really was Warsaw did not have to wait long. In a matter of days Germans announced the hostages named in the announcement were publicly executed with machine guns.

In just one month, October 1943, there were four such incidents. Varsovians were taken by the new kind of fear. Nobody could figure out any pattern in this. The hostages seemed to be chosen at random. After some time the Home Army discovered these were actions of the newly appointed leader of the SS and Police, Frank Kutschera.

His assassination and execution was suggested by the Home Army and Polish Government in Exile approved it. It was carefully planned and successfully carried out by a combat-sabotage team of 12 people but Warsaw paid high price. Germans publically executed 300 people.
But - Kutschera's successor did not continue his policies so it can be assumed the assassination had worked. On similar principles many other lower ranked Nazis were dealt with throughout Poland and while Germans had an obvious upper hand the fear of personal safety crept in to many. Germans in Warsaw felt as if they were living in the front line.

Some time in Spring Stan was late from work and Irena began to worry. Half an hour turned to hour, then two and finally she heard his footsteps approaching the door. She opened the door and he walked in, somewhat pale and silent. Matilda and Gabriela run to greet him as they were uneasy about him being so late or perhaps they felt their mum's anxiety. He gave them hugs and then embraced Irena and held her tight for a few minutes without uttering a word. He then kissed her face several times.

"What happened?" she asked softly.
"I was in łapanka" he said "I was walking on Piekna Street when

suddenly ahead of me and behind me two military trucks emerged from neighboring streets and soldiers spilled from them. It all happened with a lightning speed and I was trapped along with at least fifty others. We could only hear the doors to buildings and shops being slammed and locked One or perhaps two people managed to squeeze somewhere and thus disappear from the street. The soldiers spread out and marched on us until they herded us all against the wall. I thought they'd start shooting any second but after a while some officers appeared and they began documents check. They were asking questions and one by one they loaded people to one of the trucks. But when it came to me the German studied my kennkarte carefully and noticed the stamp and signature which was stating I was employed by a German agency. He looked at me and asked where I lived and about the address of my office and how long I worked there. I gave him the address and told him I worked there since 1933. He asked me where I was going just now and I said I was on my way home from work. He then told me I was free to go. I don't know where they took all of the others. When I looked back from some distance the trucks were driving away and the street was empty."

"Oh, Stan," Irena had tears in her eyes.

"It was close," he said "I was so scared, Isia. I thought I'll never see you and the girls again."

He then walked to a cabinet in the living room, took out a bottle of vodka, poured himself a glass full and gulped it in one shot. His nerves were so tight he felt as if it was plain water.

*

On the 1st of August 1944 Irena was on her way home with both daughters after trying to shop for food. She was pleased because she managed to buy a few potatoes at a reasonable price. She was not far from her house when she suddenly heard gunshots, some closer, some from a distance and other sounds as well sounding like small detonations. She tightened her grip on her daughters' hands and walked faster.

"What's that, Mum?" asked Matilda.

"Bombs!" screeched Gabriela "if we don't go to the cellar we are going to get killed!"

"Be quiet, Gabriela," snapped Irena, "these are not bombs, there are no planes above. These are just gun shots. Keep going."

Unexpectedly a group of ten or so young men emerged from the nearest building. They all had white and red armbands with letters AK written on them with thick paint. AK stood for Armia Krajowa which meant Home Army, the resistance.

At the same time somebody in the window on the third floor stuck his hand out and fixed Polish flag to the window sill and now the flag was flying above the street.

Irena stopped dead in her tracks. She had not seen Polish flag flying freely in five years.

"What is it, fellows?" she asked the AK men.

One of them smiled in return.

"It's the Uprising, Madam. We fight the bastards openly. Please return to you home with your daughters as quickly as you can, it's impossible to say how it will progress, it had just begun. It is highly recommended that civilians stay indoors."

Irena realized the street was nearly empty now.

"Good luck and be safe boys," she shouted after them.

When she entered the gate to her house there was a small group of people standing there chatting and commenting on what was happening. Among them, to her surprise, was Stan.

"What are you doing here?" she asked, "how come you are not at work?"

"It's the Uprising, Isia," he smiled "my duties are here."

"What duties?" she was surprised.

"I'm the local administration for the entire block. We are preparing whatever we can to dress wounds, to fight fire and otherwise be vigilant."

"You are…" she stumbled "you are…"

"I joined long time ago but wasn't allowed tell you. There was no need anyway. I am with administrative services, it's not a combat position."

Irena relaxed a bit.

"What are we supposed to do?"
"Stay home, keep away from windows and make sure the girls do the same. Gather water in the bathtub and review our food supplies. Gather anything that we have for the first aid as it may be needed. I will stay here at the gate as there may be orders coming through via runners."

"I'm sure we'll win," she smiled with enthusiasm, "four years of slavery and so many dead is more than enough. With Russians on the other side of the river Germans have no chance, they are doomed."

Stan smiled back at her.

"Certainly hope so. This is a unique and only one chance for us. The Home Army liberates the capital to show Russians and rest of the world we are capable of freeing ourselves. The only right way to liberate Warsaw is with our own hands, certainly not by Stalin and his army. Once the city is free of Germans they can come. And go."

They looked deep into each other eyes because this was not all so simple and they both knew it. It was well known that an uprising was attempted in Wilno in order to liberate the city before the Red Army

arrived. The plan succeeded and despite being outgunned by
Germans the Home Army achieved its goal. Then the first line of the
Red Army arrived and for a brief moment there was cooperation -
there were units composed of the Red Army and the Home Army
working together patrolling the streets. But it did not last long. When
the units of the infamous NKVD arrived, they began rounding up
and hunting for soldiers of the Home Army. It resulted in many
being shot, many arrested and taken to temporary camps before they
were sent away to Siberia - altogether some 6 to 7 thousands. The
Home Army Command in Warsaw was well aware of this.
Stalin and the Soviet Union were not a friend and not an ally to the
Home Army. But still, the Soviet propaganda was calling for all Poles
to raise and fight fascism. It was practically threatening that not doing
so was a betrayal and cowardice. The Home Army had no choice
really. If they would not fight, Russians would accuse them of not
being sincere in the fight against Hitler. If they fought he'd not help
them at all as the Home Army represented the pre-war Poland, the
same Poland that thwarted Soviet's attack on Poland in 1920.

The first days of uprising brought a relief and population was happy.
They were no longer hunted by Germans, Poland was back and
Polish flags were everywhere. Despite real and obvious dangers and
difficulties street markets were functioning and cheerful sellers and
buyers were haggling prices and trading their stories. Boy Scouts
organized and operated Polish Postal services and citizens could send
letters and cards within the city.

But the infatuation did not last long.

Initially Germans thought the uprising in the city was merely a
prelude to the Red Army's crossing the Vistula river and launching an
attack to liberate Warsaw. When they realized it was not the case they
regrouped. Hitler, when informed of the uprising in Warsaw flew into
rage and gave personal and very specific order to retake Warsaw and
punish the stubborn city by erasing it to the ground. The war was
now even more bitter than before. Once again Warsaw was being
bombed by the hated Stuka dive bombers. The Russian Red Army
sitting on the other side of the Vistula River did nothing at all.
Germany heavy artillery was brought in, including a railroad based

enormous gun. A rocket powered bombs were deployed which were being launched in clusters. They were not accurate but their results were deadly and destruction was enormous. Despite it all the resistance was fierce.

Krucza Street number nine survived quite a long time undamaged and for a while a local command post was operating from one of the flats, later on it was moved to another location. More and more wounded soldiers were being brought in to be initially treated before being taken to hospitals. Warsaw was fighting a very uneven fight and the Red Army on the other side of the Vistula had not moved and inch, had not sent any help at all.

Slowly the area controlled by the Home Army was shrinking and life was getting more dangerous day by day. To go from place to place one had to go from building to building through the holes made for this purpose in the external walls. Streets were getting too dangerous as Germans deployed sharpshooters on roofs of the buildings. They were also deploying tanks and the Home Army had nothing to combat them with, except bottles filled with gasoline. A bottle was filled to capacity, corked and a piece of rug was tided to its neck. Before throwing it one had to light the rug first. While primitive as a weapon it was feared by the enemy as escape from a burning tank was difficult to say the least. Death was everywhere and it was no longer possible to burry the dead in cemeteries, so they were buried on sidewalks and in courtyards. Food was scarce and so was water. From the western direction a district of Warsaw called Wola was being stormed by particularly brutal unit of SS composed of criminals, lead by a sadistic officer Oskar Dirlewanger. His unit massacred civilian population building by building, men were shot on sight, women were being raped, tortured and killed.

One day a group of people was standing chatting in the courtyard of Krucza number nine. Among them was Stan's brother who was the Home Army soldier and stopped by in a rare moment to visit his brother. Stan was walking down the staircase to join him when an artillery shell landed and exploded in the courtyard. Stan was thrown off his feet back into the staircase but when he finally emerged to the courtyard the scene was terrible. Blood and body parts were everywhere, even hanging from the tree. Stan spotted his brother on the ground by the wall. He was alive but his abdomen was ripped open by a piece of shrapnel. He was still conscious, gasping for air. Stan wiped blood from his face.

"Stan…. Stan…" he managed to utter "tell Mum, I…."

He was dead.

Irena stuck her head out of the kitchen window, screaming:

"Staaaaan!, Staaan!"

Stan looked up and shouted back.

"I'm here, I'm fine! Go away from the window, you idiot! Why are you not in the cellar?!"

She was staring in horror at her husband clutching his brother in his arms. Tears were running down her cheeks.

Another shell landed nearby and its shockwave raised a cloud of dust but mercifully there were no debris or shrapnel falling in the courtyard. She could only hear them falling on the other side and on other buildings. She withdrew, grabbed both daughters and run to the cellar. All her neighbors were already there. Few hours later it was quiet again and they all returned to their flats, some went to the courtyard to help remove the carnage and bury the dead.

Next morning there was a knock at Irena's door. She opened it and saw her neighbor Fred whom she knew and liked. She had not seen him for a while as he was with his unit fighting somewhere.

"Oh, good morning Fred!" she greeted him "come in please. Tea?"

"No, thank you Mrs. Szumska but I just wondered if you perhaps have a piece of a cable. I searched everywhere to no avail."

"What do you need it for?"

He smiled.
"It's a secret but I'll tell you – I'm trying to build a flying bomb!"

Irena looked at him.

"A flying bomb? Why? How?"

"I am stationed at the barricade at Hoża Street. The barricade is good and holds well but they are pressing their attacks and we expect they will bring a tank anytime because we deny them chance to get close. I know I can enter one of the buildings forward of the barricade. The building is in decent shape. I will go to the upper floor and fling my bomb at the tank. I don't want to use the gasoline bottle because it is not hundred percent sure. I need something that will definitely work. I will take three or four grenades, tie them together, activate one and throw it at the tank. I'll get those bastards."

"But Fred," Irena was overwhelmed "this sounds so dangerous. Besides, don't you need to have this approved by your commander?"

He smiled again.

"Well, yes, maybe I should, but what he's going to tell me? We are getting short on the little ammunition we have and we have no anti-tank weapon of any kind. If I don't stop the tank our barricade will be lost. If I destroy the tank they will have to quit because another tank will not be able to go around the destroyed one."

Irena was searching for a cable as he was speaking to her. She found one and handed it over to him.

"Will this do?" she asked "I'm afraid that's all I've got."

"It's great, exactly what I need, thank you, Mrs. Szumska," he was ready to leave.

"Be careful Fred, may God be with you. Please watch yourself and come back to tell me how it went."

"No worries, I know I can sneak into position without Germans noticing me. In fact I tried it already. I was there once to see if it is feasible. I'll be back to tell you all about it."

"When?"

"I don't know when they will bring the tank but as I said, I think very soon. We heard sound of a tank engine in the neighborhood so we know it's near, they just proceed with caution."

"Best of luck, Fred. Be safe."

"Thanks again!" he smiled and was gone.

The day was relatively quiet and about noontime she walked downstairs to have a word with the concierge. She was talking to her when an unknown man walked through the gate.

"Good afternoon, excuse me ladies, can you please point me to the Home Army office here?"

Irena and concierge exchanged quick looks.

"There are no offices here," said the concierge.

"But I was sent from the Old Town with an important message to the commander here," he insisted.

"I told you," concierge was getting impatient, "there are no offices here of any kind."

"No need to be upset lady," he was persistent, "you don't want to be guilty of sabotage do you? Because this is how it will be looked at by my superiors when I report you!"

Irena knew the commander and a couple of soldiers were resting in the flat on the ground level and so did the concierge but there was something about the man neither of them liked.

Irena interrupted with an ever so slight wink of one eye at the concierge saying:

"Oh my God! I think I left a pot of soup on the kitchen stove, I have to run to check and be right back."

As she walked towards the Home Army office to warn them she could hear the stranger saying to the concierge:

"Well, thank you. It must have been a mix up somewhere. I didn't mean to upset you. You know how it is these days. Good-bye."

Iren budged into the small room.

"An odd man was insisting he needs to see you. The concierge told him off."

"When?" asked the commander.

"Just now, he'd just left."

Three men jumped to their feet and run from the room and to the street. In few minutes they were back with the man. They brought him to the commander and one of them handed documents found on the man – a volksdeutch card along with a handgun and two grenades.

"Just as I thought," he said half to Irena half to himself.

He gave the men an icy look.

"Your masters' days in Berlin are numbered and traitors like you will not change that. You are disgrace to the humankind."

And turning to Irena he added.

"Please go back to your flat and stay there, thank you."

Irena did as she was told but she also picked through the window.
The Home Army men walked the traitor to the street side, then they
entered a building on the other side which was in ruins since
September. They disappeared from view and in a moment she heard
a gunshot.

Later on day medical services brought in two wounded men to the
court yard. One was a civilian and the other was a Boy Scout. Both
had bullet injuries but they were not life threatening. They were
treated and let go.

Few days later another quiet day came. The sounds of fighting were
always in the air but not near this time and they all had a break as
there were no wounded or dead brought in.

As they were chatting in the courtyard somebody said:

"Quiet, everybody. I hear sound of an airplane."

They waited for a second or two and Stan commanded:

"Everybody to the cellar! Air raid!"

People scurried to fetch their families while Stan was waiting to make
sure everybody was safe. He was listening to the sound and looking
up the sky. It occurred to him the sound was somewhat different; it
was not the typical droning of the German Stuka. Then in an opening
between buildings Stan spotted a plane and he thought it looked like
a biplane but it was so quick than he was not really sure. The sound
was closer now and whatever it was Stan was now convinced it was
not a Stuka.

The plane appeared again and he could observe it better. It was a
biplane indeed, with an open cockpit and he could clearly see two
heads in there one behind the other. He also noticed a red star on
the tail. So it was a Russian plane. Had they decided to help?

Irena came up to him. She disobeyed his order but at the same time she wanted to know why he had not joined them in the cellar.

"Russians," he said to her.

The plane made a pass along the street, flew away, turned around and was making another one, even lower. As it was close to them they could see an object being dropped from underneath of it.

"Good God!" shouted Stan "run to the shelter. The idiots are bombing us!" and he run after her.

But there was no explosion so they both stopped.

"What's going on?" she asked.

"I don't know," Stan wasn't sure, "a dud, maybe? I am going to take a look."

And he proceeded towards the gate.

"I'm going with you," Irena said firmly.

When they reached the street they saw a large sack which clearly burst opened on impact. It was full of what looked like some kind of a rusk.
They came closer to investigate. Indeed, it was a sack full of rusk, but since it was dropped without a parachute the contents was damaged and spilled.

Irena and Stan were pondering this unexpected drop when two men appeared from across the street walking towards them. One had a rifle of some sort and the other held a handgun. They had white and red armbands on their sleeves but when they came closer it turned out the letters on the armbands were AL, not AK. AL stood for People's Army. It was also an underground resistance organization but originating from the pre-war Workers Party with some ties to the Soviet Russia.

One of the two AL men warned Irena and Stan.
"Don't touch it, move away, it's ours!"

"We were just checking what's going on, we heard the plane and thought it was possibly an air raid," explained Stan.

"It's an air drop for us. Back off!"

Irena suddenly burst with laughter which was echoed by others who in the meantime emerged from cellars.

"You are not around to fight Germans but you are quick to claim this," she nodded towards the sack.

Clearly annoyed the man with a rifle pointed it at her and said in angry voice.

"Back off! This is for our soldiers."

But Irena did not even blink.

"Where are those soldiers? Because sure as hell they are not on the barricades along with our boys."

She turned to people on the street.

"The great AL! - two guys and the magnificent help from the Soviets in form of crushed rusk. Very useful to fight Germans!"

People on the street laughed and cheered.

"Go to Moscow!" somebody shouted.

"And kiss Stalin's ass!" another added.

The fellow with the handgun gave them unpleasant look.

"You all will be sorry. Very sorry! And sooner than you think."

Irena's face turned stern and her voice was solemn.

"You should be sorry and ashamed. The Home Army is bleeding day by day and you point your gun at me? And over what? A sack full of Stalin's crap? Go ahead and shoot me, you miserable little rat! Those who fight for Poland will never be sorry! Don't you forget that."

She turned around and walked away.

The two AL men were left alone with the sack. They tried to pick it up but it did not work because the sack was torn in several places.

The leader feeling somewhat helpless raised his voice and called: "Anyone that want some please come here, we'll be happy to share."

Although they were all hungry, nobody looked or paid any attention to him. In the end the AL men dragged the sack away and disappeared among ruins. All that was left was trace of powdered rusk.

*

Few days later Irena was in the kitchen trying to figure out how to improvise dinner this time, considering she had hardly any supplies at all when Stan walked in. She knew right away there was bad news as his face said so without words.

"What is it?" she asked.

"Fred is dead," he answered.

She recalled the cable she gave him and she knew but still she asked:

"How?"

"He made some sort of - as he called it - a flying bomb and he wanted to use it in defense of the barricade he was assigned to. Apparently he sneaked into a building next to it and made his way forward to the next one. He climbed to the top floor and intended to throw his bomb at the approaching tank when he was shot by a sharpshooter I guess. His bomb exploded in his hands."

Irena lowered her head and began crying.

"He was here few days ago asking me for a piece of cable. He needed it to build his bomb."

Matilda run into the kitchen.

"Why are you crying Mummy?"

"A good friend of mine has died," she answered.

"Was he killed by Germans?"

"Yes."

"He went to heaven, didn't he?"

"Yes he did."

"If he is in heaven, why do you cry?"

"Because we can't see him anymore."

"But when we go to heaven too we can visit him?"

"Yes."

The Uprising was fading. Several attempts to supply the resistance by air was carried out by volunteer crews, predominantly Polish, flying from Northern Italy did not help. To assure reasonable safety of the crews the drops were done at night but this made the accuracy practically impossible. Warsaw was burning, her features were unrecognizable or obscured by smoke and most drops ended up in German hands. Had it been attempted in early stage of the Uprising the success rate would be much better. But Stalin refused the request from the allies for the planes to land after the drop to refuel and rest the crews on the territory under The Red Army control.

Thus the planes were starting in Northern Italy, flying over hostile territory all the way to Warsaw, making the drop and flying back to the starting point. It was exhaustive and dangerous as they were exposed to enemy's flak and fighter attacks. Due to poor results and high losses such missions were abandoned.

But one day in September at about noon suddenly a mass of planes appeared high over Warsaw. For a brief moment all eyes were fixed on the countless colorful parachutes slowly falling down from a great height. Many were rejoicing thinking it was paratroopers being deployed to help the Uprising. But it was a massive airdrop attempted by the American Air Force.

Unfortunately slight wind scattered the parachutes over large area and in the end most of supplies ended up in German hands. Had such drop been organized earlier it would have so much better chance. Now however the insurgents controlled only pockets of Warsaw and otherwise they were pinned down by German onslaught.

Irena was watching the drop from the street in front of Krucza number nine along with all her neighbors. One of them in the excitement climbed on top of a damaged building and was waving Polish flag at the airplanes above. Soon it was over and the word was what they all knew anyway – it was too little and above all, too late. By now people were hungry practically all the time, water was scarce and medical supplies were running out as fast as ammunition. There were also rumors about particular brutality of advancing Germans troops, or rather special units consisting of merciless criminals enlisted for the occasion. Ukrainian units known as SS Galizien were not far behind in cruelty being inflicted on civilian population.

Before too long German command offered capitulation talks and Polish General Bór-Komorowski agreed. The capitulation order was signed on the 2nd of October. Germans agreed to recognize fighters as combatants and took them to POW camps. Civilian population was evacuated from the city and Germans proceeded with systematic demolition of Warsaw. House by house, street by street were dynamited and set on fire.

Civilian population of Warsaw was ordered to assemble in designated places and was were marched to a transitional camp in a small town of Pruszkow located several miles West-South of Warsaw.

Stan, Irena, their daughters, along with Irena's sister Barbara ended up in Pruszkow some time in the fall of 1944. While there was no imminent danger related to warfare, some uncertainty crept in because Poles did not trust Germans. It was good of them to let civilians evacuate severely damaged city but the rules were still the same. Germans, while possibly nervous about the Russian Red Army sitting on the right banks of Vistula, were still the enemy occupying Poland and their doctrine had not changed a bit. They were not going to suddenly show a change of heart, it was reasonable to expect some nasty developments like being sent to slave labor deep in Germany or worse – to one of the concentration death camps. For the above reasons Stan's and Irena's minds were at work. The most obvious thing to do was to run away or otherwise sneak out from the camp but this meant violating German rules and laws.

*

Irena's older sister, Barbara was an attractive woman but she was quite different than Irena and they did not look like sisters at all. Irena was relatively tall, Barbara was shorter. Irena was slim figured, Barbara had rather rounded and full figure. Also, Irena could be somewhat aloof while Barbara was easygoing and she could easily connect with strangers which Irena could not do. Barbara was also well aware of how attractive she was and she knew how to play into it. It came naturally to her. And finally, she did not have to make extra efforts to look good. She was a type of a woman that could wear anything and it always looked as if it was tailored for her. The same was with personal care. Where some women had to spend hours on their make ups and hairdos, Barbara did not need much, just some slight touch ups and she looked fantastic.
In the camp she found work in the kitchen that was set up by Germans. She volunteered when the kitchens were being set up as

she hated sitting idle doing nothing. She worked in a kitchen restaurant before the war and liked it.

One morning the camp was being reviewed by a German officer by the name Fischer who, the word had it, was in charge of the entire evacuation process.

He made his rounds among the evacuees and in the end he walked through the kitchen area. He noticed Barbara, watched her for a while and walked towards her.

"Wie heisst Du? (What's your name?)" he inquired.

"Barbara," he heard in reply.

"Verstehs du Deutsch? (Do you understand German?)"

"Ja. (Yes)" she said.

"Wie? (How come)."

"Ich mag Fremdesprachen, ich wollte Deutche lernen. (I like foreign languages, I wanted to learn German.)"

"Sehr gut. (Very good)."

"Danke, Herr Ofizier (Thank you, officer.)"

Fischer checked empty pots and with pleasure noticed they were clean. He then sat on the only kitchen stool.

„Hast du etwas zu trinken hier?" (do you have anything to drink here?)

"Nur Kaffee, aber ich fürchte, es ist nicht der Beste." (only coffee but it's not the best I'm afraid)

"Das ist egal. Gib mir ein bisschen!" (It doesn't matter, give me some).

Barbara stopped her work, cleaned her hands and wiped them in a kitchen towel, took a small metal mug, filled it with coffee from a large pot and handed it to Fischer.

"Es tut mir leid, aber wir haben keine Servietten." (I regret but I don't have napkins to give you.)

He smiled lightly and took a sip while Barbara returned to her work. He was watching her while drinking the coffee and handed her the mug when he finished.

„Du hast recht, dieser Kaffee ist widerlich. Ich lade dich zu einem richtigen Kaffee und Kuchen ein." (You are right, this coffee is terrible. I invite you for a real coffee and a pastry).

She was surprised and didn't know what to say. Private contacts with Germans were forbidden by Home Army, though there were certain exceptions as such contacts could be used to exert pressure to obtain information.

"Danke, aber ich bin hier gefangen und arbeite." (Thank you, sir but I'm a prisoner here and also have my work duties.)

He did not seem to get the allusion or just pretended.

"Ich werde früh am Abend ein Auto schicken. Fürchte dich nicht vor mir. Du bist sicher." (I'll send a car for you at the evening. Don't be afraid, you will be safe.)

He looked at her waiting for answer.

She was not naive and realized how this may end.

"Danke sehr," (thank you very much) she nodded.

"Bis dann," (see you later then) said Fischer and left.

*

"Cigarette?"

Fischer stretched his hand with a pack of American cigarettes.

They were laying in his bedroom beside his study. He occupied a villa in a pretty and quiet street at the outskirts of Pruszkow. Through the window Barbara could hear chirping birds busy with their morning activities. She was trying to think when was the last time she heard or paid attention to birds and she figured it must have been before the war so some four years ago. She puffed the cigarette. It was aromatic and fresh like everything in his impeccably kept house.
Fischer was not only good looking, he was also soft and well mannered. When the car stopped in front of the house the chauffeur opened the door for her and walked her to the house door. He knocked and opened it for her, returned to his car and left.

Fischer appeared in the hallway wearing civilian clothing. He came towards her and greeted her politely. There was something in his look that made her think of Clark Gable.

His way of talking and behavior was calm and almost soothing and she did not feel any fear or prejudice. Here in his house it seemed the humanity was what it should be, free of the cruelty of war. It was almost inconceivable he was a German officer.

"You must have had mixed feelings coming here," he said, "I'd like you to know I'm fed up with all of what surrounds us. I'd like to lead normal life without this hell we unleashed. But it's the end anyway. The Reich is finished except nobody wants to accept it. Who knows? Perhaps I'm the first that does."

"But you won," she said carefully, "our Uprising is finished."

"Oh, that was yet another madness and a whim of one man."

"Yes," he added, thinking she may not understand what he meant, "I'm talking about the Führer. All of this was madness from the very beginning."

Barbara thought it was better to keep silent, she had a feeling he needed somebody who'd listen to him.

"I am in the party because I had no choice. I was a professional officer and I believed I was serving the country but that maniac and his supporters hijacked our fatherland and replaced it with their absurd ideas. Before I noticed it was too late. Lack of loyalty was equivalent to death, we were told. I had no choice but to follow orders. You don't have to believe me, I only hope that God will be fair in his judgment for he knows I did all I could to spare lives and did not murder. I have a feeling I will be standing before Him soon."

"Can't you…" she began but hesitated because she could not figure out how to finish her question.

"No," he smiled, "you have a good heart which is whispering to you that perhaps there is a way for me and maybe you'd be even be ready to help for better or worse but there is no hope for me. If I desert I'll be caught and shot. Poles suffered from us so much that it is inconceivable to hide among you. And soon the Russians will come. They are on the other side of the river and they will drown your homeland on their way to Berlin. Caught by them I'd be either shot on the spot or taken away to their camps in Siberia and this would be the end of me, no doubt, a sure albeit slow death. I can only continue the retreat and do my best to save lives – those of my soldiers and your civilians. My only hope would be to surrender to British or Americans but they are far away from here."

He was silent for a while.

"I haven't thought I'd meet somebody like you. In normal times I'd never let you go. Do believe me, it was not that I just wanted a woman. I saw humanity in your eyes and I have not seen that for a long time anywhere in that hell, I thought it was gone for good."

He gently patted her on her cheek and kissed her.

"In a sane world I'd never let you go."

She wiped a tear in her eye.

"Is there anything I can do for you?" he asked, "anything at all?"

She considered for a moment.

"My sister and her two daughters and husband are in the camp. Can you let them go?"

"What about you?"

"I can stay, it doesn't matter."

"See? – you have a good heart, I knew it. Everybody else would care about himself or herself first and foremost. Be ready tomorrow – you, your sister and her children. I will send a car and it will take you where you want."

"What about her husband?"

"That I can't do. Men are already counted and they will be taken to the Reich to work camps. It makes no sense at all but I expect orders any day now. But - if he is clever he can sneak out. The sooner the better."

"How can I thank you?"

"It's a dangerous question," he smirked.

"Is it?" she challenged him.

"Just remember me, that's all. Under different circumstances it would all be different."

A sound of car engine could be heard outside.

"You have to go now," said Fischer.

Barbara finished getting dressed, checked her look in the mirror and walked to the door. Before opening it for her he kissed her once again.

"Where were you for God's sake?!" greeted her Irena, "we were searching all over the camp for you!"

"It doesn't matter where I was. What is really important is something else. Get the girls and yourself ready. We are getting out of here tomorrow, but…"

"What does it mean we are getting out?" interrupted Irena, "are they taking us to Germany?"

"No, just you, the girls and me!" Barbara explained.

"I don't understand. What about Stan?"

"He can't go with us but there are ways for him to sneak out."

"I still don't get it."

"Good God, what is not to get? I met a German. He agreed to take us from here."

"Why didn't you ask me and Stan for money? You know we are selling and trading trying to gather a decent amount to bribe somebody!"

Barbara was annoyed at her asking useless questions.

"Stop asking me questions. Start thinking of getting ready and be quiet about it. Don't talk to people."

"Yes, yes – of course, you are right - but… are you sure? You can't trust those German guards."

Poles did not believe in "the good German" even though there were such exceptions. Good enough was one that took a bribe for looking the other way and kept his word.

Irena's curiosity was not quenched.

"Did you…?"

"Knock it off – will you?!" Barbara lost patience, "it's not as simple as you may think and I have no intention discussing it with you. You'd better think where do we go from here because I have no slightest idea!"

"But I do!" declared Irena, „we go to Jani. Reguły is very close and as far as I know they are still there!"

Next morning Barbara went to work in the kitchen as usual and Irena finished her preparations. She worried sick about Stan but he didn't even blink an eye.

"No discussion, darling. I'm staying and knowing I don't have to worry how to get you and the girls out I can think of something. You go and don't worry about me!"

He gave her a hug and left to a place where prisoners were trading goods, information and gossip.

At about eleven German supervisor walked to the kitchen and ordered Barbara to go to the side gate to accept delivery of rutabaga. Almost simultaneously an armed guard arrived to where Irena was and ordered her to take her children and her belongings and marched her away.
Fellow prisoners watched that in silence. As he was leading Irena away somebody shouted:

"Hold on tight, Irena. We'll outlive those bastards!"

The guard turned around with an angry look but could not figure out who was shouting.

Barbara was already standing by the guards house when Irena, Gabriela and Matilda arrived.

„Alles in ordnung! Raus!" barked the guard and opened the gate for them.

There was a car with an open door standing right outside and they walked towards it. Irena sat at the back with Gabriela and Matilda, while Barbara took the seat next to the driver.

"Wohin?" (Where to?) asked the driver.

"Reguły bitte, Sadowa Strasse."

Reguły was a village near Pruszkow where the camp was, so the ride was not long, a half an hour or so. At the address lived Janina Kozlowska, Irena's classmate and childhood friend. While not really knowing whether or not she was there for sure, Irena simply had no other ideas as she did not know anyone else around Pruszkow at all. She only knew Janina and her family lived there continuously for years and they survived September 1939 but otherwise she had scarce contact with her.

The car came to stop in front of a small two storey gray house. Barbara noticed a curtain moved in the window which was a sign somebody was there.

"Somebody is there," she said.

"Good, let's go then," Irena was disembarking.

"Please convey my thanks to Herr Fischer," Barbara turned to the driver "and thank you for bringing us here. Good bye."

"Good bye," was the answer and the car drove away.

As they approached the door and knocked they were not sure of anything but the door opened and there was Janina smiling at them.

"Isia, how happy I am to see you," she welcomed them and gave them strong hugs "Barbara, Matilda, Gabriela, do come in. It's God's hand you are here."

"I hope it's all right," said Irena, "and I am sorry I could not get in touch with you. We have no place to go at all."

"You have a place here. It's a miracle you survived the Uprising, I was worrying endlessly about you. Where is Stan by the way?"

Irena had tears in her eyes.

"He remained in the camp, we couldn't get him out."

"We have to think of something. John is working it the railroad yard, it's not far from the camp and due to his work he is not restricted. Maybe we can find ways to get in touch with Stan, maybe we can find some German we could pay off."

But it turned out not necessary. Few days later Stan had just appeared on their doorstep out of nowhere. Irena and their daughters covered him with hugs and kisses.

When everybody calmed down Stan told them how he was called by the officer in command who questioned him about his profession and then told him he was being ordered to report to the railroad yard in Pruszkow. He did so, registered for work. He worked few days and was returning to camp after his shift but he quickly realized nobody was really checking his comings and goings so some day at the end of his shift he just walked to the Kozlowski's house instead of returning to camp.

Thus the family was complete and out of the camp but not out of danger. Rumors were circulating that Germans are making random checks in houses to see if there are any Varsovians hiding in there. Stan decided they needed to move as far from there as possible at once.

Since it was inconceivable to cross the Vistula River and thus cross the front line, he decided they would travel south but staying within few kilometers from the river aiming at the small town of Mogielnica where Stan had an old acquaintance.

The last time he was in contact with him was before the war so there was no guarantee he was still there but once again they really had no choice as they had no other place to think of.

A man with a horse drawn carriage was found who for certain price agreed to take them to Mogielnica and so the following day they set out.

6. THE NEW REALITY

The fellow Stan knew was a client of his from before the war. He remembered Stan and was ready to help. He installed them next door to his house in an abandoned farm house which also had a small barn. The farmer and his family were taken away by Germans a year and a half ago in the middle of the night. Many Poles disappeared in such circumstances and there was nothing anyone could do about it. As terrible as it sounds, life went on. Stan's friend who knew the farmer well assumed control over the buildings so that they would not have the abandoned look as this would encourage unwanted interests.

Mogielnica was off the bitten track and far enough from Warsaw. With Russians on the other side of the river, Germans were preparing to mount some defense for the imminent Russian attack and making arrangements for their own evacuation and withdrawal.

Barbara did not seem to be herself in Mogielnica. While happy not to be in the camp, the safe distance to Warsaw did not seem to matter much to her. The first several days she was quiet and responded to questions in almost absent minded way. Irena saw that her sister was worrying about something but guessed it must be about their mother with whom they lost touch and at the moment had no idea where she was.

Some day Barbara returned from the market and declared she was going to return to be closer to Warsaw. She was giving evasive reasons but when pressed she finally said it was to try to find mother. Irena had a feeling it was just an answer which she and Stan could not contradict. They did try to explain to her how difficult and dangerous such step would be but she remained adamant. She found already transport for the next day and was excited at the prospect of going back. Irena kept thinking she must have had a different reason but she also knew that Barbara never shared everything with her anyway.

Irena equipped her in an old suitcase, helped her pack and next morning walked with her to the town square where a horse carriage was waiting with some passengers already there. They hugged for good bye, Barbara climbed onto the carriage and off she went. Irena remained motionless until the carriage disappeared around the corner down the street and only then walked home wondering if and when she will see her sister again.

When January 1945 arrived, Russians made their move and crossed the Vistula River in several places. Sounds of artillery and airplanes flying overhead reminded Irena of September 1939 when the war had began and she fell uneasy. But the planes were searching for and bombing German positions somewhere west beyond Warsaw and the artillery was considerable distance away. Mogielnica did not have any military importance at all, so it was all quiet and the only sign of the approaching Russians was nervousness of those few Germans still visible sometimes on the streets. They were no longer that arrogant superior master race but just ordinary men being very insecure and scared.

One morning Stan and his family was awaken by an unusual commotion and when they looked outside, their yard and street was full of Germans in Wehrmacht uniforms. They were not acting hostile, so Stan and Irena ventured out. They quickly found out German units were withdrawing at rather fast pace before the first wave of outnumbering them Russians. They decided to stop to rest and dress wounded colleagues they had with them, quite a few in fact.

Apparently Russian troops were no more than some 60 kilometers away, pressing forward. Germans took any food the Szumskis had and used the well to refill their water cans. Some slept in the barn while their officers demanded rooms in the main house. Irena and Stan were not in a position to argue. Early next morning Germans were gone.

Sounds of artillery were closer now but they were not shooting at Mogielnica. There was even more airplanes in the air. Otherwise it was calm and relatively normal albeit the population was somewhat anxious not knowing what to expect from the approaching Russians. But Russians or not it meant the end of war and end of the hated five years long German occupation.

A day or two later in the afternoon sounds of engines could be heard and a couple of tanks and trucks appeared along with several soldiers. Tanks and trucks had a red star painted on sides. A small jeep also with a red star appeared, carrying an officer. It happened to stop almost in front of the farm.

 There were many people on the streets as everybody wanted to see the moment.

The officer approached Stan and Irena as they were the nearest to him.

"Greetings," he said in surprisingly good Polish, "are there any Germans in the village?"

"As far as I know – no," answered Stan.

"They were here two days ago, running away from you. They were tired and in some disarray. They rested here, took our food whatever we had and left."

"Food – don't worry about it," he turned towards group of soldiers standing by the truck.

"Volkov!" he shouted.

Soldier named Volkov promptly came to him.

"Yes, Comrade Lieutenant!"

"Bring these people some food. The German scum robbed them of all they had."

"At once, Comrade Lieutenant!" and he disappeared in the back of the truck. Few minutes later he returned with two loafs of bread and 4 cans of canned meat.

"Take it," the officer said to Stan, "is it all right for my troops to stay in your yard?"

"But of course," smiled Stan, "and thank you!"

Irena who was watching silently as she had never seen The Red Army before turned to the officer.

"Thank you, officer. We arc so happy you are here, we are finally free. Thank you, thank you so much!"

The officer looked at her and gave her an enigmatic smile which she thought was strange. He was handsome and his stare and the smile made her feel somewhat uneasy.

"Can we offer you a drink?" asked Stan "I don't have much and certainly not enough for all of your men, so it would be just for you."

"I have to give some orders first and I'll come to your house later," he replied and walked away.

They heard him calling "Starsheena!" and saw another soldier approaching him. The two of them were standing discussing something when suddenly there was a sound of a single shot and the man called "Starsheena" collapsed. In an instant the soldiers hid behind tanks, trucks and anything large enough to shield a human and shots were fired in the direction of the barn.

Carefully, in combat technique soldiers approached and entered the barn and moments later there was shouting and commotion inside. Soon two soldiers dragged someone outside holding him under the arms and the third soldier appeared carrying a rifle.

While the officer went closer some soldiers run towards Stan and

Irena.

The first one shouted with an angry look on his face:

"Is this your house, you live here?"

"Yes," said Stan.

"You fascist vermin, you will die like a dog you are!" the soldier hit Stan in his face sending him flat to the ground.

Irena tried to shield Stan from further blows, but another soldier pulled her back.

"And your bitch too!"

Soldiers dragged them both and placed them against the barn's wall.

"On your feet! Hands up!" soldiers were shouting.

Five of them lined up and were getting their rifles ready when the office shouted from a distance:

"Stop!!! Order!!! Put your guns down now or it's court martial!"

Irena recognized the officer they'd just been talking to. The soldiers lowered their guns but had not moved, waiting. The officer came closer to Stan and Irena.

"We've found a wounded German in your barn. He took a shot at me I think but missed and the bullet killed my sergeant. Were you aware he was there?"

"No, of course, not. I told you Germans were here two days ago and there were some wounded men with them but they all left early one morning. We looked around after they left but there was nobody left. We had no idea one was hiding."

He looked into Irena's eyes and could see how scared she was. Stan was just in pain but his eyes were just bewildered.

"I believe you," he said, "he was too probably weak to continue. He hid in the upper floor of the barn so that he could see the yard and what was going on."

"What is going to happen to him?" asked Irena.

"He will be shot, he'd killed one of us. I neither have choice nor do I care about one miserable fascist. Take your husband inside and don't come out. I will be there later if the drink still stands?"

"Of course it does, please do come," said Stan spitting coagulated blood and checking his teeth.

Few minutes later Irena saw through the curtains how soldiers dragged the wounded German around the barn where the back wall was facing the fields. In a moment she could hear a gunshot and the soldiers returned.

She washed blood from Stan's face and checked on Matilda and Gabriela who were told much earlier to stay in their room. Fortunately neither of them was aware of the incident that had just taken place.

Later in the evening the officer knocked on the door and Irena let him in. She prepared the bread and meat he gave them so that she could offer him some simple meal and Stan produced the last bottle of vodka he had.

"Please do sit down and eat with us!" said Stan, "once again – welcome and thank you for coming. It had not hit us yet the Germans are gone. After five years we need more time for this to sink in."

He poured three glasses, raised his and said:

"To your health! May you return to your home safe! To Victory!"

"Thank you," the officer smiled and they gulped vodka.

Only now Irena observed his hair was black and his skin had a very slight olive tone. He was wearing a thin black moustache along the length of his upper lip. He seemed to be in his late forties or maybe early fifties. He noticed her looking at him because he said:

"I'm from Georgia. My name is Sakandelidze, Grigorij Sakandelidze."

"How come you speak our language?"

"I was ordered to learn it. At some point I was transferred from my original unit to a new one. They told us we were going to be the Polish Army. But later on they moved me back to my original unit, probably because of my look," he laughed "I wouldn't make a proper Pole."

"What do you mean to be the Polish Army?" asked Irena.

"Nobody explained that. We were given uniforms with Polish insignia and officers were sent to take classes to learn some Polish. Languages come easily to me, I was teaching German before the war."

"I still don't quite understand what's the point in dressing Russian soldiers in Polish uniforms," Irena said.

"Neither do I. There is a Polish Army fighting somewhere along us. Maybe it's not big enough to impress civilians? I don't know."

Irena and Stan were silent for a moment, then Irena said:

"It doesn't matter. We are just happy you finally arrived. We thought you'd come last summer. We thought you'd aid the Warsaw Uprising."

"I can't speak for this," he answered. "I know nothing of the Uprising but then again my unit was part of the army coming from the south and in summer we were far away from here."

"No matter," Stan filled the glasses again, "to your health and safety!"

And they drank again.

The officer looked at them both carefully, lowered his voice almost to a whisper and said:

"Don't be too happy. You will yet curse us all. My soldiers and I are just the front line units. All we do is beat the fascists and liberate civilians. But the NKVD is not far behind and they may be here as early as tomorrow. They are the political units. We come and go, they come and stay. Be very careful what you say to them and how you talk to them…" he hesitated, lowered his voice even more and added "and above all - never forget they are not your friends. They never were and they never will be."

Irena and Stan were speechless.

"I haven't told you anything just now, you understand. This conversation never took place. Na zdrowie!" he raised his glass and they all drunk once again.

Next morning the Russian troops were resting. Some were cleaning their guns, mechanics were working or checking the engines of their trucks and tanks. A couple of soldiers set up a fire in the center of the yard, they placed a tripod over it and were making large pot of tea. Somebody pulled out a "harmoshka" which was a small harmonica and played what sounded like a choppy cheerful melody.

Gabriela and Matilda were allowed to go outside and they mingled a bit. What a different experience it was for them to be out among uniformed soldiers and not being afraid of them. They walked here and there, some soldiers tried to talk to them but they could not understand the language. The unpleasant situation with the German soldier was forgotten now and Irena, Stan and many neighbors were mingling with the soldiers as well. People brought in things to share with them but it was not much, mainly vodka which both sides were drinking rather happily.

 While walking by one of the trucks which was being worked on with the hood opened Irena noticed small markings under the hood which had some numbers and letters "USA" at the end.

Irena asked the mechanic what it meant.

"**Ubij Sukinsyna Adolfa**" (Kill the son-of-a-bitch Adolf), he explained and burst with hearty laughter. Few others who heard that roared with laughter too and one of them added: "And we shall do so, soon."

Another car arrived and another, what looked like officer, got out.

He had a military cap like Sakandelidze's but the color was different as it was dark blue. Seeing him, all soldiers quiet down, they instantly became less merry. The newcomer pointed at the nearest soldier and barked: "Get me your comrade in charge."

The soldier saluted and literarily run to fetch Sakandelidze. When he arrived he saluted the newly arrived man and they briefly talked about something. He then went back to the car and left. As soon as the car disappeared the music resumed and soldiers were at ease again.

After the frontline moved Mogielnica was quiet again except that every now and then Soviet military patrols drove by in a jeep but they never stopped or bothered anyone. People were trying to get on with their lives as normally as they could and the realization that the war was over was setting in.

Street vendors appeared selling things and marketplace opened as before. People were now cheerful like never before for no matter what they did or said there were no more Germans around. People could also walk around after dusk which was forbidden for years. Every now and then somebody misplaced by the war would return home to great joy of their families, friends and neighbors, and they would share their stories at gatherings. Optimism was in the air and people were speculating about end of the war being near.

Every now and then Mogielnica was visited by agitators spreading information about the new Temporary Polish Government which was set up in the city of Lublin. It was promising to make Poland a People's Republic as opposed to the pre-war "bourgeois" Poland as they said. People's Republic meant the country would be run by workers and peasant parties like it was done in the Soviet Union. It was going to be fair and better for everyone. Many locals were skeptical and did not trust such talks as they wanted Poland they way she was before the war. It was obvious that the so called "new" government" was established by the Soviets and therefore certain worries about being liberated by the Red Army substantiated. There always had been communist and socialist movement in Poland but it had marginal influence, especially the communists.

Poles they knew their history well. List of Russian attempts to subjugate Poland was long and run deep. People were also whispering about the eastern part of Poland being annexed to the Soviet Union and it was worrying, just like the rumors of the massacre in Katyn where in the spring of 1941 the Soviets executed about twenty thousand Polish servicemen who remained unaccounted for after 17th September 1939.

On the 8th of May 1944 the news spread like a wildfire - the war was over! Hitler was dead and Berlin was taken, Eastern and Western Fronts had met somewhere on German territory. People were jubilant and happy but it was not easy to be exuberant for everyone. Countless loved ones were still missing and after five and a half year of darkness it was sometimes hard to believe it was really over. There was generation of children born just before the war who hadn't known life other than under the ever present mortal danger and abuse by Gestapo. Truth about horrors of concentration camps was emerging. The population had to begin healing its wounds and learn to live in peace but - under a new order.

The propaganda spread by the communists increased its presence everywhere and stepped up it's tone. The war – according to that propaganda - was won thanks to the great leadership of Joseph Stalin and unsurpassed bravery and dedication of the heroic Red Army and the peace loving people of the Soviet Union. The workers and peasants of the new Poland were never again going to be subjected to the misery of forces which brought upon them the failures of the rotten pre-war government which brought upon Poland the catastrophe of 1939. The peace and safety of Poland was going to be guaranteed forever by the eternal friendship with the Soviet Union and Joseph Stalin, the greatest friend Poland ever had.

Stan and Irena were talking about returning to Warsaw for quite a while now as they had neither ties nor intentions to stay in Mogielnica. Their life was always in the city and so was Stan's job. In a matter of days Stan managed to hire a horse cart and they set of early morning.

The weather was fine and there were lots of people on the road moving in every direction. There was also some military traffic, going west and east. Russian soldiers were occasionally waving to people who always looked at them with some curiosity and waved back. Signs of war were everywhere. While Mogielnica survived reasonably well, other places were not so lucky. Burned and demolished buildings were everywhere, some were partially damaged and those were being worked on as sometimes entire families were hard at work trying to fix them. There were people rummaging through debris trying to find still useful things. Here and there were wrecks of German tanks, trucks and cars, sometimes debris of shot down airplanes. Most of those vehicles were burned and sometimes they could see charred remains of occupants. Nobody was in a hurry to bury them, nobody was sorry for them either.

As they were getting closer to Warsaw the air had a smell of still smoldering ruins and stench of death as bodies buried by the collapsed buildings were slowly rotting away.

After turning a corner somewhere along the way another sight came into their view. There was a German tank standing there. It looked just abandoned without signs of damage except missing one of the tracks. A bunch of boys were playing on it. Some were hanging by their hands from the barrel of the gun while others were trying to spin the turret by hand. Somebody crossed the Wehrmacht insignia on its sides and wrote "Long Live Poland!" next to them. At the back somebody scribbled with chalk: "Kiss my ass, Adolf!"

When they entered Warsaw the look of it was nightmarish and Irena began to cry. Countless buildings were in ruin, only every now and then a solitary structure was lucky enough to survive. Walls were riddled with bullets, windows were broken and roofs heavily damaged. Streets were almost indistinguishable. When they finally arrived at what used to be Krucza Street it was no better. Most buildings were torn to pieces, ripped apart and inhabitable. Their number 9 was severely damaged and did not look inviting at all. But oddly enough the chestnut tree was intact. Irena jumped from the cart, run to the tree and hugged it as if it was a live person.

"You've survived, you've made it!" she whispered through her tears.

"Isia!" called Stan.

"We can't stay here. We try John at the Poznańska Street. If we can stay with them I'll come back here tomorrow to see if we can enter. No time now."

And so they continued. They were lucky because the building where Stan's friend John lived somehow survived and John and his wife were there.

"Good Lord, Stan!" he exclaimed, "I thought I'd never see you again. Irena, Matilda, Gabriela – welcome, come in, come in! It is so good to see you all."

"John," asked Stan, "can we stay with you for a few days? We have no place to go."

"Sure, Stan, sure you can, just be prepared to live in a crowd as we have few other families already. No privacy. But don't let it discourage you – take your things and come in."

John was cheerful and optimistic.

"Now that the bastards are gone we can start rebuilding," he declared.

Stan was not sharing in his enthusiasm after freshly seeing the damage.

"It's going to be a monumental task, the city has its back broken."

"We'll make her even more beautiful than she ever was," John who was an architect before the war was confident and cheerful.

To say his flat was crowded was an understatement. The three rooms were absolutely full of people, including kitchen.

John's wife greeted them equally enthusiastically:

"Come in, come in," she said "we'll find place for you although you may not be sleeping all together. Are you hungry?"

"Thank you," Irena gave her a hug, "me and Stan are fine but I my daughters are hungry no doubt. I do have some canned meat with me though.”

“Right, we have some soup left. Girls,” she addressed Matilda and Gabriela “go straight there!” she pointed them towards the kitchen.

“Anybody in the kitchen!?” she yelled “we have two more hungry souls, give them some soup please.”

“Righto,” a woman’s voice shouted back “they shall be hungry no more!”

Matilda smiled seeing and hearing this cheerful exchange but Gabriela just followed her younger sister with a somber face. She didn’t like being among so many people.

By squeezing everything and everybody some extra space was created to accommodate the four newcomers.

In the evening the adults shared a little bit of vodka but with not much to eat as the supplies were running low.

“We’ll get some food tomorrow” declared John, “market is around the corner every day. Prices are steep but we can always haggle a bit.”

“I’m buying,” said Stan.

“You don’t have to but any contributions are appreciated.”

Later on they all chatted the evening away swapping stories and asking about friends and family members.

In the room for children Matilda easily fitted with the occupants right away but Gabriela was sitting in the corner alone. She wasn’t participating in whatever was going on.

“Gabriela!” called Matilda who was sitting with three girls more or less her age, “come to us here, we’ll play a game.”

“I don’t want to!” Gabriela shouted back, “I’m not interested in your silly games.”

“Come on,” Matilda persisted “it’s going to be fun with more players.”

"Oh, shut up and leave me alone. I hate being here."

"She can be moody," Matilda tried to explain her sister to the others, "she isn't always like that."

"You know," said a girl about Matilda's age "around the corner from here there was a heap of dead Germans. Russians poured gasoline on them and set them all on fire!"

"Really?" asked Matilda "and you were watching this?"

"Yes," she said, "as they were burning they began to move. They were moving arms and legs and faces made grimaces as if they were alive. But they were dead, just burning."

"Stop it!" shouted Gabriela "stop talking about it, I hate it. I hate it all – you hear?!"

"They were bad, you know," the girl tried to justify it, "they made war with us and destroyed everything."

"I don't want to hear it, understand?" Gabriela was angry and they changed the subject to appease her.

"What's wrong with her?" another girl asked.

"I told you, she is like that sometimes," repeated Matilda, "she was afraid of bombings when the war began. But I wanted to see them."

Next day Irena was helping in the kitchen while Stan walked to Krucza Street number 9 to see the condition of the building up close as he was hoping to be able to move in no matter how bad it was. He figured as long as the structure was stable they could reclaim their flat and begin fixing things. Perhaps by the end of summer they could be reasonably settled. But it was not meant to be. While the front looked not that bad, the inside was very uninviting. Weakened walls with large holes in them, staircases on the verge of collapse and practically no roof – it all looked hopeless. Stan was no expert but he just could not imagine how long it would take to clean up the rubble then possibly reinforce damaged areas, rebuild the roof and do all sorts of other things before work on his flat could even start. It looked overwhelming. But he decided to consult John who as an architect and would be able to give a valid opinion. Stan turned around and was going to walk away when he was stopped by somebody shouting his name.

"Stan? Stan Szumski?"

Stan looked back and in a thin and old looking figure he recognized his boss from the bookkeeping agency.

"My God, you survived!" Mr.Zalewski exclaimed.

"And so did you," smiled Stan as they exchanged handshakes.

"And your family?"

"My wife and my daughters are fine but I lost my brother in the Uprising. What about you?"

Mister Zalweski's eyes filled with tears.

"My wife was a nurse in the hospital in Wola district during the Uprising. Have you heard what was going on there?"

Stan felt shivers down his spine. Nearly everybody heard about particular cruelty and bestiality of SS German and Ukrainian SS Galizien units that took place in Wola.

"Good God, Mister Zalewski… I don't know what to say."

"I cry every day, Stan. When the evening comes I begin crying until it exhausts me and I fall asleep."

Stan was silent.

Mister Zalewski sighed.

"But the rest of my family was lucky. I don't count the wounded ones. One or two cousins ended up handicapped, that's all. What are you doing here may I ask?"

"We lived here before the war. I came to see if it was safe to move back but it looks hopeless, there seem to be too much damage. I can't even access what used to be my flat."

"Most of Warsaw is like that. They say the three quarters of the city is just a heap of ruins."

"It certainly looks that way," agreed Stan.

"If you have problem with finding a place to live my long time friend has flats available but it is in Józefów. It's a village not that far from Warsaw on the train line which before the war was electrified and equipped with modern trains. It was part of a bigger plan to connect the city with suburbs. Once the bridges and tracks are repaired it will be a short ride. I understand it may not be what you want but it is better than nothing."

Mister Zalweski jotted down the name and address of his friend and handed the piece of paper to Stan.

"Thank you, Mister Zalweski!"

"There are many Varsovians living there. Józefów was getting popular before the war as a summer getaway so people settle there now either for good or as a temporary measure due to shortage of places to live in the city."

"I will try hard to find a temporary place in Warsaw before we can return to Krucza, but if it produces no results I will contact your friend."

"If you talk to Jankowski please be sure you mention my name. He will give you a better deal. Do you have work?"

"Of course not. I'm happy to be alive and we've literally just returned. Yesterday. I haven't though of work. I was buying and selling things for a while, I also know some carpentry."

"It's hard, I know, but we have to think of the future. We will be needed and I will be organizing my firm again, our services will be needed no doubt, it's only a matter of time. You can have your job back, the only thing is that it's obviously not imminent. And you can't be paid until we make some money."

"Thank you, that's understandable. If you mean it please count me in. How do I find you?"

"I live at the Filtrowa Street. There's a decent part of it that survived in reasonable shape. I am at number thirteen. Please stay in touch every month or so."

"I will - thank you so much Mr. Zalweski!"

Stan felt as if somebody injected him with a dose of optimism.

"Good-bye then and see you in a while."

"Bye," replied Stan and walked back to John's.

For the next several days while Irena was helping in running John's household, Stan was frantically searching for a place to live but to no avail. Simultaneously he was looking for some work but that had not produced any results either. He knew they could not stay at John's forever. It was time to move.

"Isia," Stan began.

"Yes?" Irena could sense it was important.

"You know we can't stay at John's indefinitely, we just can't. We also can't go back to Krucza Street because the building is unsafe and most likely will be demolished. I'm also unable to find any other place in Warsaw for us to live. There are people everywhere and there is nothing available at all. Not having work doesn't help either."

"So what we are going to do?" she worried.

"I've met Mister Zalewski on the street and he gave me name of his friend who rents flats in Józefów and the word is he has a flat available."

"Józefów?" asked Irena "where is that?"

"Józefów is on the train line going east from Warsaw. I don't know if you recall but there was a big news about this line being modernized between 1936 and 1938. New stations were built and the line was electrified which ended up making very efficient mode of transportation. One could ride from Józefów to Warsaw in under one hour even though it's a long distance by road. Once the trains are running again it will be the same or even better."

"But I want to live in Warsaw!" objected Irena, "I'm a city girl, I always loved the city, it's in my nature and in yours too. I don't want to live in some village!"

"It's only temporary, Isia," explained Stan, "once I get my job going again, we will have steady income and I will find us a place in Warsaw, I promise. I will do my best to go back to Krucza when it is rebuilt."

But Irena was sad.

"Also," added Stan, "think of the girls. God knows when they will set up schools here. It will probably be quicker on the outskirts. No matter how you look, education is the key to success. They will need to start school as soon as it is feasible. And I heard that many Varsovians are in Józefów."

Irena was as if she was given bad news.

"You are right, I'm sure" she said, "children first, that's how it is and should be. But I know I won't be happy there."

"It'll be only a temporary measure, Isia, I swear. It will also do Gabriela some good. She seems to be withdrawn at times. Matilda adjusts easily to everything, she has this bubbly personality. Gabriela seems either angry or upset or both and I can't figure it out."

"These are the scars of war. Remember how first in September and then in the occupation time she was unwilling to go out, even to the yard? I think it is still the same. I keep telling her the war is over for good and I encourage her to go and play with kids her age. She does but rarely and with some difficulty. She says she hates looking at the ruins and the damage all the time but there is no escape from it."

"Well, there you go. Change of environment will be good for her. It will help her bounce back."

"Yeah, I suppose," agreed Irena but without much enthusiasm.

Stan looked at her face trying to find even the slightest trace of that spark she always had. It was no longer there but Stan thought it was all due to what they went through in the past five years. Five years was a long time and it was going to take long time for scars to heal. He was sure of it. He loved her just as much as when he first fell in love with her, and he was going to do anything to make her happy. *Time* — he thought - *she needs some time and everything will be all right again.*

Józefów - as Stan explained — was a village not far from Warsaw. The area was full of pine trees and the soil was very sandy therefore the climate was generally dry and for this reason even before the war there were several homes built for people suffering from tuberculosis. They were usually away from the beaten track here and there.

There was a lovely church built in the twenties in a style resembling gothic. During the war Germans constructed several defense bunkers which were hidden and spread out at a distance of several kilometers from the Vistula river north up to the road connecting Warsaw and Lublin. Well hidden among houses or in woods they served as an unpleasant trap for the advancing Eastern front and some fighting took place here.

Being part of the pre war design for a commuter line Józefów had it's own train station, one of the several identical ones built in a modern and appealing Art Deco style. Some well to do Varsovians had their summer houses here even before the war and with Warsaw in ruins many lived here now and more were arriving as the word had spread about Józefów being a pleasant place.

Early in June 1945 Stan, Irena, Matilda and Gabriela took the precarious trip across the Vistula River on a small boat and once on the other side they hired a horse cart to take them to Józefów. Before they set of Irena looked back at her beloved city and tears were falling down her cheeks as the horse cart was drawing away. The view was depressing. It seemed the only building standing above the ruins was the only sky-scraper in Warsaw built in Art Deco style in early thirties and known as Prudential as it was the home base for the British insurance company of the same name. The building sustained damage in the war and further heavy damage during the Warsaw Uprising. It was hit by about 1000 artillery shells including a single hit by a 2 tons mortar shell from the Karl the Great self propelled siege mortar brought in by the Nazis.

The Prudential survived it all and was still standing although it was slightly bent sideways by that mortar shell.

On the very first day of the Warsaw Uprising, Corporal Cadet Jerzy Frymus alias "Garbaty" climbed to the top of the Prudential despite his respiratory problems and placed the Polish national flag there. It remained there for a long time flying over the fighting city and was a subject of admiration of the proud Varsovians.

Irena was staring at the Prudential until it disappeared from view. Forced by circumstances beyond her control, she was leaving Warsaw for the second time and she was unable to contain her sadness, she was almost physical pain.

7. JÓZEFÓW

Mister Jankowski owned two properties in Józefów, one of them at the Church Street, a walking distance from Church and this was where Stan and his family ended up. Unlike most houses in the area which were constructed entirely from wood with pine needles as insulation between walls the building at the Church Street was built of bricks and it contained 6 flats. Two on the ground level, two on the first floor and the fifth was actually converted attic. The ground flats had lovely terraces on the street side and the first floor flats had corresponding terraces but these were more like balconies as they had no roof. Comparing to where Stan and his family lived before, the flat in Józefów was a luxury. They had a small entry hall, kitchen, two rooms and a full bathroom with bathtub, sink and toilet. And all plumbing was functional as the house had its own pump to circulate fresh water. They were told there is also a water heater for the whole house but it needed repair which was being dealt with. Even with cold water on demand, just from a faucet was something they hadn't had for a long time. Kitchen window was looking out to considerable backyard with mature trees and bushes while both rooms and terrace were facing the street side which had trees and bushes as well. You could see neighboring houses but only partially as they were hidden by bushes and shrubs. It seemed to be a peaceful and private location.

They did not have many belongings so initially all they had was just spread on the floors. Gabriela and Matilda enjoyed the terrace as they had not had anything like it before and they spent lots of time there. Irena and Stan went about searching for some basic furniture. They contacted neighbors and followed up on tips and hints they were given.

One day Irena stopped at church. She was pleased it was so near. It was obviously not like her church in Warsaw. She couldn't stop comparing everything with what she had lost.

The church was not locked so she walked inside. It was a bit dark as the stain glass windows were narrow and tall but in a moment her eyes adjusted and she could see better. The floor was tiled with black and white tiles. Along both sides were nicely carved pews. Just before the altar to the left was the pulpit which was also carved. It was raised and it had a matching roof. The priest had to climb six curved stairs to get there. The altar had a pretty tabernacle and a large painting above it portraying Mary Magdalene kneeling before the crucified Christ.

Irena was contemplating the painting when she heard footsteps from the sacristy and a priest appeared. He looked middle aged with closely cropped hair almost military style. He was a bit stocky.

"Hello," he said, "may I help you?"

"Praised be Jesus Christ," she said.

"Forever and ever," he replied.

"I've just moved in here," Irena explained, we live two or three houses away. I came to see the church."

"I'm Father Wincenty Malinowski," he introduced himself, "welcome to our parish."

"Irena," she said, "Irena Szumska."

"We have services every day at seven thirty in the morning and at six in the evening. Sundays have different schedules — eight, ten, twelve and five in the evening. I celebrate them all regardless on how many people come," he smiled.

"Well, you've just gained a new sheep, father" she said cheerfully as she felt at ease in his presence.

"I have to go now but I will see you again or otherwise you will see me at Masses."

"Stop by any time even if only to chat. The vicarage is behind the church. You can't see it from the street but it's there. I have a number of books if you wanted to borrow something to read. Some day I am going to set it up as library for all interested in borrowing books."

"Thank you, I'll remember that. Good bye, father."

He watched her leaving and returned to the sacristy.

*

Among population of Józefów there was a number of teachers and they were instrumental in setting up a school. Gabriela and Matilda were signed up and began attending classes almost immediately. At first it was just one group of kids of mixed ages but as the word spread more kids were joining and the school divided them by grades.

Local authorities were not interfering so the teachers worked out schedules and subjects based on the pre-war program and schoolbooks they managed to gather. It was a step that turned out to be a catalyst towards the normalization of life for kids and adults alike as life had a different rhythm now. Kids were quick to form friendships and associations and by this default parents got to know each other too so this was how some people got acquainted. Most of the children were from Varsovians families, there was a group of locals who were raised in Józefów and there were some kids whose families were misplaced either by the war or the new order brought in by the Red Army. Along with ideas of communism came things like nationalization of property. Factories were taken away from their rightful owners and they belonged to the state now. In the same fashion landowners were removed from their properties and told to go away. Their land was subdivided and given to peasants – such was result of the Agrarian Reform carried out by the communists.

The school was in – how we'd say today – a full swing when the authorities moved in. Teachers were told to toe the line or else. By toeing the line they had to be carful what and how they were teaching. Scientific subjects were in the clear but history was heavily manipulated by the government. Pre-war Poland was now presented as a bourgeoisie and rotten state where working class and peasants were being used and abused by the upper classes that were to blame for the failure of the Polish defense in September 1939. Teaching about the 17th September 1939, the day the Soviet Union attacked Poland and effectively partitioned it together with the Hitler's Germany was strictly forbidden. The massacre in Katyń, forced relocation of millions of Poles, mass arrests and sending Poles to camps in Siberia or Kolyma were taboo. Joseph Stalin was the unsurpassed genius who saved the entire world from fascism and was the best friend Poland has ever had. The United States and their allies were the enemy looking for an opportunity to attack the peace loving Soviet Union and its friends. The Home Army was a group of hooligans nearly as bad as Nazis and the Warsaw Uprising was an act of provocation by the disgusting reactionary Poles from London.

Some teachers refused to teach this grotesque and were promptly sacked and new ones, properly indoctrinated by the authorities were sent in. Police force was established and their presence was quite wide. Only tiny villages had no police stations, any substantial villages, small towns and cities had them now. Initially set up to keep order police was generally snooping around and was always on lookout for subversive elements. Propaganda was full of warnings of foreign spies sent by the imperialistic West led by the United States of America. The secret police was hunting for the members of the Home Army. The People's Republic of Poland declared the Home Army was in fact an enemy of the people and it did very little in fight against fascism. It was the People's Army that was carrying the resistance and fight. Many Home Army officers, especially those from the high command were arrested, accused of treason, put on fake show trials and sentenced to death. Countless lower rank officers and soldiers were executed without trial in cellars of secret police buildings. Poland was slipping deeper in deeper into the abyss of a totalitarian system driven by insanity of Stalin and his cohorts ruling Poland. What to the West was known as the "Iron Curtain" hid the madness of state sponsored murder and torture on a massive scale. Till this day many families are searching for graves of their loved ones who disappeared in those years as the secret police was frequently burying its victims in unmarked graves or just out in the countryside.

While Stan was trying to look for work and concentrated on practical matters, Irena was despising the new order with all of her mind and soul. She took care of the household and Gabriela and Matilda and knowing how perverted the "new" history program at school was, she took time to talk to them about the past to make sure they would know how it really was. It wasn't really hard as both girls remembered a lot as they were big enough. Irena only made sure they understood that saying certain things to classmates or teachers could have unpleasant consequences. But both were surprisingly clever to be able to filter what they knew from what they were supposed to know officially. Such modus operandi was not exactly new to generations of Poles in general. Between 1795 and 1919 when Poland was partitioned between Russia, Prussia and Austria, people learned to be careful and vigilant. In fact many say that Poles are quick to oppose whoever governs them because of the historical precondition. Generations of Poles lived under foreign and hostile powers so by this default they've learned that whatever was coming form the "above" it was no good and was to be opposed.

Irena's longing for Warsaw was by now deeply rooted in her. She hated the new reality which seemed to promote primitive and arrogant people as long as they were aligned with the obnoxious new system and she feared that Warsaw as she knew it may never return. She did not like Józefów either, to her it was just a rural setting foreign to her and while it may have had certain charms she did not like them at all.

One day Stan returned from yet another trip to Warsaw and he was visibly pleased.

"Isia," he said, "I will have my old job back, it's a matter of a week or two. The office is just about to be set up, there are few clients already lined up."

"Fantastic!" she was happy for him, "I'm depressed with all that goes on around us, maybe it's a sign of a better life for us."

"I hope so," Stan was optimistic, "perhaps that nonsense will cease or at least subside. I also have another piece of news."

"What is it?"

"I bought a radio from Kowalski. It was too big for me to carry it with me but later today his son will bring it here on some push cart."

"Oh, that's great," she smiled, "music will be a nice break from the otherwise boring life here."

"Is it that boring?"

"It's not what I am used to and you know it. On the other hand I met our neighbors who live in the flat above us – they are Halina and Marian. They are very pleasant and classy. He was in military and she has some German ancestors but she is Polish of course. They live here for couple of years now and told me to ask if I need anything."

"It's good then – isn't it?"

"Well, - yes, of course."

The radio was a very impressive looking device with nicely finished wooden box. When switched on, the scale would light up and the loudspeaker would come alive.

"It's German!" Irena exclaimed with a note of disapproval in her voice after she examined it.

"No," contradicted her Stan, "it is Swedish origin, but it may have some German parts I suppose."

"Thank God!" she sighed.

The two of them fiddled with the radio for a while like children, wandering with the dial from station to station trying to see what can be picked up. While browsing through the short waves despite a lot of static and odd noises they could suddenly hear a voice saying in Polish "this is the Polish Broadcast of the Radio Free Europe."

They looked at each other.

"I know what it is," said Stan, "the communists hate it and in fact one can get locked up for listening to it."

"It must be good, then," declared Irena, "and it most likely tells the truth. I'm going to listen to it!"

She thought of the time when she was working for the resistance listening to broadcasts during the occupation time.

"Good God - how odd," she commented, "it's like in a twisted mirror. Back then I was listening to foreign broadcasts for our underground Polish free press. Now I am listening to Polish broadcast from a foreign country talking to us from the free world because we are occupied once again. What have we done to deserve this?"

"We haven't done anything wrong Isia," there was slight sadness in Stan's voice "it's politics and our unfortunate location between Russians and Germans. Both hate us and both are bigger and stronger. This time the West sold us to the Soviets. It's actually that simple."

She had not responded as there was nothing she could say. Objectively speaking he was right. But she promised herself to listen again to that radio station. Whoever was behind the programming, made it sound normal in sharp contrast to the obnoxiously hyped pro-Soviet propaganda being trumpeted by the communist Polish Radio Warsaw. This Radio Free Europe resembled the times before the war and Irena could almost time travel to those days. It made her feel better and sad at the same time.

"Just remember, Isia" Stan reminded her, "last week an entire family was arrested after somebody sent an anonymous letter to the police saying they were listening to the Radio Free Europe."

"I'll be careful. If Gestapo didn't catch me, the communists won't either. I'm hungry to know what is happening in the world, I mean the truth, not that crap they keep barking here day in, day out."

Stan's job materialized and they were happy as finally they were going to have a steady income and it was a big step forward. But the flipside was Stan had to travel to some bigger and smaller towns, which made him absent from home for stretches of time. But the money was good and to ease travelling Stan could afford to purchase an old motorcycle so he did not have to rely on trains.

Life was becoming stabilized and while Irena recognized it she had her longing for the city she loved so much. Nice interruption of her daily life were chats with her neighbors Marian or Halina or both of them. On their way to or from their flat they had to walk by Irena's kitchen window and they had to pass her door before they went up on the staircase. All she had to do was to open the door and had a brief chat right there or ask them in for a cup of tea. Marian was considerably older than her and older than Stan. He was an old fashion gentlemen, always well dressed even if it was modest. He was also very polite and when Irena chatted just with him without Ann present he made her feel so good and light hearted. Her face would light up and she felt weightless, in similar way as when she was dancing so many years ago. Sometimes, while talking their eyes would lock for a moment and Irena felt a strange vibe.

In the meantime Matilda and Gabriela were making progress at school. Matilda was frequently talking about becoming a doctor some day and Gabriela was interested in commerce. They both hoped to go through the higher education to achieve their goals. They struggled a bit with the official indoctrination at school which they both hated and branded as stupid.

Outside school they had a group of friends. They were all a nice bunch of kids, boys and girls. Irena knew most of them as they all lived nearby and at times they were coming to her house. Among them was somewhat moody and quiet, good looking boy named Jurek. He was a bit older than the rest of them and Irena knew he was in the Home Army during the Uprising. He was very lucky for he was never discovered by the secret police or perhaps they decided he was not important enough. Jurek seemed to like Gabriela, Irena thought, as she saw them talking more and more and it seemed when talking to him Gabriela was unusually engaged in conversation. Matilda was attracting boys attention too as she was way more outgoing and cheerful.

Bearing her own experiences in mind, Irena was making her observations and trying to monitor the situation. She was aware that sooner or later there will be time to talk to both daughters about relationships, such moment was clearly approaching. She was not looking forward to it though. Being in her late thirties she was still at odds with herself and not quite sure of herself at times. Sometimes she felt being less mature than everybody else same age as her. Her relationship with Stan was not what she thought it should be. Physical aspect of their marriage was precarious to say the least. One day she felt guilty, the next day she thought he was to blame. After so much they went through together they were very close, as close as two people can be, but in her mind they were not lovers anymore. Come to think of it perhaps they never were from the very first night. It was not what Irena thought it would or should be. If she had any passion at all, it was gone. Sometimes she wondered how it was that she had never felt certain strange vibe with Stan but was getting it when talking to Marian. The vibe was so unspecific and vague but sometimes it gave her a funny ever so slight itching in the lower part of her body. She didn't know what it was and why it was happening. She was a wife and a mother and she was doing her best to fulfill both roles but her best was not necessarily what other people would consider as best. But she was doing what she could and she was finding consolation in her faith which was one or perhaps the only thing she had with her that was solid as a rock. Listening to the mass every Sunday she felt free of problems that were thrown at her by fate or circumstances which more often than not she didn't like. In church she found consolation and the only direct connection to her past. Listening to songs and prayers she could be at any time in her past or perhaps in the future because the world around her was different, but here in church everything was the same as always. Halina and Marian, the neighbors from upstairs were regular churchgoers too and sometimes after the service thy walked home together. During special holidays when the chief priest would walk under a canopy carrying the Holy bread he would be supported by two distinguished members of their parish and Marian was usually one of them. One such day was Corpus Christi. It was a rare occasion when communists would not dare to interfere with the show of faith by the nation. The procession in Józefów marched around one block stopping at every turn to pray at improvised altars. The last stretch before returning to church was leading in front of Irena's house. It always looked as if entire population of Józefów was there.

The worst moments she had when she'd recall her leaving the ballet. During the war she hadn't had time to dwell in the past much, but now, as life was somewhat normalized sometimes she was haunted by that. She was convinced her life could have been completely different had she not had that pregnancy back then. Perhaps such thoughts somewhat contributed to decline and disappearance of her passion for Stan.

Stan returned from work in a cheerful mood and during dinner he said he had rather big news. Irena, Gabriela and Matilda went silent and looked at him with anticipation.

"Well," he began, "after trying hard for a very long time I finally managed to secure a flat for us in Warsaw. We can pack up and move immediately."

Irena jumped from his chair, hugged and kissed him several times.

"Oh, Stan this is the happiest moment we have since the war destroyed everything! Good God, you can't imagine how happy you've just made me."

Matilda was all in smiles too.

"I shall miss my friends here but it's going to be great to be in Warsaw again!" she declared, "I can always write letters to my friends here or come for a visit."

Gabriela however sat silently and had not uttered a word.

"What's the matter, Gabriela?" asked Stan, "we are returning to Warsaw – aren't you happy?"

"Where is the flat?" asked Irena, "Krucza hasn't been possibly rebuilt yet?"

"No, Isia. Krucza – who knows when it will be rebuilt and it's hard to say what chances we'd have to be back at number nine. The flat I found is at the Pankiewicza Street. I saw it and it's not bad - not bad at all, considering how monumentally difficult it is to find any decent flat."

The three of them – Irena, Stan and Matilda were not paying much attention to Gabriela as they were happily chirping about the anticipated move.

"When do we move?" asked Matilda.

"I have to organize some transport for our belongings and off we go – in a couple of days I hope," explained Stan.

"I don't want to move to Warsaw," declared Gabriela with a stern face, "I want to stay here!"

"But Gabriela," Irena was surprised, "Warsaw is our city, our true home. We are all born there and we are here only because of the war."

Gabriela gave her mother a defiant look.

"I want to stay here. There will be another war and we will all die in that wretched cellar we sat in during bombings and during the Uprising."

"Nonsense!" exclaimed Stan, "the war is over. It's peace time and there won't be another war. It's really absurd to think otherwise."

"I don't want to move to Warsaw!" Gabriela raised her voice "I will never go there, I hate moving."

"Gabriela…" tried Irena.

"No!!!" screamed Gabriela, "leave me alone! I won't go, I don't want to go! There will be war again. You can say what you want but I know it will be and it is only going to get worse. I don't want to die like a rat locked in the damn cellar, do you hear?! I won't move!!!"

She pushed her chair from the table, run to the other room and slammed the door behind her.

There was a grave silence in the room. Matilda was looking at her parents. Irena and Stan were surprised by the temper tantrum and they were not sure what to do.

"She can't do this to me," whispered bewildered Irena half to Stan, half to herself.

Stan embraced her and looked into her eyes.

"I know what it means to you, Isia. Don't worry, she will come around. Perhaps this is just a reaction to what she's been through for the past six years. Sometimes people react in odd ways. Maybe I shouldn't have said that quite so suddenly, I'm really sorry. I do have that flat on hold. I paid some money up front so we don't have to move immediately. We just can't take forever, that's all. Let's give her a day or two."

Irena nodded and got up to clean the dishes after the meal. Matilda collected the utensils and brought them to the kitchen, then went to the bathroom to get ready to go to bed for the night. Gabriela did not emerge from the room the girls were sharing.

Before falling asleep Matilda tried to talk to her sister.

"Are you asleep Gabriela?"

"Leave me alone!"

"Why are you like this? Nobody did anything to you."

"Don't bother me, just leave me alone and go to sleep."

"Good night, then" said Matilda but there was no answer.

On Sunday Irena and Stan arranged for Matilda to go to a friend's house for a while and they tried to talk to Gabriela. So far they had never had any problems with either one of their daughters but they were aware that the war, long years of occupation, the Warsaw Uprising and the exodus from the destroyed city must have made some scars on them. There were occasions that Gabriela seemed to be scared more than anyone and did not want to leave the cellar after an artillery shell or a bomb fell somewhere close, but back then there was no time for analysis. In fact, anybody who survived it all must have some scars – no question about it. But for young children it was worse. It is not normal for young ones to see death, destruction, maltreatment of population by foreign soldiers, beatings, even mass executions. Stan and Irena figured Gabriela had such emotional scars, signs of which were showing back in September 1939 when she would not want to emerge from the cellar even after the air raids were called off. In the chaos of those days they were not spending extra time explaining things to her as it was just not something that was the most important thing to do. As she was growing up she was somewhat more serious and moody than her younger sister but they did not perceive it as a problem. They'd just accepted it as sisters being different. Otherwise she was a good kid and a good student which is really all a parent wants. The sudden resistance and anger was something new and they were not sure what to make of it. They could simply choose to just ignore her resistance and literarily order her to do what was necessary but at the moment they decided to reason with her.

She was sitting on her bed with her back against the wall, knees bent high and feet resting on bed so that she was supporting a book resting on her knees.

"We need to talk to you Gabriela," Irena said in a soft voice as she walked into the room and sat on the corner of Gabriela's bed.

Gabriela looked at her.

"What about?" she asked.

"Our move to Warsaw," said Stan who'd joined them now.

"I don't want to talk about it," Gabriela was looking at her book.

"Gabriela, you are mature enough and we expect you to be sensible. Can you tell us if anything happened to you that we don't know?" asked Stan.

"No," she said.

"I can understand you may not want to talk to me, I can leave so that you talk to Mum," Stan continued in reconciliatory mood.

"I'd rather talk to you."

Stan and Irena exchanged looks.

"All right," Irena got up "I live you two to it."

She walked away and closed the door.

"I think you've just hurt Mum," said Stan.

"I don't care," snapped Gabriela "she doesn't understand me at all."

"How can you say that? Mum loves you very much."

"She loves Matilda better and I know it. Everything spins around her."

"Matilda is younger than you and has to be treated differently sometimes. By the reversed token we expect you to be more mature and understand more difficult things."

"She has different faces for different people."

"Look Gabriela, this is not about your sister. I need you to understand that us being here in Józefów was from the very beginning only a temporary measure. We moved from my friend's flat only because there were too many people there, not because we wanted to move out of Warsaw. Mum and I are city folk, our families have deep roots there. Mum always loved Warsaw and I know she'll never be happy anywhere else. I love Mum and I want her to be happy."

"More than me?"

"This is childish Gabriela and I hope you realize that."

"I like Józefów. Warsaw is a pile of smoldering stinking rubble."

"I can understand that what you saw in the last six years made a deep impression on you, but things change. The city will be rebuilt, it is being done as we speak and will be great again. And the flat is quite nice, you'll see."

"They will chuck us out and we will be nowhere again."

"Nobody will chuck us out."

"Yes they will. Original owners can return or the communists will do so. You were talking about things like that taking place. I even have a classmate whose family was thrown out from their home. The father was arrested and taken away and the mother was given a horse cart and one hour time to clear out. They had no place to go. It will be the same with us or new war will come and it will be all over the same."

"Gabriela, I do hope you are not falling for the idiotic propaganda about western imperialism."

"I'm scared of being thrown out again, I hate not having place on our own."

"We are just about to move to our own place."

"I'm not going anywhere!"

"Look, I'm the head of our family and I'm trying to explain things to you as if I was talking to a mature person. Mum and I decide what we do. You and Matilda need to adjust one more time. I will always protect you as long as I live. In case you really have some fears in your thoughts I'm telling you they have no substance whatsoever."

Seeing things were not going her way, Gabriela looked at him with anger and replied:

"I'll run away. I'll go to an orphanage and tell them I have no family. They will take me in. You all can go."

"Would you hurt Mum and me that much? How could you even think of that?"

"You are hurting me!" she hissed, "and you don't seem to be

troubled by it."

"I'm trying to explain things to you."

"I will not move!" she shouted "I'm sick of it all! If you move it means neither you nor Mum love me, I will then know for a fact you don't care about me!"

This conversation was going nowhere and Stan was sensing she was pulling away into some sort of psychological shell. But his patience was also running thin so he decided to throw his weight about.

"Look, I tried hard and I work very hard for our family and this obviously includes you. Mum and I love you both equally and do all we can for you but I won't have a child telling me what to do. Until you are an adult we tell you what you do. We are moving in three days and you'd better be ready!"

He walked to the kitchen where Irena was, poured himself a glass of cold water and drank it in one gulp.

"How did it go?" she asked.

"She is so stubborn," said Stan, "I can't understand where it's coming from. Please try to make some sense with her when I'm at work."

"I will try," she said, "but for a while now I feel she has more respect for you."

"Thank you," he put his arms around her and tried to kiss her on the mouth but she twisted her head so he just kissed her cheek.

"I love you Isia," he whispered.

"I know."

Her answer sounded a bit mechanical but he hadn't noticed.

*

The spotlight was focused on her as she went into the *fouetté en tournant en dehors*. Suddenly, after the third revolution the trapdoor under her feet opened and she dropped into the darkness but did not hit the floor. She was just falling freely and couldn't see anything around her except occasional single sparks which looked like distant stars. After the initial shock and expectation of hitting some hard surface the feeling was almost pleasant now. A bright light appeared in a distance and was growing slowly and steadily. It seemed like an end to a dark tunnel through which she was falling. It was not approaching fast and she had no fear at all. She was surrounded by light now, which after the darkness moments ago was blinding and it took her a while until her eyes adjusted and she could see where she was. She found herself standing in front of a tall stone wall. The stones were color of sand. She looked around but there was nothing but sand, not a single tree or anything growing there. The sky was intensely blue and free of clouds. The wall seemed reaching the horizon on both sides, it had no end at all. Only now she noticed a small wooden door right in front of her. As she was trying to comprehend her situation there was a sound from the other side as if some rusty mechanism squeaked pressed or forced by somebody or something and the door opened. There was a young girl standing there framed by the door. She had straight long blond hair parted on top of her head. Her slender figure was covered in a simple white linen robe.

"Hello Irena," she said with a sad smile.

"You know me?" asked Irena, "who are you?"

"I'm your aborted daughter."

Instantly everything went impenetrably black as if somebody switched off the light.

Irena opened her eyes. She felt sweat on her forehead and her heart was beating fast. She was lying in her own bed. Stan was sleeping next to her breathing rhytmically.

*

Stan went to work on Monday thinking about Gabriela. He'd said what he'd said but he generally detested when a person, even as immature as Gabriela was forced to do something. That is, in a clear situation it would be all right to use the parental authority. But he worried she may have had some problem that was making her acting the way she did. If the problem was genuine and defined then it could be addressed and solved. But if she was just being stubborn it would be okay to just force his will. He felt insecure about this and he had nobody he could talk to.

He rearranged his day so that he could go home early. He told Irena he'd be back sooner then usual. On one hand he hoped that without him around Irena may be able to sort it out with Gabriela but on the other he wanted to be there. His family was in a crisis and his place was home.

Irena expected him at about four in the afternoon. The four o'clock came but there was no sign of Stan. Irena kept the dinner warm on the kitchen stove hoping he'd show up any minute but sound of his motorcycle was not heard. Then an hour went by and yet another.

"Mum, when is Dad coming home?" inquired Matilda.

"He should be here now, something must have kept him. Dad works very hard," explained Irena.

The evening came but still there was no sign of Stan and Irena began to worry.

At about eight in the evening she heard a sound of an engine but it was not Stan's motorcycle. The sound was different, somewhat lower and she thought it was a bit like the sound of police motorcycle with a sidecar the local station was using.

The sound was coming closer and closer and then it was cut. In a moment there was a strong knock on the door.

She walked to the door and without opening it asked:

"Who is it?"

"Police, Mrs. Szumska, please open up. It's about your husband."

Irena opened the door. There was a uniformed policeman standing in front of her.

"I'm sorry to tell you," he said, "but we received a phone call and were asked to tell you, your husband had an accident while riding his motorcycle. He is in the hospital in Grochów."

Irena felt a shiver running through her and for a brief moment was thinking whether or not it was actually true. Maybe they arrested him and this was just to mislead her for whatever reason.

"How is he?" she inquired.

"I don't know," the policeman replied, "but you can go visit him tomorrow. He is injured so they need to keep him for a while."

"Thank you."

Irena closed the door and turned around. Gabriela and Matilda standing there in front of her.

"What happened to Dad?" asked Matilda.

"You heard the man," she said, "I don't know anything else. I will go to the hospital tomorrow while you are at school."

"I don't want you to go there while we are here alone," demanded Gabriela.

"There is no other way. You are not going to be alone, you are going to be at school and when you return home and I'm not here you go upstairs to Halina and Marian."

"I want to go with you," Gabriela insisted.

"No, you go to school with your sister like usual."

"No!"

"You'll do as I say!" snapped Irena.

Gabriela turned around and walked away to the room she shared with Matilda.

"It's okay Mum," said Matilda, "she can be like that you know."

Irena sighed.

"I know. I just wish she wasn't, that's all."

*

The hospital was quiet. Irena gave her name and asked where her husband was. She was pointed to a long corridor and went on to look for room number 126. She found it without difficulty and opened the door.

Stan was lying on bed with his right leg immobilized and wrapped in bandage or cast, it was hard to tell. His forehead was also dressed in a bandage.

"Stan!" she run to him and kissed his face several times.

"Isia!" he was happy to see her, "it's so good of you to be here."

"What happened?" she looked at him up close.

"I… I don't know. My motorcycle must have slipped on something I haven't noticed. Suddenly I was out of balance, falling."

"Were you riding fast?"

He looked at her.

"I wanted to be home as soon as possible so I was not riding slowly but I didn't do anything out of ordinary. I was just riding like I always do."

"What's with your leg? Because it seems to me more serious than your head."

"Oh, head is just a scratch but the leg…"

"How bad is it?"

"They are not sure if they can save it."

"Good God, Stan. But don't worry. You made it through the war, this is just a scratch. I'll talk to the doctor to get better idea."

"You think he'd tell you more than me?" Stan was skeptical.

"Do you want anything? Do they feed you here?"

"I'm not exactly hungry but yes, they give me meals."

"I will go out now and try to buy some fruit for you. Will be back within an hour or so."

"Okay, thank you."

"All right then" she walked towards the door.

"Isia?"

She turned around.

"If I am handicapped I may loose my job. Mobility is the key to it."

"Don't worry about it now," she said, "it's going to be all right. It could've been much worse."

She smiled and walked out of the room but as soon as she was in the hallway her mood sunk. Without Stan's job it was going to be hard again. She'd have to pick up sewing to keep the household going at some minimum level.

She found the doctor, thanked him for what he'd done so far and asked about the future.

"The prognosis…" he hesitated for a moment, "the damage to his knee is extensive. I will do all I can to save your husband's leg. I don't like to amputate unless I have no options left so you can rest assured I will do my utmost."

"I understand. Thank you, doctor. Thank you very much."

"You haven't recognized me, have you, Irena?"

She looked at him.

"No, I'm afraid not. I'm sorry. Have we met?"

"I am Jan Kowalski, I was your partner at Lidia Jastrzębska Dancing School."

Only now her memory kicked in.

"Oh my God, it is you!" she smiled, "but…"

"I was wounded in the Uprising. My beard hides ugly scars but never mind that, I am so pleased to see you. I was shocked when I learned you quit dancing back then."

"I… I got married, you know, and everything changed."

"You've never said good-bye."

"It was not so simple, quite opposite in fact. It wasn't done the way I would've wanted, I'm sorry."

"I was quite smitten with you back then, you know," he smiled.

"I didn't know," she lied.

A nurse appeared some distance away and called him to a patient.

"Sorry Irena, I have to run. Perhaps we'll have a chance for a proper chat some day."

"That'll be nice, good-bye!" she said and watched him disappear in the hallway.

As she was walking out of the hospital her head was spinning. It was not a tragedy for a tragedy would be if Stan died. It's just that Stan being handicapped was at least for the moment difficult to think of. Irena had no idea or experience with any form of handicap. She did not know how it was when someone partially looses mobility and what – if any - psychological consequences could be. For the moment she thought of just the physical aspect and look and something like a shiver went down her spine but she immediately pushed it aside and scolded herself. But how Gabriela and Matilda would take it? Stan was not going to change - he was going to be the same he always was.

She walked a block or two and found a small shop that had some apples. She bought a few and returned to Stan, sat with him for an hour or so, promised to return the next day and left as the journey to Józefów was time consuming.

Few days later she was sitting in doctor Kowalski's office.

"I'm afraid I don't have the best of news," he said.

She felt frightened.

"What is it?"

"Your husband's leg will be saved, but his knee will be locked permanently. We had to operate it, but the trouble is there is so much damage that we can't restore it."

"You've frightened me," she said, "for a moment I thought it was something worse."

"I'm sorry, I didn't mean to. But we did hope to get him back to normal so it is disappointing."

"It's all right," she recovered, "I was prepared for such outcome."

"The thing is though," he continued, "he will need a long time to heal so he will be bed ridden for several weeks. He'll need help getting to the bathroom. Eventually he'll get better and then it will take time and patience to get used to having a stiff leg."

"Several weeks?" she echoed.

"Yes, it could be around three months, maybe more."

Irena's face changed.

"Obviously, he won't not be able to go to work for some time as his mobility will be limited."

"When can I take him home?"

"In a week from today. I will make arrangements for an ambulance. Where do you live?"

"In Józefów. It is about – I don't know - fifty kilometers from here."

"I see. How will you manage?"

She looked at him.

"I'll manage. We have two daughters."

"You may need assistance from a nurse at the beginning."

"I know a nurse who lives in the neighborhood."

"Good," he gave her a faint smile, "I'm sorry I could not do better."

"Thank you in any case. I will go to him now, if that's all."

"Of course."

She stepped outside of his office and sighed heavily: *Oh, God - why?*

She then walked to the ward where Stan was.

*

Stan was out of bed and walking again nearly a year later but he gained some weight and was not happy about it. He was also irritable as he was still adjusting to being handicapped. His job was gone as his employer could not keep his position for him that long. There was work that needed to be done and it required travelling so they hired somebody in Stan's place and Mister Zalewski promised to see if there would be anything for him to do once he recovered after the accident.

Early on Gabriela and Matilda had to quit school and went to work to help Irena maintain the household as the costs were mounting. Without Stan's job the family had no money to live on and Irena had to be home for him practically all the time. Both daughters were unhappy about having to quit school because this practically meant no continuation and no further education. Matilda was taking it harder as she dreamed of becoming a doctor some day.

Both girls continued to see their group of friends which was by now crystallized and there were few pairs among them and it looked as if they were going to marry within few years or so. Gabriela was seeing Jurek, a boy she had met at school and Matilda was attracted to Gabriela's classmate, Teodor. He was son of a landowners who were thrown out from their home by the new authorities in the process of implementing the agrarian reform in 1946. Their land was taken away from them and Teodor's mother was given about an hour to gather her most necessary possessions, load them on a horse cart and leave. Her husband, Teodor's father was arrested and taken away without any explanations. Not only he was considered "bourgeoisie" and therefore an enemy of the state, they also knew his oldest son was in the Home Army. It was enough to arrest him.

Teodor had three older siblings – two brothers and a sister. Life was hard for them as his mother had never worked in her life apart from running the household but she always had help in form of a servant or two. She was fortunate to get to Józefów where she knew somebody from the times before the war and she secured a small flat to live in. Some merciful soul let her stay without charging her for rent for a while. Being reasonably resourceful she began sewing things as sewing was the only marketable skill she possessed. With time she had some number of clients who usually needed repairs. Hardly anyone was ordering completely new articles, not in Józefów anyway.

Teodor and Matilda were not really walking out but they liked each other's company and they did spent time together. Teodor's older brother was locked up in prison in the Lublin Castle for his activity in the Home Army. His other brother was bent on getting higher education and so was his sister. Teodor himself was not exactly academic and had his doubts concerning education. The current political system was all about the working class and workers were praised and cherished by the authorities, they were also considerably better paid than engineers. Additionally, those who joined the workers party were paid better than those who did not. The system was looking down at intelligentsia while praising peasants and workers. Young Teodor had no intention of joining the party which robbed his family of their home and land but was thinking about taking a job as a worker rather than continuing education. Finances were also an important factor. Education was free but he would need to be sustained by his mother and with money being tight it was problematic for three kids. He was sensing that he would have to be sacrificed anyway so to speak. But he had certain self esteem as he was good with tools and could repair nearly anything he got his hands on.

One evening Gabriela walked to see Jurek who lived nearby but she returned within few minutes crying.

"What's the matter, Gabriela?" asked Irena.

"Jurek was arrested last night by the secret police!" she was sobbing uncontrollably.

"Why?"

"Somebody must have reported him to the police!" she said through the tears, "the bastards knew he had a handgun."

"Why on earth he had a gun?"

"You don't understand, Mum. This gun saved his life in the Uprising when he was cornered somewhere by Germans. He loved it for this reason. But knowing guns were made illegal now he made it useless by damaging the firing chamber or whatever it is called. He drilled a hole through it so it rendered it useless. But the bastards did not care. His mother told me they busted in late at night shouting "Where are you hiding the gun you son of a bitch?" and beat him up. She tried to protest and they shoved her to another room. They found the gun and took Jurek away."

Irena felt silent for a moment. She despised communists and she was aware of the abuses by the feared secret police.

"Crying will not help you," she said, "try to focus on something else of practical nature. I will go and visit his mother to support her. I will encourage her to go to the police station seeking information about her son. The bastards pretend to obey their own laws, so within a reason they owe answers to citizens."

"I love him Mum," Gabriela was crying hysterically.

Irena never heard her saying that so she was surprised a bit and she added in a softer voice.

"Don't worry. We'll get him back."

But deep down, she was not that sure. Stalin's obsession with foreign spies trickled down to the communist Poland and the secret services had practically card blanche. There were rumors circulating about individuals and families being arrested on suspicion of listening to foreign radio stations. The public trials of the so called "enemies of the working class" were staged and death sentences were nothing less than state sponsored murders. Fear among population was nearly as strong as during the war. Police was acting even on anonymous accusations. Neighbors were growing weary of neighbors they thought they knew. Only those who openly embraced the communism seemed not to worry much but the rumors had it they were not exempt from suspicions either. Looking for foreign spies and agents the system was encouraging denunciations which in turn released dark sides of human's mind and in some instances people lied for their personal gain or to get even. The farce was complete and there was no escape.

8. EVIL DEEDS

Ever since the train service to Warsaw was restored Irena was taking the ten in the morning train to the Warsaw central station every Thursday but the pre-war impressive and modern main station opened in 1938 was gone though. It survived the September 1939 in reasonably good shape hit only by a single bomb. After capitulation Germans repaired the damages so that the station remained operational throughout the occupation time but after the Uprising it was demolished with explosive charges during systematic destruction of the city by the Germans. After the war the new authorities decided not to rebuild the station. The rubble was removed and its place was left empty for years to come. Duties of the central station were delegated to another pre-war station which was small, old and seriously outdated.

From that central station Irena would walk along the Aleje Jerozolimskie Street for a distance of two blocks then she'd turn to Krucza Street and proceeded to where the number nine used to be. In early years after the war it was all rubbles for a long time until clean up began and rebuilding process commenced.

But Irena was not going to the number nine to see the progress of work. She was going to visit the chestnut tree which somehow survived the mayhem of war, the Uprising and liberation and remained full and pretty as it always was. Irena would touch its trunk and pat it like people pat their beloved pets. She'd whisper greetings to it and tell it about her worries and sorrows. More often then not she'd just cry with her tears falling down her cheeks and land at the bottom of the tree. She'd spent about half an hour or so and then, depending on her plans, she would either visit the Aleje Ujazdowskie or go to some café and meet with her only childhood friend, Janina Kozłowska. Sometimes, after visiting the tree she'd return to the station and take a train to Reguły where Janina lived and where Irena, Stan, Gabriela, Matilda and Barbara had stayed for a while after the Uprising. Janina was the only person Irena could openly talk to about everything that was on her mind.

During Stan's recuperation from the accident and elongated process of him adjusting to being handicapped Irena had to put her visits on hold and was unhappy about it. All that was left of her deeply private life that she was not sharing with her immediate family were those Thursdays and she missed them a lot just like she missed the pre-war Warsaw.

"Hello Jani."

Irena wasn't in very cheerful mood. She was always like that after visiting her tree but she loved meeting her friend.

"Isia, it's good to see you as always," Janina seemed calm as usual, "how are you doing?"

"We are managing. Stan is used to his new situation and any day now he is going to venture to Warsaw to his former employer to see if he can find some work. The girls are working steadily. How about you?"

Janina began to cry.

"What is it, Jani?" asked Irena.

"It's Wiktor," she said through her tears.

"What's going on?"

"You know he can't get used to living in England. At the same time the "new" Polish Embassy is encouraging all Poles to come home and help in rebuilding the country. They put quite an effort to get people to return."

"That's not what our government in London says. They say Poles who return, military personnel especially, get arrested as soon as they set foot on Polish soil," said Irena, "you know that, don't you?"

"Yes, I heard rumors."

Irena was firm.

"These are not rumors Jani, these are facts."

"How can you be so sure?"

"I listen to the radio. That's what the BBC said and the RFE confirmed. Secret police here grabs them all, the higher the rank the worse it gets. Some people just disappear, they are never heard from again. It's a nightmare!"

"But… but he misses the country, the family, he is just homesick and he doesn't like England at all. Next time we meet I will show you his letters. He says that while the Battle of England was raging on, the Polish fighter pilots were the heroes and the public over there couldn't get enough of them. Newspapers were writing stories about them and publishing their photos. They were the celebrities. Strangers were inviting them for dinners and parties and buying drinks in pubs. But once the war was over they almost overnight became like unwanted guests. Even people on the streets sometimes seeing men in Polish uniforms tell them "the war is over – go home". Some got married so it is easier for them I guess, but immigration is not for everyone. That's what he writes to me. He visited the Polish Embassy and he says the people there were so nice to him, so enthusiastic and appreciative he considers returning."

"Good God, Jani! This is just a perverted propaganda for the show, don't you realize that? He places himself in at a grave risk. They may lock him up here for years, they can accuse him of being a spy, they can even shoot him and you will never know."

Janina was crying again.

"I wrote him that. Not quite so openly, of course, but still. Nevertheless his last letter says he'd practically made up his mind. I'm so afraid, Isia. I never worried so much during the war or during the Uprising. As long as I knew he was there, I was calm even though I knew he could have been shot down any day or any hour. But now it is just so scary. Why do they hate us so much?"

"Because we know the truth, Jani, because we want to be free, because we kicked their ass in the 1920 and because they always wanted to enslave us. They hate us, the Home Army and our boys who fought in the West, they are afraid of them - that's why. Anything that comes from Russia is venomous. That includes the government here. Whoever they really are they are not us, they were taught to be so deceiving. Don't ever fell for it, Jani."

"Oh, Isia, it feels so much better talking to you."

"We must be vigilant, Jani. Those who fought for the real Poland and survived the war are being now eliminated and prosecuted by communists. They want to change the nation into a herd of cattle and then they can drive the whole population as they please with a whip. They despise church because it stands in their way to destruct families and moral values. Once the respect for family and values are gone, people have nothing to go by and are easily manipulated and controlled. That's what communism is really about. I tell you – they will make us pay for eternity for the dead Russians killed fighting Nazis on our soil but they will never even discuss Eastern Poland which they took away from us and they will never admit how many Poles they killed or sent to Siberia."

"You are right, Isia, I know you are."

"Write him a letter, Jani and use strong words. Hell – give me his address and I will write one myself. We used to…" Irena hesitated to continue.

"I know," Janina interrupted her, "I always hoped you two will end up together."

Irena had a flirt with Janina's brother before the war. He was a handsome boy with a look of a film star, somewhat similar to Rudolf Valentino, who for countless of young and not so young girls was an icon. Irena and Wiktor were flirting a lot while meeting at parties or whenever they met. It all came to an end when he decided to pursue a military career in aviation and consequently enrolled to the Air Force Academy in Dęblin which removed him from Warsaw by about 100 miles. Busy schedule and intensive training made seeing Irena impossible and as it happens with many young people placed considerable distance away they drifted apart. It did not help that fighter pilots carried certain aura around them which was rather magnetic for women. Wiktor was visiting Warsaw rarely and if he did he was spending time with his parents and sister and he was always in a hurry to get back to Dęblin. He was proud to fly his "Eleven" as the Polish built PZL-P11c was affectionately called by its pilots. It was in its time a wonderful machine but by 1939 it was outdated and no match for the Messerschmitt BF-109.

Still, Poles took to the skies in their "Elevens" and managed to score victories before the war was over. But in the end, outnumbered and with fuel and supplies exhausted, Wiktor, like many of his fellow pilots sneaked out of Poland and via Romania and Hungary to France where the Polish Air Force was reformed and equipped with modern Morane fighters. Unfortunately – France, despite her strength and potential, when confronted by German onslaught lasted even shorter than Poland and Polish pilots had to flee once again. This time they fled to England where during the Battle of Britain they wrote their most beautiful chapter ever and Wiktor was one of them.

*

Wiktor Stoczyński was looking down at Warsaw from the window of the plane carrying passengers from London to Warsaw. The city looked horrifying and depressing. It was a ruined city full of skeletons rather than houses and in many areas streets were symbolic really, just bulldozed through the rubble.

Once the plane was lower Wiktor could see people down there and some traffic. In many areas clean-up was in progress but it was not really rebuilding as yet. It was sad and depressing but his hopes were high. He was happy to be back. England was not for him and in fact it was not for many others even those who decided to stay there. The weather was bad, the rationed food terrible and the habits among population were difficult to get used to.

The hardest and painful though was the dramatic difference in attitudes towards the Polish servicemen. During the war in general and during the Battle of Britain in particular Poles were liked, admired, almost cherished. Poles were ever ready to fight Germans and they did so with bravado and fury. They demonstrated flying skills that nobody quite expected of them. On the ground they were gallant, charming and ever ready to party. Many were handsome and some were photographed and their images were used for propaganda purposes to support the war effort.

But the Battle of Britain was the peak of their popularity. When later in war Americans began arriving to England they were the news which pushed Poles to the back burner. American crews flying bombing missions from countless bases throughout England were now the hot topic. They brought with them a lot of things like different kind of supplies and sometimes new and attractive products which were either in dramatically short supply locally or never even heard of. They also brought new and cheerful music everybody wanted to dance to. With Battle of Britain won and being over Poles were now flying support missions of all sorts which were so much less spectacular. The newspapers were writing about Americans now.

When the war ended it got even worse. As people and nations were happy the war was over, Poles had no reason to celebrate as their beloved country was overrun by the Red Army and one did not have to be an expert to know that once the Red Army comes in, it never really leaves. As if this was not bad enough, a large part of Poland – in fact all eastern territory was not even Poland anymore. It was now the Soviet Union and countless soldiers who came from there had no place to return to.

In the victory parade organized in London where all nations who participated in the war effort proudly marched with their flags to celebrate the victory over Nazism there was no room for the Polish contingent. British Government specifically excluded Poles from the parade in order not to annoy Joseph Stalin and the Soviet Union.

The plane carrying Wiktor and other passengers lined up for landing and in few minutes its wheels touched the ground. Wiktor was happy. He was finally home. It was his homeland and his people now. Yes, the country and the city were in ruins but people would rebuild it just like they rebuilt it after 150 years of slavery when it was partitioned and removed from the map of Europe by Russia, Prussia and Austria.

One by one the passengers disembarked. Wiktor took his beaten up suitcase and before stepping down he looked around – damage was visible everywhere but it was home. He smiled and stepped down.

A man in a leather coat standing at the bottom of the stairs.

"Wiktor Stoczyński?"

Wiktor looked at him and replied with a smile.

"Yes, it is me."

"Come with me please," the man said without any emotion, turned around and walked towards a car waiting nearby. There was a driver behind the wheel and another man in a coat standing next to the car.

"My sister may be waiting for me somewhere here, can we look for her?" asked Wiktor.

"She's not here," he was told, "get in there please."

"Are you going to bring me to her then? I have no other place to go."

Wiktor was maintaining normal conversation but thought the situation was odd.

Both men sat on his sides and shut the door. As the driver started the engine one of them said.

"You are arrested on the suspicion of being a foreign agent sent to destabilize the government of the Polish People's Republic."

"It must be some mistake," replied Wiktor, "I'm returning home from war. I was a fighter pilot in England."

"We know who you are and what you did for the reactionary government."

"I was fighting for Poland. I have documents issued by the Polish Embassy in London and my service record is certified by them."

"Your documents will be reviewed at the station."

"Where are you taking me?"

"Police station."

Wiktor could not believe his ears.

"I demand to be taken to the military authorities at once. You have no right and no jurisdiction over me."

"We are the authorities that deal with spies like you and we have all the jurisdiction we need. I have nothing else to say to you. If you resist or try to escape I will shoot you like a dog you are, understand?"

Wiktor fell silent. He suddenly realized that all the warnings he was told in England and which he disregarded came painfully true.

The car came to a stop in front of a gate with sentries. Driver waved some card at them and inn a minute the car stopped in front of some building.

"Out of the car!" barked one of the men, "and don't even think of trying anything."

With suitcase in his hand Wiktor followed the order and after few steps was inside a room standing in front of a desk manned by a uniformed man.

He looked at Wiktor.

"Name and documents!"

Wiktor gave his name and rank and handed him his documents.

"Name only," the man said, "you have no rank here, in fact no rank at all."

"I have my rank and I earned it in combat. I don't think you are in a position to contradict my military record", he snapped back.

"Open your suitcase!" the man ordered.

He then looked through Wiktor's belongings.

"Put it back together and close it!"

Wiktor did as he was told.

The men at the desk labeled the suitcase with Wiktor's name and called:

"Stockroom!"

Another man appeared.

"Take it away!" the man at the desk ordered.

"Where are you taking it? These are my things and I need them!" protested Wiktor.

"If you don't shut up I will show you your place now!" barked the man and raised his voice again.

"Sentry!"

Another uniformed man appeared.

"Cell number 21!"

"Can you… please…," asked Wiktor "there must be some mistake. I'm a servicemen returning home. I'm a decorated fighter pilot and officer of the Polish Air Force. My record is certified by the Polish Embassy in London. It's all there in the documents I've just given you. Why are you doing this to me?"

The man looked at him with icy eyes.

"You were sent here by the rotten reactionary forces looking to carry out subversive activities in order to undermine and destabilize the Polish People's Republic. You will have a chance to talk but not now and not to me. Take him away!"

"Can I at least notify my sister?"

"She doesn't want to have anything to do with enemies of the state. Sentry, take him out of here before I loose my patience!"

The sentry placed a heavy hand on his shoulder and led him down the corridor.

"We have plenty of other vermin like you here," the sentry said, "I look forward to the execution day. I usually volunteer to be on the squad. We do it every Monday, four a.m. sharp. Stop!" he ordered Wiktor when they arrived at a metal door with number 21 painted on it. He opened it with a key and pushed Wiktor forward.

"In there, you fascist pig!"

Wiktor only managed to notice there were already several men in the small cell before the heavy door was slammed shut and locked behind him.

*

Stan adjusted his tie and turning towards the kitchen called:

"I'm leaving, Isia."

She appeared from behind the door.

"Good luck, Stan!"

She then grabbed him and gave him a peck on the cheek.

"Not sure when I'll be back," he said and left.

Irena watched him from behind the curtain as he walked around the house to the gate and then left towards the station. He walked slowly but steady and firmly. He wasn't using a cane, he did not need to and he hated the idea anyway. Apparently his exercises paid off and at no time he disappeared from her view. He gave himself plenty of time to catch the ten o'clock train and she had no doubts he was going to make it all right.

She also hoped his meeting with his former employer will bring up some prospects for work. She prayed for this so hard and believed it was going to be okay. She returned to the kitchen where she put the radio on and carefully navigated to BBC but after a while she changed to the Voice of America.

It's been so many years since they got married but still every now and then she'd think about her doubts. It was a recurring process and she didn't know if it was her own sense of guilt for marrying him without loving him at full hundred percent or if it was just some external splinter like thoughts tormenting her. Being deeply religious she confessed that long time ago but was told she gave her word during the wedding ceremony and was expected to keep it. She never thought of a divorce and had no other reasons. Stan loved her dearly and loved both daughters and in this sense he was a shining example of a family man. He liked a drink like any other man and sometimes he'd get tipsy but that was it. He was always calm and had no violence in him at all. The only thing about Stan was that sometimes he could be stubborn and unable to see somebody else's point of view. And finally, there was the thing with their intimacy. While he always had a strong drive, she had it at a different and by now much lower level and since the first time she had a slight problem with physical attraction and perhaps as a consequence she had never really enjoyed sex. With time she was slowly growing cold but did her best to at least appear affectionate. It worked but she had a sense of guilt about that too as she was faking things for years.

But the family as a unit was functioning well. They went together through so much and it seemed they bonded rather well. The only exceptions were occasional arguments with Gabriela who, perhaps like her father, could be stubborn and uncompromising. As long as both girls were just children it was never a problem but now with Gabriela and Matilda being in their teens the tensions were high.

Matilda was seeing this Teodor kid who appeared to be all right. He was polite and nice but it seemed he was avoiding coming to Irena's house. He would only come to pick Matilda up and they were off. Very rarely he would come and stay so it was hard to get to know him better.

Gabriela was clearly waiting for Jurek to return and she was edgy and explosive about the tiniest detail but Irena understood it was all about him.

Knowing the madness of the dictatorship of the proletariat being in charge of Poland and their hatred for the Home Army, Irena feared the worst. She even thought of preparing Gabriela for the worst but talking to her was impossible as she would get hysterical and unreasonable. Irena wanted to help her so much but she couldn't find a way to approach her.

Based on her own experience she wanted to make sure her daughters run their lives better or at least the decisions they'd needed to make would be carefully thought through. Inhibited by her own past she felt somewhat trapped between Gabriela's outbursts and Matilda's boyfriend avoiding their home. If he was doing so now when he was so young, it was only going to be more pronounced later. At the same time Matilda was going to and spending time with his family more and more. Every parent hopes to continue seeing children in the future even when they have their own families. While always caring about having her own time and her own privacy, Irena worried about family relations in the future.

Stan returned home about eight in the evening. He was tired as he tried to walk fast from the station so he was a bit out of breath but he was clearly pleased.

"It's not immediate Isia," he said, "but I talked to somebody about accounting job in some organization that is being set up to oversee a federation of several sport clubs. It's being formed and organized as we speak and the man said he'd be happy to hire me. He needs to submit my candidacy for his boss' approval and if it all goes well I could have a job in two weeks or so!"

"My God, Stan, it's a fantastic news!" Irena hugged him and kissed him on the cheek.

"Would it be in Warsaw?" she asked.

"Yes, they are talking about having the office somewhere close to the city center. It means, of course, I will have to commute every day. I am guessing I will be taking the six twenty train every morning."

"Will it not be too exhausting for you?" she worried.

"Nonsense!" he declared, "I am sick of being on the backburner for such a long time doing nothing. Because of me the girls had to drop out of school. I am feeling absolutely great. The only thing is I don't have the speed I used to have because of my leg. Other than that I feel strong as an ox and ready to go!" he smiled and hugged her again trying to kiss her on the lips but she escaped. He just gently touched her bottom.

"Stop it!" she said.

"Later perhaps," he smiled again.

*

The heavy metal door opened with a squeak of old hinges and the guard appeared.

"Nowak!" he barked, "get your ass ready!"

One of the eleven men in the cell got up to his feet. He was in his late twenties but he looked like an old man. His jet black hair he always combed back was gray at the temples. His nose was broken after the last interrogation and he could not breathe through it well. His front teeth were knocked out by a brutal punch of his interrogating officer. The jacket he had on had blood stains on collar and lapels. He was weak from eating a piece of bread in the morning and watery soup in the evening.

"Get moving!" the guard barked and motioned with his head towards the dimly lit hall. As soon as Jurek crossed the door the guard slammed it shut and turned the key.

"Where am I going?" inquired Jurek.

"Shut up!" ordered the guard.

He led him up the stairs which made Jurek think he was going for yet another interrogation. His body was still sore after the last one yesterday and he could not walk very fast.

When they arrived to the top of the stairs the guard ordered him to open the door. Jurek only observed that this was not the door to the room where he's been interrogated last night. Obeying the guard he opened the door and found himself in a well lit area. He had to squint his eyes to see where he was. It looked like the area where they brought him in when he first got arrested.

"To the desk!"

Jurek approached the desk where a man was sitting writing something in a file – he had a stack of them.

"Name?" he asked.

"Nowak, Jerzy Nowak."

"Place and date of birth?"

Jurek gave the men his date of birth and place.

The men wrote something in the opened file, then turned it around and placed it in front of Jurek.

"The government of the working class is showing you how forgiving and merciful it is by releasing you. Not that you are not guilty you little shit. Personally I think you should be shot along with your lot. But the law is the law and you can go and crawl back to where you came from. Make sure you don't give us reasons to bring you back here because it will end far less pleasantly. Sign here!" he pointed at the bottom of the document in front of Jurek.

"What am I signing for?"

"You are signing to confirm you will never, ever disclose anything you were asked, anything you said, anything you have seen or heard here. You are also confirming you were treated and fed very well. If you breech this contract you will be arrested and sentenced for treason. Understand?"

Jurek nodded.

"Sign it!"

"I can't use my right hand," Jurek's forearm and fingers were hit repeatedly with a baton during the last interrogation and were hurting badly.

"Do it with left you imbecile!"

Jurek took the pencil and after struggling for a while produced his first and last name in the space indicated.

"That's it!" barked the man, "what do you say?"

"Excuse me?" asked Jurek.

"You say thank you, you moron or I will kick your ass through the main door!"

"Thank you," whispered Jurek.

"Here are your papers," the officer threw some folded papers towards him, "now get out!"

Slowly, because of his pain but as fast as he could Jurek walked the few steps to the door where sentry checked his documents and then he stepped outside. He was finally free and out of this torture chamber. What a joy it was to take a breath of fresh air! It was getting dark and he wanted to check the time but his watch was damaged during initial beating and stopped working long ago. He realized he had no money and was standing on a street in Warsaw. Getting anything to eat was out of the question. He had to walk to the train station and try to go on the train without ticket no matter what the consequences were going to be. Even if they throw him out of the train he was going to walk to Józefów. Thinking of seeing his mother and sleeping in his own bed he mustered some energy and began the long walk towards the station. Some pedestrians on the street gave him a look and moved aside. He knew why – his look, his clothes and his smell made them think he was some unwashed for weeks drunk trying to make it to his miserable destination.

"Why the police won't arrest creeps like that?" some woman said to her companion referring to him, "it's a disgrace to the humankind!"

*

 "Mum, have you heard that Jurek is back?!" Gabriela's voice was echoing happily through their flat, "I'm going to go and see him!"

Irena knew he returned last night and knew his condition.

"You may want to hold off for a day or two, Gabriela. Think of him, not of yourself. He's exhausted no doubt."

"I want to, I need to see him and I need it now."

"I have dinner on the table!" Irena was trying to talk her out of it.

"Dinner can wait, he needs me!" and before Irena could think of anything else Gabriela was gone.

For some reason Irena never get along with Jurek's mother even though they were neighbors and by now they knew each other for quite a while. They never moved beyond typical pleasantries. Perhaps there was no chemistry between them. But in any case she told Irena with details how beaten up he was. Like every mother she deeply cared about her only son and she poured her frustrations and sorrow at anyone who'd listen. Thus Irena knew how he was dragged in the middle of the night and mercilessly beaten for keeping his hand gun from the Uprising. It did not matter he intentionally disabled the gun. The police accused him of being a bandit first and then of being a member of some imaginary subversive organization aimed against the workers state. The beating continued every few days because he was denying the accusations. Some day they decided he was not guilty of anything at all and perhaps somebody realized that nobody can shoot a bullet from a permanently disabled gun. So for a while they just beat him up for the sentiment he had for his gun and for the fact he was in the Home Army and in the Warsaw Uprising. He was probably lucky he did not have a high rank as this would possibly land him either a long prison term or execution without a trial. Irena also knew he was not in shape to see friends but Gabriela did not give her a chance to explain anything.

Gabriela was back almost as fast as she disappeared.

"That bitch would not let me see him!" she snapped as soon as she marched in.

"You should not be taking in such words about anyone!" Irena had a disdain for bad language.

"That's what she is. How dare she?"

"She is just a mother protecting her son while she is nursing him back to health."

"Protecting against me?!"

"Look, Gabriela, he'd just returned and he is obviously in bad shape. He may not even want to be seen like that. You need to look at things from different perspective, not just your own."

"What do you know about different perspective?" Gabriela challenged her.

"I know more that you can fathom and I'm telling you to stop placing yourself first. You can be very selfish and if you don't work on it you may get seriously hurt some day."

Gabriela looked at her unpleasantly.

"Oh yes? It's like you are an expert on how people should live and love one another? Where do you have the expertise from? Your own life maybe?"

Irena was not ready for this and felt hurt. But she was not an explosive type so she had just said calmly:

"How dare you speaking to me like that? I run my life how I run my life and I will not have my daughter challenging me like this."

"You'd rather have me acting like Matilda, wouldn't you? Always sweet and happy!"

"Keep your sister out of this. Neither your father not I have any preference between the two of you so stop this now and if you don't know how to talk to me be quiet, understand?"

Gabriela had not responded, she just turned around, walked to her room and shut the door.

"Dinner is ready now!" shouted Irena "if you don't come out you will go to bed hungry."

Few minutes later Gabriela emerged.

"I'm sorry Mum" she said, "but she made me really mad."

"It's all right," Irena said "I can understand but I'll never accept lack of respect. There is too much of it everywhere as is, with that rabble that governs us. That's where it all comes from and I will not have it in my house."

*

Sound of the key unlocking the mechanism in the cell's door woke up the men inside. Some blinked their eyes as the light from the hallway was much brighter than the single and weak light bulb in the cell.

The guard called for Wiktor and he got up on his feet.

"Step outside!"

Wiktor did as he was told.

"Turn left and move forward."

"Where are you taking me?"

"Documents check, shut up!"

Wiktor was lead down the corridor to the staircase, one level down and then through a door to another one and finally the guard ordered him to stop in front of an unmarked door where another guard was waiting. He then knocked on it.

"Come in!" they heard.

The guard opened the door and ordered Wiktor to go in. There was a man behind a small desk with a piece of paper in front of him.

"Name! First, last, date and place of birth!"

Wiktor gave the details.

"Step aside, face to the wall!" the man pointed to the wall on his right hand.

Wiktor did as he was told. He noticed the tiles on the floor were wet.

Unseen by him, another man who was quietly standing behind the door made one step towards Wiktor, raised his hand with a handgun to the back of Wiktor's head and fired a single shot while simultaneously kicking Wiktor in the back.

Wiktor's body collapsed forward. Blood rushed out from the entry and exit wounds in Wiktor's skull and for a brief moment it formed a small fountain until the pressure decreased.

"You have to kick them in the butt when you fire, otherwise the blood squirts on you and your wife will be bitching while washing your shirts," said the executioner to the man sitting at the desk.

"Guards!" he called.

The guards walked in and pulled Wiktor's body by the hands out of the room.

The executioner took a short water hose and rinsed the floor where Wiktor's body fell. Water mixed with blood disappeared in the drain and the floor was clean again. The tiles were wet and shiny as when Wiktor looked at them moments ago.

*

"I don't know what else I can do, Isia" Janina was depressed, "just look at this – The International Red Cross wrote to me stating my brother is residing in London and gives me his address. His last letter says he decided to return to Poland and he was working on documents with the Polish Embassy in London. But that was half a year ago. I wrote a letter to him but it was returned to me saying there is no such person at this address. I wrote to the Polish Embassy and I have no response."

Irena thought for a moment.

"Let's go to the police headquarters now and see what they say."

"Is it wise to go there?" asked Janina.

"Well, the propaganda keeps trumpeting about how superior and fair our new government is. If you have a missing person you go to the police and report. Let's go."

It took them good forty five minutes to reach their destination. At the entry they explained what was it about. The sentry told them to wait and disappeared for a while in his booth. When he returned he told them to go to room number 101. Janina and Irena walked into the big building and found their way to room number 101 where they knocked on the door.

"Enter!" a sharp men's voice called.

They opened the door and walked in.

"I understand you want to report a missing person?" said the man in civilian clothing, "I'm comrade Kręźlewicz. Please sit down."

"Yes," replied Irena.

"Who is it to you?"

"He is a brother of the friend of mine here," Irena pointed at Janina.

"Can't you talk yourself?" he turned to Janina.

"My friend is rather distressed," explained Irena, "and she asked me to help."

"Tell me then."

"This is Mrs. Janina Kozłowska," Irena began, "her brother Wiktor Stoczyński was going to return from England. He was a pilot in the Battle of Britain."

"Was going to?" he interrupted.

"Half a year ago her wrote this letter," Irena handed Wiktor's letter to the man, "as you see he wrote to his sister he decided to return to Poland, made contact with the Polish Embassy to obtain proper documents and was expecting to leave soon. That was half a year ago and we have never heard from him again. Her letter sent to his address was recently returned as undeliverable which seems to suggest he left the place he stayed in London, but it seems he had never returned to Poland."

"Well, you know, there can be different circumstances."

"Like what?"

"He could have changed his mind, go somewhere before leaving or… find a lady friend – you know, this could put different ideas in his head."

"No, not Wiktor," Janina interrupted him, "Wiktor would tell me if he changed his mind. He did not like England, he missed Poland he wanted to come home."

The man smiled lightly.

"There are things a man would not tell even to his sister."

"No, not Wiktor," repeated Janina, "he really wanted to be back here. He hated being in England, he wanted to come here and help rebuilding Poland. We want people to return, don't we?"

"Yes, of course we do. We need all the help we can get."

"So can you do anything to help us find Wiktor?" asked Irena.

"Do you wish to file a formal request then?"

"Yes, please."

"All right," he said and took some form to fill out. He then went on to enter all relevant information. When he finished he asked Janina to sign the petition and when she did so he said:

"This may take a very long time, as missing persons are not the highest priority. There are still thousands of people looking for families displaced by the war, so you must be patient. You also have to consider possibility that something happened to your brother."

"Like what?" asked Janina.

"Oh, I don't know, it's impossible to say but accidents do happen. Also murders. England and all rotten capitalist countries have a high crime rate. If a person is robbed of everything including documents and then killed it is nearly impossible to find out who that person was. Even for the Scotland Yard."

He smiled which Irena thought was crude.

"You are not very positive about this," she remarked.

He looked at her with surprisingly cold and penetrating eyes.

"We live in still difficult times. Our enemies are determined to see us fail and they would not stop at anything. Preventing people from returning to help build socialism is one of the things we know they are doing. It's a fact. It was not enough to fight and conquer the fascism, now we have to fight enemies of the state – foreign and domestic. It's a struggle and as in any struggle there are sacrifices and victims. I am only saying this to make you understand how rotten the West is. I wish you and your brother well and I hope I will find him for you but you have to be realistic and prepared for the worst. Half a year is a long time."

"Thank you, mister…" Irena hesitated as she did not remember his name.

"We are not "mister" here. I'm comrade Krężlewicz."

"Thank you comrade," Irena managed "how should we leave it then?"

"As I said, you have to be patient. If we find out something we will contact you."

Irena hated the new nomenclature and addressing people as comrades was ridiculous to say the least. But the communists, in their disdain for the upper classes and in an attempt to reengineer the society were formally using comrade instead of Mister or Misses.

After Irena and Janina left, comrade Krężlewicz took the file he has just created and walked into the room next door.

There were four young women in military uniforms working at their desks. Along walls there were endless bookshelves full of files.

"Comrade Wolińska!" he addressed one of them.

"Yes, comrade Kreżlewicz!" the short woman with curly dark hair stood up.

"Take this file and in three months time send the standard reply to that bourgeoisie bitch saying that despite our efforts we were unable to locate the missing person."

"Thank you comrade, it will be done."

9. EBBS AND FLOWS

Matilda waited until her sister went to friends' house to play bridge. She needed to talk to her mother but wanted to do so one on one as what she had to say was of monumental gravity.

"Mum?" she asked to get Irena's attention.

"Yes," Irena turned away from the kitchen countertop to face Matilda.

"Teodor asked me to marry him."

"What?"

"I said Teodor had asked me to marry him."

"I heard you the first time. Why?"

"We love each other."

"My God, you are young, too young. You are merely twenty and he is what – twenty two or three?"

"Twenty four."

"It's too early Matilda, way too early."

"Too early for what? – what's the point in waiting for something unspecific."

"It's not about something unspecific but about making well considered decision."

"I made such decision and I accepted."

"Where are you going to live?"

"At his parent's."

"They are – as far as I know – in a bit precarious position. His father only recently returned home and he is in fragile health."

"There is nothing precarious about them. They are renting the flat. His mum is running the sewing business, Teodor is working in Warsaw and his siblings will be out on their own, it's only a matter of time. His sister is juts about to marry her boyfriend Andrew, his older brother is already married and moved out. His oldest brother is going steadily with that girl Vera and they are talking about living together soon so there will be room for Teodor and me."

Irena fell silent as her own past suddenly appeared to her like a film. She was older then Matilda when she decided to marry and till now she thought she was not old enough or mature enough or whatever it was. A prospect of her twenty years old daughter getting married was not something she was ready for.

"And there is one more thing…" said Matilda.

"What's that?"

"I think I'll have a baby."

"What???"

"A baby, I will have a baby."

"You think or you know?"

"I… I have morning sickness for a while now."

"Good God, Matilda. Didn't you have a brain to watch what you were doing?"

"I told you before, we love each other."

Irena suddenly moved to the door and took her coat from the rack.

"I need to go to church."

"Right now?"

"Yes, right now. A mass begins in five minutes. I need to talk to God."

And she walked away.

Matilda was baffled by her mum's reaction. She was prepared for her to be upset she also remotely hoped she'd be happy. But Irena was neither, she'd just walked away. *Or perhaps* thought Matilda *she went to be alone.* When she was a child she had no means to understand what she could articulate now – her mother was somewhat aloof at times. She was never excessively sweet like so many other mums happily demonstrate. She did all things a mother would and should do and she did it all well, she was protective and loving but she was not exactly showing her emotions much. What she thought as aloof while she was younger she now perceived that perhaps her mum was a bit more self-centered than she ever knew. Matilda was always puzzled by the scene she witnessed once being a little girl. There was a moment she quietly walked into the parents' room and she saw her mother standing naked in front of a large mirror. She only had high heel shoes on. Not knowing what to do Matilda quietly withdrew.

But she was wondering about that moment ever since. Perhaps if she had a towel as if she came from the bathroom it would be different. The high heel shoes were such a contrast and perhaps that's why Matilda remembered that scene so well. Being young adult now Matilda thought that perhaps after all, her mother loved and cared about herself at least as much as about her family.

Matilda heard a sound of somebody opening the door and went to see who it was. It turned out to be Stan returning after work.

"Hello Matilda," he smiled and pecked her on the cheek.

"Hi dad!" Matilda returned the smile and the kiss.

"Where is mum?"

"She went to church for the evening mass."

"Right," he said.

"Dad, I have something to tell you," she began.

"What is it?"

"Teodor had asked me to marry him and I agreed."

She was a bit nervous as she was saying this to him but it turned out to be ungrounded for he smiled to her.

"You love him?"

"I do, dad and I know he is the one."

"That's great, kiddo. You're perhaps on the young side of things but..." he smiled again, "I trust your judgment."

"That's not all, dad."

Now she had doubts again.

"Oh?"

"I'm going to have a baby…"

He looked at her carefully and quickly glanced down at her stomach which was flat as it always has been. Then he suddenly burst with laughter:

"So I will be a granddad! I love it! Give me a hug!"

Matilda embraced him with all her might.

"I thought you'd be upset."

"Why would I? This is your life. If he didn't want to marry you it would be different but as is…"

"He is not marrying me because I'm pregnant."

"That's good, that's very good. Do you worry?"

"No, not at all."

"Did you tell mum?"

"Yes."

"How did she take it?"

"Well… she went to church."

"Don't take it wrong and don't worry. I'm sure she is happy for you. She may just not like the prospect of being called grandmother, that's all. Many women struggle with that. Trust me."

The door opened and Gabriela walked in. She immediately noticed the two of them in the embrace and was a bit annoyed right away.

"What's the matter with you two?"

"You are going to be an auntie!" declared Stan.

"It's a stupid joke, dad," she snapped.

"It's not a joke at all. Matilda is getting married and she will have a baby."

Gabriela stopped dead in her tracks.

"Married?" she repeated "to Teodor?"

Matilda nodded.

"You could do better," she said flatly.

"Aren't you happy to be an auntie to be?" teased her Stan.

"She's getting married, dad. That doesn't make me an aunt."

"She's having a baby too."

"What?"

"That's right," said Matilda.

"Its ridiculous!" said Gabriela, "I told you to watch out for him but as usual you have your own ideas. They obviously made him marry you."

"How dare you? And besides, what do you know?"

"I know what I know."

"You know nothing. He asked me to marry him."

"Yeah, only because you are pregnant."

"No, you idiot. He asked me not knowing it."

"I wouldn't do it."

"What?"

"Get married."

"Unless Jurek would ask you – then you'd do it as fast as possible."

"Keep Jurek and me out of this!"

"You started it."

"I can say what I want."

"But you don't have to be mean to your immediate family. We are not mean to you!"

"Leave me alone!" snapped Gabriela and walked to her room.

"Easy, easy, girls," said Stan "no need to argue. Let's celebrate. If you are happy, darling, I'm happy and so are mum and Gabriela!"

While Irena was living Thursday to Thursday in anticipation of her regular trips to Warsaw, Stan was living week-end to week-end as this was the time for him to see his grandson Michael. Matilda would usually come to her parents on Sundays. She was visiting her Mum during the week as well, once or twice. Teodor and her lived one train stop away but it was actually easier for her to walk with Michael in his pram. Especially in good weather it was a nice walk, about half an hour one way. Grandpa Stan was very much looking forward to weekly visits and he loved playing with Michael. When Michael grew up a bit he loved holding him on his lap and he'd let Michael do anything he wanted. It led to some arguments with Irena who basically thought her husband had a screw loose over the little kid.

Stan would let Michael rummage though any drawer in their flat – whether it contained underwear or kitchen utensils (apart from knifes). Under Stan's watchful eye Michael could take everything out, check it out and put back together – more or less. It wreaked havoc on Irena's sense of order and she would get upset but Stan's was unmoved: "let the child play" he'd always said.

He'd let Michael play with his tool set, shuffle his papers, fan through books from the bookshelf, play with liquid glue (Michael would be gluing pages of newspapers together which rendered them useless), play with and destroy cigarettes and even play with matches – and this Irena hated the most.

Bu whether she shouted in anger or appealed softly Stan's answer was always the same: "a child needs to have some fun and I watch his every move, he's safe with me."

It all went safe indeed until some day Stan let Michael refill his cigarette lighter and then try it. Michael flipped the lighter and suddenly the lighter and his hand were on fire because Stan hadn't noticed that Michael spilled the highly flammable liquid. Stan was quick to extinguish the flame but Michael's hand needed an ointment.

He called Irena and told her what happened as he needed her to fetch the ointment and some bandage.

She exploded.

"You stupid old fart!" she was shouting with real anger, "I keep telling you not to let him do anything he wants and you don't listen to me! He could've burned to death, you idiot, and so could you, me and the entire flat!"

Stan was quiet because he was really scared and very much upset at himself, but his methods hadn't changed a bit. One hour later he was back to normal and little Michael was rearranging Irena's shoes in the closet.

Stan just loved his grandson to pieces and he was spoiling the little kid rotten. But to be fair Michael was surprisingly sensible and well behaved little boy as Matilda was raising him with maximum attention so in the end everything was properly balanced.

The only thing that was not in balance was Matilda's husband, Teodor. The earlier doubts Irena had about him came true. He was never eager to visit his in-laws, he'd always prefer to go to his parents and in fact he quite frequently would go to visit his mother after returning from work. He'd just say "I'm going to my mum" and leave Matilda with Michael. On Sundays after church he would sometimes go with Matilda and Michael to Matilda's parents who lived really close to church but he'd stay half an hour or so and then go to his parents.

Matilda and Michael would sometimes go with him but not too often. She sometimes felt she was not quite welcomed there. That is, the other grandparents loved Michael too and wanted him to come for visits but it was just that Teodor's mother was a bit cold. His dad liked Matilda and was showing it clearly by being always cheerful towards her. He was also coming to visit Matilda and Michael every other week or so. She'd give him some lunch and they'd sit at the kitchen table and talk. But the rest of Teodor's family seemed to keep her at a distance. Perhaps these were politics of Teodor's mother but Matilda didn't know. She just felt being slightly snubbed.

The hardest times for Matilda were holidays like Christmas or Easter. Well ahead of time there were discussions and planning where they'd go – that is to which grandparents, and Teodor always wanted her and Michael to go to his parents. Matilda would usually let him have it his way as long as there was time allocated for her parents as well. But still - Teodor was biased. When they were going to go to his parents he'd be ready well ahead of time and would be pestering his wife to get her and Michael ready. But when it was time to go to Matilda's parents Teodor would not be ready until it was late, sometimes very late. No matter how early Matilda would remind him he did his own thing – whatever it was and it looked as if he was doing it on purpose. Matilda was worrying about things like that because they were only getting worse.

Teodor would also easily collide with Irena and Gabriela. With Irena he'd contradict whatever she said. With Gabriela he'd try that as well but she was more intelligent, more eloquent and way better articulated than him so she could run circles around him. She could make him look almost stupid or bad and if she did that he'd became angry and would say something unpleasant.

He also sometimes collided with his father in-law who had certain specific way of joking which at the face of it seemed crude but he never really meant it, it was just his way of teasing people. But Teodor would take it at face value and on occasions he'd just get up and leave. Matilda would than cry which would usually prompt Gabriela to comment on her inability to put her husband in his place. Matilda would sometimes fight back by saying at least she had one which would immediately infuriate Gabriela and then the quarrel would really take off until Stan or Irena would put a stop to it by telling Matilda to knock it off. Matilda always wondered why she was always the one asked to stop, not Gabriela but that's how it always was.

Being a young adult now, and having her own family, Matilda felt torn apart at times. On one hand she thought it was no longer fair but on the other, for a while now, she could see Gabriela's personal life wasn't going anywhere so she felt somewhat sorry for her and such thoughts were enough for Matilda to back off and appease her. But the trouble was Gabriela was aware of that and she'd sometimes used it to her advantage.

When Stalin died the government declared mourning for the entire country and the newspapers were outdoing one another in writing ever more absurd eulogies. But people on the streets were quite happy. The tyrant and monster was finally gone and they were hoping life would get better.

But it was not exactly so. The monstrous machine had its own momentum and the enslaved nations had no choice but wait. Few years later people in Hungary openly attempted to overthrow the communist regime. In Poland, workers in the city of Poznan organized protests and demanded better conditions, better treatment and better pay. In Hungary the communist party member named Janos Kadar asked the Soviet Union for help which gave Russians excuse to enter Hungary with soldiers and tanks and quench the rebellion in blood.

In Poznan the government pacified protesting workers with the use of special police forces and army units which included 400 tanks. About one hundred protesters were killed and six hundred were wounded. The top of the Polish Workers Party was shuffled a bit and a communist by the name of Wladyslaw Gomulka who was imprisoned by the Stalinists was set free. He assumed the post of the chairman which meant he was the new face to run the country. His triumphant speech in Warsaw promising better life to everyone was cheered by the crowds. Since it was known he was imprisoned by the Stalinist regime people thought he was by this default on their side and had high hopes. But the promises were one thing, the reality was something else. The Soviets invited him for the official visit to Moscow from which he returned a different man. There was no doubt he must have been told by the Russians to toe the line or else. While the Stalinism was officially branded as "period of warps and errors" there was nothing in the official line to indicate change or improvement of any kind. Hopes disappeared in gray reality of the state run country which in turn was run from Moscow.

One day Gabriela returned home with a beaming face after being out with Jurek and she announced:

"I'm getting married to Jurek! He'd asked me!"

Irena jumped up, run up to her and gave her a big hug and kiss.

"Finally, darling, I was beginning to worry for quite a while."

"He needed time after what he'd been through."

"I can certainly understand that."

Irena knew from his mother what the secret police did to him. She liked this boy even though she was not on particularly good terms with his mother but she felt strong sense of solidarity with her. Mrs. Nowak's husband went to war in September 1939 in the rank of an officer and he was in eastern part of Poland. She had not heard from him ever since and her fear was he was among the twenty thousand officers shot by Russians in Katyń. Her daughter was a messenger in the Home Army and died in the Uprising. She was left only with her son. The poor woman went through a lot and Irena hated what has been done to her and her family. But on personal level the two women were not getting along, they were just neighbors and kept their distance. The fact that Gabriela was walking out with her son had not changed anything.

"When?" Irena asked.

"We thought we'd do it in the spring when the weather is nice."

"Excellent," Irena was pleased "you could choose to have the wedding ceremony at the outdoor altar."

"I suppose we could," agreed Gabriela.

"Let's wait till dad comes home. He will be so happy for you!"

Stan, who like Irena was worrying about Gabriela, was truly pleased and Gabriela thought he showed the same enthusiasm as few years back when Matilda was getting married.

Since childhood she was suspecting both parents of favoring her younger sister and eve now was she couldn't help it.

Matilda, always cheerful and easygoing by nature seemed to be getting cheerfulness from everyone. Gabriela was failing to notice it was not favoritism but simply action and reaction. Her failure to understand that made her jealous at least at times. But now she was truly happy. She was in love with Jurek for a long time, she was in pieces when he was arrested and happy when he returned. But what she did not know was that Jurek's mother did not like her at all and Jurek had not told her about his proposing to Gabriela.

For the moment everything was fine and as soon as Matilda came for a visit to her parents she was told the news. Ever since she got married, moved out and had Michael she was not seeing Gabriela that often. She did not work while Gabriela did. She was taking early train to Warsaw and she was returning late in the evenings.

Matilda was usually visiting her Mum during the day so the only time the sisters could see each other was Sunday if Matilda was coming for a visit. Naturally, Matilda was happy for Gabriela because just like her parents she worried about her. Waiting for Jurek took a long time and while her devotion was certainly commendable, just the length of time waiting or hoping for the proposal was really long and sometimes Matilda thought nothing would never happen. But when she once expressed such thoughts to Gabriela it ended in a row.

Irena was pleased too. With both daughters married she thought she'd be able to make a step towards reclaiming her own life. She looked forward to her motherhood being over. It would be a bit like before Gabriela and Matilda were born, she would have her independence again. She felt she completed her duties as a mother more than enough because she did so in extraordinarily difficult circumstances. She was so much older now and she was also a grandmother but the more she thought about it the more she wanted to have her life back. She was convinced it wasn't too late to do things.

*

Janina handed a piece of paper to Irena.

"Look what they sent me" she said.

Irena glanced at the letter. It was a formal response to her missing person report she helped her file a while ago. It stated the investigation produced no results at all. There were no records of her brother ever entering the country. It confirmed he obtained all necessary documents from the Polish Embassy in London.

"It's a dead end," said Irena "the bastards are obviously washing their hands."

"Does it mean he is…?" Janina couldn't finish.

"Maybe not," Irena did not want to believe he was dead "perhaps we can write to the International Red Cross in Switzerland rather than relay on its branch here. Why don't you do that?"

Janina brightened up a bit.

"All right, I will do it. How are you Isia?, I'm sorry I never seem to care about you. All I talk to you about is Wiktor."

"Don't worry Jani," Irena loved her friend dearly and was not paying attention to little things like that.

"I'm all right," she added "looks like Gabriela is getting married with that boyfriend of hers."

"Oh my, Isia," exclaimed Janina "this is really great news! I know you worried about her."

"Yes, it is good news and yes you are right, I was worrying about her. We all did, but…" Irena hesitated "I don't know what it is - I have a bad feeling about it."

"How can you?"

"I don't know - I just do. Perhaps because I have no connection with his mother. Not that I have particular connection with Matilda's in-laws, you know. But at least it is – how should I say it? – civilized. They even sometimes stop by at our house after Sunday Mass. They drop by, have a tea and make some small talk. But with Jurek's mother it is just cold. I feel terribly bad for her with her husband most likely killed in Katyń, daughter dying in the Uprising and Jurek arrested and so badly maltreated by the bastards from the secret police. But still – I have no common platform with her, no connection at all."

"Perhaps it will change once they get married?" Janina said without much conviction.

"I doubt it. I wish it was better but it is – how do they call it? – chemistry, or rather lack of it. Sometimes you meet somebody and you are interested in that person so you start talking. But sometimes you meet somebody and there is nothing at all. No attraction, no interest of any kind."

"Well, there are no rules about in-laws having to be on good terms."

"No there aren't, but it would be nice."

Janina smiled.

"We can't have it all, can we?"

"Yup," agreed Irena.

"How is your pastry?" Janina asked.

They were sitting in the café at Krakowskie Przedmiescie Street which was always a popular destination for the Varsovians even before the war.

"It's all right" replied Irena "but they have no clue how to do it right, you know. It's not the same what we are used to."

"Yes," agreed Janina.

"Just look at the shop windows," said Irena "it's a far cry from how vibrant it was before the war. And the pedestrians – it's a mob now. You should see how it is on the train. I always try to avoid the long distance one – it smells like a dead fish!"

"What do you mean?"

"All of those peasants coming from the God forsaken villages don't seem to wash themselves every day. Judging by the odor it is once a week! But they go to the city like that. That's what the government wants. They encourage people to come to the city to be workers. They do not teach them anything, they just want more and more uneducated working class. But then again - how could they teach them, they have no class themselves. All they want is to further dismantle our society so they can just herd us just like they did it in Poznań not so long ago!"

"Don't talk so loud, Isia," Janina was uneasy a bit "somebody can hear you."

"I couldn't care less. If we don't resist they will squish us completely. I hate those Moscow pawns!"

Irena glanced at her watch.

"I have to go now I'm afraid. I need to catch the seven p.m. train or I will ride with that populace again – I can't stand it!"

Janina stood up too.

"Same time next Thursday?"

"Of course, Jani," smiled Irena, "as usual."

"Yes, please. Good-bye!" Janina and Irena exchanged hugs and parted their ways.

When Matilda gave birth to another son, Stan only shifted gears to overdrive and found even more energy and love to pour on both grandsons. Irena, by now used to being a grandmother, welcomed the newly arrived Gregory with much enthusiasm. The baby was cute and to everybody's delight was healthy unlike Michael who ill at birth and there was a moment when his survival was questionable. Things in the family run pretty much the same way, perhaps even a bit better in fact as the relationship between Teodor and Matilda's parents had somewhat improved.

 Certain tensions were relaxed because with two children now Michael could go with his dad to his parents while Matilda could simultaneously go with Gregory to hers. Holidays remained a perennial problem as before but at least non-holiday week-ends and visits were somewhat easier to handle.

As Michael was growing up Irena was telling him stories about the Warsaw Uprising and introduced him to the Radio Free Europe. She figured he was sensible enough to see and understand the difference between what he was taught at school versus what she had went through during the war and later.

Teodor did not particularly liked her doing so, but on the other hand he never uttered a word of protest as he had his own frustrations with the political reality of the Polish People's Republic. Deep down he knew Irena was right even if she was too emotional about it at times.

*

"Thank you for coming to see me, Gabriela. I need to talk to you."

Mrs. Nowak always had a stern face so it was impossible to guess her mood and Gabriela had not even tried. She had just arrived to her house at her request. Apparently she invited Gabriela specifically when Jurek was not around.

"Would you like to have some tea?" asked Mrs. Nowak.

"No, thank you."

"It's about Jurek," Mrs. Nowak said, "as you know he means the world to me and it's not just a metaphor. I lost my husband in September 1939 and I lost my daughter in the Uprising. Jurek is all I have left."

"I know," Gabriela acknowledged.

"I am aware of your plans," Mrs .Nowak continued, "happiness and well being of my son is very important to me."

Gabriela was silent trying to figure out where she was going with this.

"Ever since they let him go he is…" Mrs. Nowak thought for a moment, "not himself really and I worry about him a lot."

"What do you mean by not being himself?" asked Gabriela, "he hadn't mentioned anything to me."

"He is sleepwalking which he never did and he screams in fear in his sleep. He doesn't want to talk about his dreams but they must be really bad. He also has some fears and is afraid he may not be able to keep his job."

"I'll talk to him," said Gabriela thinking she was asking her for help to get Jurek to a doctor, "perhaps he should see some specialist and go through a treatment of some kind."

Mrs. Nowak looked at her.

"What is he going to say to a doctor? That he was severely beaten up by the secret police and has anxiety because of that?"

"Perhaps it is the war first and foremost."

"It's not the war and not the Uprising" said Mrs. Nowak, "it's the beatings by the police."

"Well, still – I'll talk to him and if necessary I can go to the doctor with him."

"I'm afraid you do not understand, my dear. I am not asking you for anything like that. What I'm telling you is that I think your plans should be postponed."

Gabriela was stunned.

"I see no reason for that."

"But I do. Weddings and preparations are stressful. Also, being married changes a lot, people need to make adjustments and have to recognize different sense of responsibility."

"Of course, that's all understandable - it's life, that's just how it is for everybody. As to preparations it is way more stressful for a woman than for a man and I will do everything I can to make him feel at ease. I am well aware of what he went through. Perhaps even more than you do."

That jab was unnecessary but when agitated, Gabriela's tongue was sometimes quicker than her brain.

Mrs. Nowak did not like that at all. She looked straight into Gabriela's eyes.

"As I said, this is my son and his well being is the most important thing in the world for me."

"I could say almost the same, Mrs. Nowak."

"I'm very glad to hear it, but if this is really the case you'd have no problem agreeing with me."

"I do have a problem because in the end it is our life and our plans. He made conscious decision and asked me to marry him. I love him, I want to marry him and I agreed. I see no reason to postpone anything."

"Sorry dear, but I do and I insist."

Gabriela thought for a moment.

"Out of curiosity - for how long?"

"Until he is fit."

"This is very vague Mrs. Nowak. You want me to wait unspecified amount of time?"

"If you love him you shouldn't have problem with it."

"No woman wants to wait indefinitely. Especially for vague reasons!"

"These are not vague reasons! I am seriously concerned about his well being."

"You think I'm not?"

Mrs. Nowak was silent.

"I…" Gabriela hesitated, "I'll discuss it with him."

"You will not do anything like that, I forbid you."

"You are not telling me what to do. Also – have you thought of me and my interests?"

"As I said, my son takes priority for me."

"It's the same for me so it's a quid pro quo!"

"Except that I'm his mother and I still know better what is best for my son."

"And I'm going to be his wife. I also know what is good for him and I will be caring for him for the rest of his life. I'm sorry to say this to you but your role is coming to an end. Perhaps the sooner he's out from under your wings the better!" snapped Gabriela.

Mrs. Nowak stood up.

"I think this conversation leads to nowhere. I've tried to explain certain things to you but you refuse to look at them from a different point of view than your own. I think you should leave now."

"I quite agree. This is pointless. I will talk to Jurek whether you like it or not. Good-bye!"

Gabriela got up and left the room. She tried to close the door gently or at least normally but it didn't quite work, it sounded as if she slammed them.

She was fuming. She'd never liked Jurek's mother but always doubted herself thinking she was somewhat prejudiced for some reason. Now she knew she was not. She felt sorry for her loosing her husband and a daughter in the war but that was it. She wasn't alone as millions of Poles lost their loved ones in the same way. The woman was clearly screwed up and bent on running Jurek's life and making decisions for him.

When she stormed into her home Irena knew something was going on. She could read Gabriela like an open book by now. It was enough for her to hear the pattern of her footsteps or the way she opened and closed the door, even the way she hung her coat on a peg.

"Are you all right, Gabriela?" she asked knowing it was not so.

"Do you know what that bitch told me?"

"Mrs. Nowak?"

"Yes, her!"

"What?"

"She wants me to postpone the wedding because Jurek has some nightmares and insecurities! Can you believe that?"

"Look, you may not like it but she is his mother, she lost her husband and a daughter. And you know what happened to Jurek."

"Oh, I know it all, but this is the past and it can't be changed. I need to move forward, we need to move forward. The sooner, the better."

Irena did not particularly like Mrs. Nowak either but on this occasion she sympathized with her. Her tragedy was undisputable and what the communists did to Jurek was terrible and cruel to say the least. But Irena was no expert on human psychology. If Jurek's mother thought he had some sort of problem perhaps she was right.

"You know, she may have a valid reason and it's not like you have all arrangements made and ready. It is not going to kill you to postpone it a little."

"A little?!" shouted Gabriela with anger, "how do I know how little is little? The old cow says it may take a long time! This is my life and I can't wait forever."

"If he needs some time to recover so be it. You love him so for his sake, for his well being you should consider it."

"I made my plans and I already prepared myself. I hate changing plans."

"This is not a big deal. A plan can be modified and also you keep talking as if you were the center of it."

"I am, these are my plans and I will not be pushed around!"

"You should calm down and think of the man you say you love."

"Stop saying it as if you were questioning that."

"I want you to be happy Gabriela, but you are a bit too self centered and you need to change that."

"How dare you telling me something like this? I can't believe my own mother criticizes me like that. Do you understand what it does to me? You're making me feel like crap. Not only I had a shitty talk with that old bag, you are acting as if you agreed with her. You only make it worse!"

"Stop being hysterical Gabriela. It's time to grow up and have a mature perspective on life. You are not the center of the world and sometimes you must make an adjustment. Your childhood is over long time ago. I regret giving in to your demands in the past – perhaps that's the result."

"I can't believe you are saying things like that to me! I don't want to hear it and I don't want to talk to you!"

Gabriela marched to her room and slammed the door.

Irena stayed in the kitchen looking out the window at the back garden. How was it that her daughter was so disrespectful and so selfish? Has she missed something in the turbulent years of war?

Irena was trying to see what had she done wrong and the only thing she could think of was what she'd said to Gabriela – perhaps they as parents were giving in too much instead of demanding more from her. The most drastic example was when they decided to stay in Józefów after Gabriela threw the fit over the prospect of moving to Warsaw. Who knows – maybe Stan's accident was caused by him being shaken by this episode? But the worst for Irena was that deep down she felt robbed of Warsaw forever and she resented it.

It was a sunny day but the garden suddenly looked as if it was getting dark. Irena turned her head away for a moment and then looked back again. The garden looked colorful and cheerful again.

There were days when Stan felt exhausted for no apparent reason. Sometimes upon returning home from work he had to sit down for a while just to rest for half an hour or so before he could do anything else. Irena kept saying he should see a doctor but he'd always wave her away.

"I'm just getting older like everybody else, that's all" he'd say.

But deep down he worried because with time he noticed he had to stop half way between the train station and home just to catch his breath. He quit smoking years ago and gained a bit of weight soon after so for a while he thought his extra weight was making him more tired. But when he noticed he was spitting blood he signed up to see a doctor.

He was told he had developed tuberculosis and he was immediately sent to a hospital for treatment and then to a sanatorium. It was a shock for Irena, Gabriela and Matilda, but mercifully the sanatorium was not far away from Józefów so Irena could visit him quite frequently, three to four times a week except Thursdays of course, as Thursdays were reserved for her trips to Warsaw.

Stan was asking about his grandsons as he was missing them the most. Michael was visiting him every now and then, not as frequently as he'd wished but Stan understood Michael had his life, friends, school and homework. Matilda was coming as much as she could but not always with Gregory because Teodor insisted it was dangerous for a young child to be in contact with a man who had tuberculosis. Matilda understood this but she also knew how much her father loved his grandsons and how he missed them so perhaps not very wisely she sometimes would take Gregory with her and made sure he'd keep the secret from his dad. The border between common sense and love was in this case not easy for her to navigate.

If her husband did not have the history of avoiding his in-laws perhaps she would obey him but as it was she had no means to say whether or not Teodor was just using the circumstances. She had no proof either way and what's more she knew that when Teodor's father was diagnosed with tuberculosis long time ago his contact with his children was severely limited and the plates, knifes, forks and spoons he used were washed and kept separately for the duration of his illness.

Gabriela was visiting Stan as well but during the week she was leaving home early and returning after work late so she could do it only on Sundays which she did alone or with Irena and sometimes with Matilda. Within several weeks Stan was making good progress and prognosis for his recovery was favorable.

*

Irena was sitting and talking with Matilda in the kitchen at Matilda's house. While Stan was remaining in the sanatorium, apart from visiting him an going to Warsaw on Thursdays Irena was coming to see Matilda once a week or so. Matilda was quite busy running her household and taking care of her two sons and all that in a flat with no running water. Only recently they acquired a simple two burner LPG unit which made daily cooking easier but if Matilda needed to bake anything she had to start fire in the old kitchen stove which needed coal to get the heat going.

Teodor's miscalculation from the early days of the Polish People's Republic when he saw simple workers being much better paid than engineers backfired and by now he was working two jobs. One was full time work where he was a technician assembling elements of aircraft instruments and after hours he was working as a dental technician making crowns and bridges. Most of his work was for his sister who was a dentist and lived and practiced dentistry in the same house. He also did a bit of work for few other dentists.

He'd usually returned from work at about five in the afternoon, had a meal and set to work. Sometimes he worked till midnight. He only had Sundays for himself and his family. Running the second job allowed him to save money for two things – main purpose was saving for a car and the second one was vacations. He loved skiing and he taught both of his sons to love it as well so winter vacations was a must every season. Summer was also time to go somewhere and he'd usually take his family to the seaside. But both winter and summer vacations were subsidized by his father-in-law who worked for sports organization and was in a position to get reduced rates for rooms at various sport clubs. It was a bit odd situation because the two men were not exactly getting along but at least in case of vacations they had common interest which was well being of Michael and Gregory. Grandfather wanted to do just anything for the boys and for his daughter whether he was getting along with his son-in-law or not.

Matilda and Teodor lived in a modest small flat which had just one room, kitchen and entry way. Matilda kept it clean as a button at all times and it was very pleasant and cozy.

Irena and Matilda were sitting at the kitchen table having tea.

"How is dad?" asked Matilda.

"He's all right" Irena answered "he is getting better and better and the doctor said he will be able to go home next month."

"Oh, that's good!" Matilda said with relief in her voice, "I keep worrying about him."

"He says he is thinking about taking early retirement."

"He's exhausted, I know but I don't know how he'll handle that," said Matilda, "some people deteriorate quickly because they can't find anything to do."

"I heard that too," agreed Irena, "but with his illness I don't really know how feasible it is for him to return to work."

Matilda glanced through the window and saw Gabriela approaching her house.

"Oh, look Mum," she said, "Gabriela is coming. I didn't know she had a day off."

"She hasn't," replied Irena.

The door opened and Gabriela burst in. She was wearing not very tidy sweater and some old trousers. She was pale and her eyes had an odd glare.

"I'm going to kill myself!" she exclaimed.

"Sit down, Gabriela," Matilda made room for her "what's the matter with you? Why are you so pale? Aren't you supposed to be at work?"

"I don't care about anything anymore!"

"What happened? Calm down and tell us."

"It's Jurek!" she began crying hysterically.

"What happened?"

"He broke off the engagement!" and she threw the engagement ring on the floor with such force that it bounced off the floor and disappeared under the cabinet in the corner.

"Look what you've done!" Matilda bent down trying to see where it was.

"Stop it!" said Gabriela "I don't want it!"

"Why are you so pale?" asked Irena.

"I took sleeping pills and I hope I fall asleep and never wake up."

"Good God!" Irena exclaimed "how could you be so stupid?"

Gabriela looked at her with anger on her pale face.

"That's just what kind of mother you are! My life is going down the toilet, it's not my fault and you call me stupid? Me?!"

She was sobbing again.

"How many pills you've taken?" asked Matilda.

"I don't know!"

"Pull yourself together! How many? Ten or a hundred?"

"Half a bottle, whatever it was."

"Come with me now!" ordered Matilda.

"Where are you taking her?" asked Irena.

"Outside!" explained Matilda, "she needs to puke."

"I can't do that," resisted Gabriela.

"You will. Come!" she said in a commanding voice.

Matilda was mad and could not believe that her sister who always acted as if she was the most intelligent, know it all person in the world could be so stupid. Yes, what happened to her was terrible but to respond by swallowing sleeping pills was just plainly idiotic. Typical hysteria as Matilda witnessed many times before.

They walked outside to the corner of the garden by a large jasmine bush.

"Okay," said Matilda "stick your finger down your throat!"

"I won't be able to do it!"

"Do it now!"

Gabriela bent down a bit and awkwardly tried but she was only coughing and spitting.

"Try harder!" ordered Matilda.

Gabriela tried but with the same result. Without wasting more time Matilda grabbed her head with one hand and shoved her own hand as deep into Gabriela's mouth as she could. Gabriela was fighting back and making terrible noises but then finally the reflex kicked in and she threw up.

Matilda glanced at the vomit and thought she saw what looked like white pieces of not quite digested pills.

"Okay, back into the kitchen!"

Gabriela sheepishly followed. Matilda made very strong black coffee and handed her a full mug.

"Drink!" she said.

"I like it with milk," said Gabriela.

"This isn't about what you like or not. Drink it! I want to make sure you won't be sleepy."

Gabriela drank the coffee.

"How do you feel?" asked Matilda.

"Terrible," replied Gabriela.

"That's not what I mean. Are you sleepy?"

"A little bit."

"Nauseous?"

"No."

"Good. You can't go to sleep, understand?"

"Yes."

"Mum," Matilda turned to Irena, "make sure she will not fall asleep until later in the evening."

"Shouldn't we call a doctor?"

"At this time of a day the surgery is closed and she is not in a condition to ask for the ambulance. The only thing you could do is take her to the emergency."

"I don't want to go there," Gabriela interjected.

"I don't think she needs to go," said Matilda, "but if she gets some symptoms within few hours or at night you will need to get her to emergency."

"That's all right, I can call from Marian and Halina's."

"Okay then. I think you need to take her home now, I have to start dinner," Matilda glanced at the clock on the wall, "I also don't want Michael, Gregory and Teodor to see her like this."

"Thank you, darling" Irena seemed to be somewhat detached throughout this ordeal.

"Thank you, Matilda," said Gabriela whose face was getting some color back.

"I'll see you as soon as I can," Matilda gave her a little smile, "and don't do anything stupid. It is unpleasant but after all it isn't the end of the world."

"Easy for you to say!" snapped Gabriela getting ready to leave "it is the end of my world as I thought it would be."

"Don't get me wrong," said Matilda with slightly softer voice.

 "I'm well aware what he meant to you and I don't want to sound cynical but he's not the only man in the world."

Gabriela did not say anything.

"Bye!" Matilda gave hugs and kisses to Irena and Gabriela and watched them walk away towards the gate.

Gabriela recovered in several hours but was devastated and furious for the following weeks and months. Some days she was just angry, some other she was exhausted and devoid of energy. She withdrew from her circle of friends. Being dumped was so obviously unpleasant and in a way had a certain stigma about it. She did not want to meet and talk to anyone who'd feel sorry for her. She concentrated on her work instead.

She was working for one of the foreign trade enterprises in Warsaw and by now she was a seasoned professional.

In the communist run Poland foreign trade was strictly controlled and was carried out only by designated offices created for that purpose. It was all arranged by industry groups so for example textiles and related products were being offered for international sale by a foreign trade enterprise specific to this industry.

Gabriela worked in a section that dealt with transportation of goods. She was monitoring contracts and making arrangements for shipments to their ultimate destinations. The work was interesting as it required coordination of tasks between clients, manufacturers and a transportation company. The work was never really boring as half of the work load was always the same between the same suppliers and clients but the other half was a bit unpredictable because many contracts were one time deals so clients varied. This way she was working with clients from many countries of the world. Additional bonus for all who worked in such enterprises were opportunities for business trips. It was not easy to get one as there were several factors coming into play. When a need for a business trip occurred it had to go through the chain of command so to speak. It was also politicized as Workers Party members had certain preference, but if one had a really good record, sooner or later he or she would end up travelling. Needless to say any destination in the western world was always the most attractive and lucrative. A person going for such trip would be given certain amount of hard currency per day for expenses and hotels. This would be on top of the regular salary. Usually people sent for business trips would go out of their way not to spend the hard currency on feeding themselves and would also search for the least expensive hotels. This way they would realize savings which were theirs to keep. And hard currency was always in demand. It could be sold for profit on black market or it could be used at state operated stores which were selling western goods for foreign currency only. Such stores have better prices for certain goods than compatible goods in foreign countries. Finally, if one accumulated enough one could purchase a car in such stores and this was almost a money making scheme. There were never enough cars available back then. New ones were expensive and there were long waiting lists in state run stores for them. Used cars commanded high prices. A new car purchased at nominal price off the waiting list could be privately sold with considerable profit. Sometimes potential buyers were literally waiting out on the street. In the state run stores that accepted only hard currency one could acquire a foreign made car without waiting at all. Selection was very limited but still it was an attractive proposition.

Basically most people were trying to save for a car Gabriela was not interested in cars so she had no motivation to save for such purpose but any foreign trip gave her a chance to get away from her usual life and acquire some foreign goods of her choice. She worked with a nice group of people and she liked most of them. She never joined or even considered joining the Workers Party as she detested communism and all that came with it. Like all non members she was routinely invited to join but she always declined.

Eventually she had more or less recovered after the break up with Jurek but it left a permanent scar or perhaps it was a wound that never really healed and she was not looking to find somebody. She was just going with the flow. If somebody would come along her way she would give it a consideration but that was it. She threw herself into the whirlpool of work and she was content with her colleagues at work. Every now and then they would go places in various groups or to restaurants to celebrate names days or birthdays. It was a bit hard to return home to Józefów after late night dinners. Last train was leaving Warsaw few minutes past midnight but it was not really her preferred way of returning home. The last train was a bit creepy as at this time of the night it would be nearly empty and then of course a walk from the station would be an unpleasant and scary too. She'd be home at about 1.20 at night and she'd have not even five hours to sleep as the morning train she needed to catch was at 6.20. More often than not Gabriela would return from such events by taxi at a considerable expense as the distance was about fifty kilometers and taxis had night rates which were higher than during the day. Irena and Stan worried about her blowing money away on taxis but any comment about it would immediately turn into an argument. Gabriela would not let anyone criticize her whether it was justified or not, especially her parents. Nobody was going to tell her how to run her life.

*

Stan and Irena decided to make a birthday party for their younger daughter, Matilda. She was born in May so good weather was almost guaranteed as May in Poland is usually nice, flowers are blooming and everything is fresh and green after the Spring. It was not going to be a big party, just a festive family dinner for Irena, Stan, Gabriela, Matilda, Teodor, Michael and Gregory. Irena prepared the entire dinner herself – tripe soup for starters and steaks with baked potatoes and green beans and red cabbage salad with marinated pears on side for those who liked it. The menu was geared towards Matilda's husband who was fond of steaks, baked potatoes, marinated pears and he particularly liked the red cabbage salad alas – only when it was made by his mother-in-law. Whatever the reason she had some special touch. Matilda took recipe from her and countless times precisely followed it but to her frustration, Teodor's conclusion was always the same: "it's good but not as good as when your mother's." In the end Matilda quit trying.

Oddly enough, while not getting along with her mum, Teodor absolutely loved Irena's red cabbage salad. It was one of the cases when two people seem to get on each other nerves as soon as they exchange their greetings for the day. But somehow, Irena's red cabbage salad was exempt. The marinated pears were not bad either and as with the salad, Matilda was unable to produce the same result. Matilda's marinated pears were always mushy while her Mum's were always crunchy.

The day was gorgeous and before dinner they sat on the terrace drinking and chatting. Irena was in the kitchen with Gabriela while Matilda, her husband and both boys along with her father were lounging on the terrace enjoying the liquor made by Matilda's dad. Stan was busy chit chatting and joking with his grandsons and only every now and then he would exchange a word or two with Matilda and Teodor.

"So," he asked, "what are the plans for summer? I can get you to the seaside as usual."

"Thank you, dad" said Matilda "but this summer we may skip it altogether."

Teodor was silent.

"Why? I know you like it so much and it's good for the boys. Mum and I could join you this time, I thought."

"Well…" Matilda seemed somewhat uneasy, "Michael is going for a month to a summer camp."

Her dad looked at her with some surprise.

"What camp?"

"You know," she explained, "same as most other kids do every year. Summer camps are organized by parent's employers. Teodor had signed Michael up."

"Michael," asked Stan "are you looking forward to this?"

Michael looked at him.

"No I don't. Dad wants me to go."

"Why are you sending him then, Teodor?" inquired Stan.

"That's what all kids do every summer. They go to summer camps. He will learn how it is, make new friends and spend time with his contemporaries."

"Parents who send kids to those camps do so because they can't provide anything else for them and they both work. So without such camps kids would be stuck all summer at home day in day out with nothing to do. Michael is not in such situation. Matilda doesn't work, and Michael can come and stay with us for a while and I'm sure he can stay with your parents for a while too. I can also arrange for your family to go to the seaside for a month like we usually do. What's the idea then?"

Teodor had not answered.

Gabriela walked in with a bottle and offered refills of the liquor.

"Well, Teodor?" prompted Matilda's dad.

"There is nothing wrong with such camps," replied Teodor, "countless of kids go and have a good time."

"But you know how it works – peasants' or workers' kids have their camps in nice places at the seaside or in the mountains. In other words kids from god forsaken factories in the middle of nowhere and villages you've never heard of go to lovely places. Kids from cities and suburbs end up going to the middle of nowhere. That's one of the unwritten rules of our government. It's their equalizer for the future generations. Where is the camp may I ask?"

Teodor did not like the direction in which this conversation was heading. He knew his father in law would do anything and everything for his grandchildren and would no doubt pressure him not to send Michael to the camp at all.

"It's somewhere near Słupsk, some 40 kilometers away and the seaside town Ustka is about 80 kilometers or so."

"Not exactly walking distance to the beach then?"

"No."

"How and where is the camp located then, do you know?"

"I believe it is on the grounds of what used to be some German landowner's mansion. You know, the "recovered lands" where people from what used to be eastern Poland were resettled. The farm lands were nationalized and part of it is the national farm, some parts were divided and given to the new settlers. The main building is serving as local school throughout the year."

"So what is Michael going to gain or learn from being stuck in such place?"

"Self reliance to begin with," Teodor was getting itchy, "they will go places, have games – I don't know. He'll meet kids of people I work with, at least some of them. He will make new acquaintances or friends. He'll do whatever kids his age do."

"This sort of thing" said Matilda's dad "is yet another form of them - the government, to re-engineer the society, to mould them to the communists liking. What they offer as subsidized or employer paid vacations for your kids is nothing short of trying to drive a little wedge into families. They will have no doubt some lovely bonfire nights with war stories about the Polish Army but mind you – the one aligned with the Red Army, not the Home Army. They will sing patriotic songs but only those with communist tint and they will be taught and otherwise indoctrinated how lovely the communist motherland is. Don't you get it?" the last question was said with a strong emphasis.

"Whether I get it or not," Teodor was getting irritated, "is one thing. The other and perhaps more important is the reality. This is what my kids are growing up with. They need to learn to live with it."

"This would be possibly okay if you were teaching them the other things."

Stan knew his son in law was apolitical which was odd because if anything he should have been bitter – after all, his parents were robbed of their vast land by the communists and everything else they had. Teodor witnessed it all but yet he seemed to be so resigned to the present circumstances and he seemed to be practically complacent.

Matilda's dad was apolitical in a way as well but he had his convictions and he loved Poland how she was before the war.

"He'll be all right," said Teodor as if to defuse the awkward conversation.

"What are you trying to prove Teodor?" asked Gabriela who so far was sitting silently.

"I'm not proving anything," he replied, "it's my son and I decided to send him to the camp."

"Michael is sensitive," said Gabriela, "and the camp may make more damage than anything worthwhile."

"Since when you have experience in raising children?" he asked with slight venom in his voice.

"You're hardly around home, so don't tell me you have plenty!"

"Whether I'm around or not it's none of your business. I work a lot and I'm commuting to and from work by public transport", he retorted not quite pleasantly.

"And it takes much more time than a taxi," he added.

She knew what he meant and it stung a bit but she hadn't showed it.

"I'm only saying I think it's not going to be neither good nor fun for Michael and you actually don't seem to have any sensible reason for sending him there."

"Nobody is going to tell me how I run my family," snapped Teodor. His face was tense and eyes squinted which in his case was a sign of anger.

Irena walked in asking everybody to the table.

"Dinner is ready!" she announced.

They all followed her to the dining room and it seemed the situation was defused.

10. INTO THE DARKNESS

Gabriela and Matilda were sitting on the terrace of their parent's house in Józefów. Irena and Stan took Gregory for a walk to the ice cream shop which was about half an hour walk. Michael was by now a late teenager and he was home either working on his homework and listening to the music or sneaked out to see his girlfriend. Girlfriends were not a popular subject within the family. For one reason or another nobody talked to Michael about his feelings, adventures or misadventures with the opposite sex. Sometimes he wished it was not so but on the other hand he was happy he was spared possible embarrassments. It was easier to talk about such things with his friends.

Gabriela and Matilda were sipping home made cherry liquor.

"I've met somebody," said Gabriela.

"Oh?" asked Matilda, "who is he?"

"I've met him half a year ago actually, when I went for the business training trip."

"Wasn't it that trip on a ship?"

"Yes. He was the captain of that ship."

"How exiting!"

Matilda was genuinely pleased for her sister. She really wished for her to find a partner.

"Tell me more. What's his name?"

"Stefan Borkowski. There isn't much to tell. He isn't the most handsome man I've ever seen but he is fun to be with and he's good in bed."

"I wasn't asking about that," Matilda made a face, "your private moments are just yours."

"That's life and it's important if two people want to be together."

"I asked about him as a person," Matilda, like most people considered such subjects as very private and therefore inappropriate to discuss.

"We hit it off almost from the moment I set my foot aboard his ship really. The very first evening we began talking about quite personal stuff. He's divorced and lives alone."

"Where is he from?"

"Gdynia, he's got a house in suburbs."

"A flat you mean?"

"No, a house."

"Wow – that's something."

"Captains make good money. He must have lost considerably in the divorce but he kept the house and the car."

"What car?" Matilda was curious as cars were more of a status symbol than houses.

"Wartburg" I think, Gabriela was not into cars but happened to remember the brand.

"Nice," Matilda was impressed, "do I get to meet him?"

"He'll be coming for a visit in two months or so. He can't obviously stay with me and mum and dad so he'll be in the hotel in Warsaw. He really wants to meet the family."

"It's unusual, I'd say."

"He works on a tight schedule which means that he is at sea much more than home. He's not sure when he will have another chance and he'd really like to meet us all."

"What a comfortable life you'd have then!" laughed Matilda.

"How do you mean?"

"You'd have house to yourself for stretches of time and you could do what you please."

"Unless - like any proverbial seaman he's got a girlfriend or wife in every port."

"As long as it's only one in each and they are not wives," said Matilda and they both laughed.

"How is he, jokes aside?"

"He's a nice guy but he's not sophisticated."

"Do you love him?"

"I don't know really but I do love spending time with him. He makes me feel at ease."

"Does he love you?"

"He said so, yes."

"So?"

"I don't know."

"I don't want to tell you what to do…"

"So stop right there. I can guess what you wanted to say."

"I only want to help. Time is not exactly on your side."

"I'm well aware of that," Gabriela was annoyed, "but it's my life, not anybody else's."

"Look, Gabriela, you got hurt once long time ago and such things leave scars. The point is your other associations were not exactly fortunate - were they. Don't measure him against Jurek, he's just another human being. Not better not worse, just different."

"I'm not asking for your advice," Gabriela turned less pleasant, "people who give advice usually do it for their own benefit."

"I'm your sister and I'm not looking for any benefits, I want you to be happy, that's all. Everybody wants to settle down, don't you?"

"With the right man, yes."

"Isn't he?"

"I told you, I'm not sure."

Matilda sighted.

"All right, time will tell then. Just don't blow it."

Gabriela said nothing. She was just staring into the late afternoon sun.

"All of you are the same. Just want to get rid of me it seems," she said.

"How can you say something like this?" Matilda was hurt, "we want you to be happy."

"That was taken away from me the minute Jurek dumped me and I can't get over it."

"Look, Gabriela. I'm trying to understand you but the simple fact is sometimes people dump each other. It's a fact of life. It's unpleasant, it ruins your self esteem but in the end it isn't the end of the world."

"It was to me!" said Gabriela with anger in her voice.

"All the enthusiasm I had for life back then was suddenly crushed like a broken glass. I picked up the pieces but it isn't the same. Sometimes I think that no matter what I'll do or who I end up with, Jurek will remain as a point of reference."

"Was he that special?"

"Yes. Do you know the expression "soul mate"?"

"Yes."

"Well, we were perfect soul mates. I was always happy and always at ease with him."

"I had that with Teodor."

"You are using the past tense," Gabriela was quick to notice.

"Yes. It used to be like this but over the years it diminished and evaporated. I'm raising two boys and Teo is working two jobs. We are just a married couple now."

"You let him walk all over you and you've got the result."

"Even if what you say is true, my life is stable and I like it that way. More often than not passion settles down with time."

"Maybe so," Gabriela was staring at the sky.

*

Irena was walking from the terrace towards the kitchen when somebody in the room above where Marian and Halina lived distinctively knocked on the floor three times. It was an agreed sign there was a phone call for Irena.

Phones in the communist Poland were hard to get and Marian and Halina were one of the few lucky ones that had one.

Seemingly it was simple – one had to apply for a phone with the local administration but waiting time was measured in years. Typically it was about seven years which was always explained by not enough exchanges. Somehow they were not being built as they were not on the priority list. Communism was struggling with shortage of flats for growing population. Phone exchanges were of lesser importance.

Irena ascended the flight of stairs and knocked on the door.

She could hear the commotion, then there was the mechanical sound of the door being unlocked and Marian appeared.

"Hello Irena," he greeted her and stepped aside to let her in.

"Thank you, Marian," she was catching her breath.

"It's your beloved daughter for you!" he announced.

Irena grabbed the phone.

"Gabriela?"

"Aaaa – I always suspected that," laughed Matilda on the other end of the line.

"What are you talking about?" Irena pretended nothing happened.

"Which one of us is the beloved one," chuckled Matilda as she found it really funny.

"No, she isn't"

"Can I tell her that then?"

"No. Oh, Matilda – knock it off. What are you calling about anyway?" Irena distanced herself from the charade.

"I haven't seen you and dad for a while so I just wanted to know how you were."

"Fine, we're fine."

"Also, I wanted to tell you we can't come this week-end. I promised you we'll come for a visit – remember?"

"Oh, yes – right."

"We can't. Teodor is going to see his childhood friend – he does it few times a year and I have some overdue housework to do. Gregory has lots of homework and Michael – I don't know what he's up to."

"All right, I understand. Pity though as I have dinner for all of you all prepared."

"How's Gabriela?"

"You know – as usual. She comes home late and sometimes I'm already asleep. Next morning she goes to work early so for the past few days I hardly see her."

"All right, Mum, I'll call again in a few days and I will come definitely next Saturday even if I'm to do so by myself."

"All right, Matilda."

"Bye, Mum."

"Bye."

Marian returned to the room while she was finishing her conversation with Matilda.

"I'm sorry I've set you up," he smiled.

"No need to be sorry. They are not little girls."

"But there is some natural competition isn't it?"

"Oh, I don't know. Perhaps it is but I don't pay attention really."

The radio was on and one of the popular songs from before the war came in.

"Good God!" exclaimed Marian, "I haven't heard that in years!"

"Yes," Irena agreed, "it's surprising the communists hadn't banned it for good."

He made a step in her direction.

"Would you do me the honor and dance with me?"

"What?"

"May I have this dance please?" he looked serious.

"But… Halina?"

"She will not be back until tomorrow. Please dance with me!"

He stretched his hand to her. Late afternoon sun was filling the room with shafts of rays coming through the windows at an angle and mixing with shades in a three dimensional crisscrossed pattern which seemed to be filling entire space. The room lost its usual properties and seemed to be like an impressionist's painting.

Irena forgot everything around her. The room, the walls, the entire environment dissolved in the sunny haze. There was only this wonderful music and Marian's arm waiting for her.

She stepped closer to him and accepted his stretched hand. He then reached with his right arm and placed it around her back and led her to the music. Irena felt transported back in time. It was a ball somewhere in Warsaw before the war. The lights were shimmering and she could hear other pairs dancing and chatting around them. Her partner was wearing a black tuxedo with impeccable white shirt with a white bow tie and he had a white carnation in the button hole. He pressed her gently a bit closer and palm of his hand slid down and was now resting on her waistline. It sent slight tingling down her spine and her heart accelerated a little. He was a very good dancer and Irena felt as if she was flying in space. She felt alive perhaps like never before. She lived for dancing, she was born for it and every step she took was infatuating and getting her ever closer to her destiny.

*

Teodor was sitting at his worktable where he worked on his second job making crowns and bridges for his sister's patients. Even though his little workshop was of miniature size he could produce any dental fixture from a single crown to a full set of false teeth. He had unusual talent which allowed him to repair anything from a simple alarm clock to a car's engine. But despite encouragements from Matilda and his friends he was reluctant to venture into potentially lucrative car repairs. He would do it only as a hobby and for friends who never offered to pay for his work and time so he did it just for a "thank you" or a vague advice sounding like "you could make lots of money if you do that for a living. Should you go for it I'll sent you everybody I know who has a car or a motorcycle."

Teodor considered technical dentistry more predictable and stable. It was also portable enough and he could do it in the kitchen's corner. Repairing cars would have to be done outside or he'd have to rent a garage somewhere. But quitting his regular job and renting a garage would not work as he would not have money for the rent. Teodor and Matilda lived on a tight budget. Matilda did not work as she was raising two boys. Even if she wanted to, Teodor being old fashioned wouldn't let her. She actually had a job for a while before Gregory was born and she liked it but at that time Michael was under care of her grandmother who'd come and stay in their flat. The scenario worked but only until Matilda got pregnant with Gregory.

He looked at Matilda who was tidying things up after the supper and said:

"Can you please tell your mother to stop telling Michael about the Radio Free Europe?"

"She doesn't."

"Yes, she does!" Teodor was annoyed knowing she was denying the truth.

He heard his mother in law telling Michael countless times how the RFE had a segment for young people with the chart of top ten or twenty hits updated every day. She was also telling him how the RFE reports on current sports events and the real news, not filtered or otherwise manipulated by the communists run national radio.

"But she only…" began Matilda but he cut her short.

"No she does not. I know what I'm talking about and I heard it myself!" he snapped.

"Michael is sensible and he wouldn't…"

"Look," he was now angry, "this is not about what Michael is or isn't. I want her to stop for good and you first deny it, then try to change the subject. It was the same with her giving him wine in this miniature mug. I was asking her not to do it and she'd juts say it wouldn't do any harm. The woman ignores me completely and if I open my mouth you accuse me of being mean to her."

"Because you are unpleasant to her."

"If I am frustrated I can't help it! She is undermining my authority all the time. I ask, but when I have to repeat it several times I get pissed-off. Your father can be the same sometimes but mercifully less so. It's only a matter of time before she does the same thing to Gregory."

"She loves her grand children to pieces. That's what grandparents do, they love and spoil them."

Teodor was fuming by now.

"Not by telling them about Radio Free Europe! Don't you get it?! It's almost the same with you. I'm not asking for much and you keep giving me arguments. This is not a conversation, I'm telling you what to do! Do you understand?!"

He raised his voice and at the same moment the knife he was working with slid and went deep into the base of his left hand thumb. Blood squirted from the narrow but deep cut. Teodor threw the knife and the piece he was working on against the wall and hurried to rinse the cut.

Matilda followed.

"Let me see, I'll dress the wound," she said.

"Get out of here and leave me alone!"

Matilda returned to the kitchen. She picked up the knife and placed it on his worktable. She then reached for the piece he was working on. It was broken in half. She knew it took him four hours to make it and it wasn't possible to mend it. He'd have to do it all over again. It also meant the patient was not going to had it fitted the following morning because there was no time. Teodor had to go to sleep and get up at 4.30 in the morning to go to his daytime job.

Teodor was seemingly apolitical and never engaged in conversations about politics like his fellow countrymen did. He was just unable to sort things out. He despised the system which robbed his father of the land and thus robbed Theodor of his future but he was resigned to his fate. He thought that talking endlessly about what ifs and criticizing the government was just waste of time and energy.

When he was nineteen he was drafted to the mandatory military service and as any recruit he had to go through the boot camp and then serve two years. That of course included indoctrination on daily basis. Not that Teodor sold his mind and soul to it – not at all. But he drew his own conclusions. The communists controlled everything but above all the army, the police, the press and the radio. In other words they controlled life. And the Polish State was controlled by the Soviet Union which had military bases in Poland and in all other countries belonging to the so called Soviet Block, just to be sure.

An individual like his mother in law with her memories of the pre-war Poland constantly complaining about the present and spreading whatever she picked up from the Radio Free Europe was going to nowhere.

Every few years the workers who in theory were in charge of the country would protest against the government's inability to run economy and every single time the government sent police and sometimes army to pacify the protests. On each such occasion people were killed and injured because the police was told to beat the protesters mercilessly and sooner or later were allowed to use live ammunition if just beating people was not enough. In the aftermath the government always announced it was some hooligans who hijacked a rightful protest of the working class to disrupt the peaceful demonstrations. It was the hooligans that got killed and injured and more hooligans were arrested. That was the pattern. People were whispering that in many instances the government sent provocateurs who were young policemen in civilian clothing to instigate violence by smashing shop windows which then was used as the excuse to send uniformed police units specially trained for crowd control. They were equipped with extra long batons, large shields and heavy helmets.

Deep down Teodor hated it just as much as his mother-in-law did but he felt there was nothing that could be done to change the reality. Teaching kids about the Radio Free Europe could only land them in trouble if not now, perhaps later in life. It could in fact land the parents in trouble as well. As resigned as he was Teodor would not join the Workers Party despite being invited many times. He refused every single time just like he refused when he was offered to join the police. That happened towards the end of his mandatory military service. He was physically fit and apart from the idiotic political indoctrination he actually liked all the military stuff. He earned rank of a corporal and his service record was outstanding.

About a month before the discharge he was called to report to the officers barracks. He knocked on the door and was surprised to see a civilian in there. It was a middle aged fellow who asked him to sit down and offered Teodor a drink. He produced two glasses and a small bottle of vodka. He asked Teodor how he was, complimented him on his good record and asked about plans for the future. Teodor was quick to observe the fellow knew about him a lot. He then said a career in the police was available to Teodor along with considerable perks – notably an elevated pay, access to special shops not available to general population and retirement at full salary. Teodor could even choose the branch – general, criminal or political. There was even a hint at secret services with either police or military. This fellow was very much unlike Teodor's superiors.

He was laid back, easy going and not projecting his superiority at all. It was almost like talking to an old friend or a distant family member.

He didn't expect immediate answer. He suggested that Teodor takes time to think it over. In fact he did not even ask for any commitment. If interested Teodor was to knock on that door or otherwise he could just continue as if the conversation never took place.

It was tempting and Teodor could imagine how many others would go for it. But Teodor knew rather well that this man represented the same force that imprisoned his older brother for being in the Home Army during the war, imprisoned his father for being the landowner, took away the land and the family home and left them with nothing. The land and buildings were subdivided and given to peasants because this is what communism was about. Land was given to those who hadn't had it and factories were taken over by the state. The original owners were the rotten bourgeoisie which only used and mistreated the working class and peasants.

Teodor's father was a broken man for the rest of his days and his eldest son was slipping into alcoholism. Teodor hated it all and there was no way he would align himself with the system which robbed his family of life as they knew it and reduced them to nothing. No way.

*

The spotlights were blinding and she couldn't see anything beyond the nearest musicians just after the row of lights at the edge of the stage. She could only feel the presence of the audience. The acoustics of empty theater were distinctively different when compared to the same auditorium filled to capacity. The spectacle was coming to an end. Few more steps, few more measures of music, the final pirouette and it was going to be over. With the corner of her eye she noticed the ballet director standing right by the curtain watching her. In the grand finale she was taking the center stage alone while the cast was lined up in half circle behind her. As she went into the last pirouette she suddenly felt a jolt of pain going straight into her toe as if there was a needle in the toe box of her pointe shoe. She screamed with pain, slipped and fell down. The music stopped and there was a dead silence. The pain in her toe was excruciating. She glanced at her right foot and saw how the dark red stain was rapidly growing in size, spreading on the fabric and was now expanding towards her ankle. She touched the it with the tips of her fingers and looked at them – the blood was now spreading fast from her fingertips to the palm of her hand and further into her forearm. Irena screamed in horror and woke up breathing heavily.

She was in her bed and the clock hanging on the wall in the kitchen has just ringed two o'clock at night. Stan was sleeping flat on his back snoring lightly. She got out of bed and went to the bathroom to get a drink of water. She glanced at her face in the mirror and noticed her eyes being unnaturally sparkling.

The cold water was soothing and refreshing. She looked into the mirror again and her eyes were normal now. She quietly returned to bed but was twisting and turning for a long time being unable to fall asleep again. She heard the clock striking three, three thirty and four. After that, exhausted, she finally fell asleep.

*

Gabriela walked into the hallway of the flat in Józefów where she lived with her parents and slammed the door. It was Saturday afternoon and Irena, Stan, Matilda, Teodor and their two boys were there waiting for Gabriela and Stefan. The family was eager to meet Stefan and the dinner was carefully planned and prepared by Irena and Stan.

Irena rushed to the door and was surprised to see Gabriela alone.

"Where is Stefan?"

"He's not coming!"

Dining room was close enough for Stan, Matilda and Teodor to hear it.

"What happened?"

"I broke it off."

"You WHAT?!"

"I've just told you," snapped Gabriela, "we're through. I broke it off and we'll never see each other again."

"But - why? What happened?"

"He's crude and unsophisticated – that's why."

Matilda appeared and Gabriela gave her a look telling Matilda to stay away but she ignored it.

"What has he done? Are you all right?"

"Oh, I'm fine."

"So?"

"Okay, I tell you – we went to the theatre late last night."

"Yes, I know."

"It was a ballet actually, the Swan Lake."

"Right," Matilda and Irena said simultaneously.

"He fell asleep after half an hour!"

"And?" prompted Matilda.

"What do you mean "and"?, Gabriela was irritated, "that was it!"

Matilda was still not quite getting it.

"What then?"

"Nothing," Gabriela was winded up fast, "what else do you want? Snoring? I jabbed him and he woke up. I didn't want to make a scene during the show. I broke off in the intermission!"

"Why?" Irena was beside herself but this question only tripped Gabriela off.

"Are you both stupid?! Don't you get it? How can one fall asleep in the theatre at all, let alone with a fiancée???"

Stan and Teodor remained in the dining room but they heard it all.

Stan raised his voice so they could hear him.

"Didn't you say he travelled overnight to come here?"

"Yes! So what?" asked Gabriela.

"And you basically dragged him straight into the theatre?"

"I haven't dragged him anywhere!"

"Did he have time to rest after his journey and refresh?"

"Gabriela?" Stan did not hear the answer because there was none.

"No, he hasn't. But it doesn't matter. What he did is unforgivable!"

"The man was tired," said Stan, "you told me yourself he'd returned home from the sea and practically instantly caught the train to come here to be with you. You haven't given him time to catch his breath and you are upset he fell asleep? Hell – I'd fell asleep at the bloody Swan Lake even if I was well rested!"

But Gabriela wouldn't give an inch.

"It only means you are just as unsophisticated as he is."

Teo who was sitting silently throughout the entire exchange joined now.

"Well, you are just so high above us all, or everybody else for that matter."

"You keep out of it!" hissed Gabriela, "all of you are the same! Don't you get I want somebody to be on a certain level! How hard it can be to understand?!"

"I've got a news for you, Gabriela" Teodor was calm, "nobody ever will be on your level – including prince charming from a fairy tale. You'd find something wrong in him too. Unless you change and get real you'll be on your way to be an old maid! It's happening already."

"How dare you?! How can you let him talk to me like that!" screamed Gabriela, "who do you think you are, you peasant? No wonder you don't understand what it's about!"

And turning to Matilda she added:

"I told you before - you failed to raise him. Once a boor - always a boor!"

"Calm down Gabriela, and apologize to Teo," her father attempted to defuse the situation which was spinning out of control, but Teodor already got up and walked towards the coat rack in the hallway.

Reaching for his coat he said:

"It's all too posh for me. Insulting guests is rude to say the least – I believe I heard it somewhere."

And turning to Matilda he added:

"You can stay if you like - it's your sister and your parents. I'm leaving."

"Teo, wait, please don't go!" Stan pleaded with him.

But Teodor put on his coat and walked out of the house closing the door behind him.

"You should apologize to Teo and call him back!" said Stan angrily, "do it now!"

"He is what I said he is," Gabriela was defiant, "and the same goes for Stefan. I've done nothing wrong."

"What you did is selfish, self-centered and stupid!"

"And you call yourself my father?!" screamed Gabriela.

"I, we – your Mum and me, gave in too much to your hysteria before, each time we thought about it and we did so hoping we are helping you in difficult times. We hoped you'd appreciate it. But it obviously doesn't work because this is what we are getting in return."

"What is really obvious is that you don't know me at all!" shouted Gabriela "and so I don't know you either, Mister!"

She rushed to her room and slammed the door.

Irena tried to follow her but as she began opening the door Gabriela shouted at her.

"Get out! Leave me alone! All of you!"

Matilda gathered her sons.

"Let's go, boys," she said to them, "we have to go home."

"No Matilda, please stay, let's have dinner. We need to eat no matter what, you must be hungry," asked Irena.

Silent all of this time until now Michael looked at his Mum.

"Let's have dinner, Mum. We'll go home later."

Matilda looked at him.

"Yeah, all right," she said.

Gregory who all of this time was drawing something in the corner of the room turned to his grandpa.

"Look what I drew!" he said.

Stan looked at the piece of paper. It seemed to be filled with featureless people. Above them was a thick cloud of fog or smoke.

"What are these people doing?" Stan asked.

"It's all of you arguing just now," replied Gregory with a sheepish smile.

Stan examined the drawing again.

"Very good", he said, "very good indeed."

*

Stan was not feeling well for a while now. Being a former smoker, handicapped for number of years now and getting older like everybody else he thought his shortness of breath was easily explained. He was no stranger to a drink either. Over the course of time he made changes – he quit smoking long time ago and he never was a heavy drinker but with doctor's advice he was careful about drinking and by now he limited it to a glass of wine with dinner on week-ends and only occasional hard drink.

One day in February he walked from the flat early in the morning as usual to catch the commuter train to Warsaw. He kissed Irena good-bye as he always did and left. Irena saw top of his head from her kitchen window. She always had breakfast sitting at the kitchen window looking out at the backyard. Stan walked around the building to the gate leading to the street but when he reached for the handle to open it he suddenly felt a piercing pain in his chest. Looking to support himself he reached with the other hand to grab the gate but he missed and fell forward. By the time his body hit the pavement he was no longer aware of the world around him.

About five minutes later a neighbor who was taking the same train left his house next door and found Stan lying on the ground by the gate. The neighbor thought Stan had just fallen and tried to talk to him wanting to help Stan stand up but Stan was not responding. The neighbor run back home and called for the ambulance which arrived in about fifteen minutes but there was nothing the paramedics could do. Stan was unresponsive and he had no pulse. He must have died instantly.

Irena who was completely unaware of what was going on was called in before the ambulance arrived and she was crying uncontrollably. Halina, her neighbor from upstairs placed her arm around her and led her away. Police was called by the paramedics and arrived within minutes and after not finding anything suspicious they called undertakers to take Stan's body to the mortuary. In the meantime Marian called Gabriela who was at work. He also called the neighbor of Matilda's who notified Matilda. Teodor and Matilda did not have a phone service at their home, they were on the waiting list five years so far.

Halina, who was calm and practical, gave Irena a dose of Valerian drops to drink which had a very mild sedative effect and people typically used them to calm their nerves. With that Irena fell asleep for a couple of hours and Halina made arrangements for her to stay overnight at her flat rather than Irena's own. She also called the chief priest and invited him to come later on day to talk to Irena.

Irena was sitting in the pew of the Our Lady of Czestochowa church in Józefów, staring at the painting of Mary Magdalene which was hanging above the altar. The painting was actually a cover, hiding the main painting which was portraying the Black Madonna of Czestochowa. It was not an original as the original is the Jasna Góra Monastery in Częstochowa.

The church had a clever mechanism which allowed the picture of Mary Magdalene to be lowered almost to the ground level to the point it was not visible to the congregation thus exposing the revered Our Lady of Czestochowa as the Black Madonna of Czestochowa is also known. The Jasna Góra Monastery has a similar device but there is also a beautiful hymn played when the picture is being uncovered.

Irena spent probably about an hour on her knees praying but now she was just sitting looking at the altar and the painting. There was only an old woman in church except her. She was in front of the altar on her knees whispering the rosary. There were also sounds of some commotion coming from the sacristy located to the right of the main altar. There was probably one of the young priests there doing something or preparing himself for the upcoming evening service.

Thoughts in Irena's head were spinning. It was a mixture of snippets from her life with Stan, experiences during the war and the Warsaw Uprising but every now and then she'd think of more recent events.

Stan's funeral was going to take place the following day and Irena was still in shock trying to recover. In times of crisis she always looked for peace in church and always found it there - but today was a bit different. She was struggling with everything and she was unable to calm herself down. The prayers she said helped and seemed to be working but once she finished the spinning returned and her brain was playing flashbacks from her life at complete random. While unable to stop it, being in church was somewhat soothing and Irena found herself as if suspended somewhere halfway between reality and illusion. She wished she could just stay where she was. The life outside had just caught her completely unprepared, the void seemed like a horrifying chasm and even thinking about it and trying to absorb it made her feel sick. As long as she was sitting here in church she felt exempt and protected from the horror. Yes, the more she thought about it, Stan's death had qualities of a horror. She realized now she was taking him for granted all of those years. He was always there, whether she was in a good mood or a bad. Whether he teasingly pinched her bottom – or front for that matter, which she really hated, or not - Stan was always there. Now, as of two days ago, the sometimes stubborn like a donkey, unwilling to compromise on anything Stan was no longer there and nothing could change that. He always wanted her, even at the older age, and she denied him countless of times. They discussed it and they argued over it. She hated either but now it was all irrevocably gone. Forever, for good, for the eternity.

Suddenly Irena realized what it was all about – the widowhood was waiting for her outside and she despised it, she hated it, she was afraid of it, she did not want it. It seemed as long as she was sitting here in her pew she was safe. But she could not sit in the pew forever and she knew it.

The day of the funeral was cold and unpleasant. The sky had this unattractive color of concrete stretching from east to west and from south to north. It was even and depressing. The service was a typical funeral mass, about half an hour long. After that the undertaker's crew carried the coffin outside and placed it on a four wheel cart, while all the guests lined up behind it and as soon as the priest took position in front they began the long walk to the family grave. Irena, Gabriela and Matilda were all dressed in black with Irena wearing a simple bonnet with a black veil. She looked very dignified. She was too exhausted to cry or show any emotion, her face was just fixed somber. Gabriela was just stern and Matilda's eyes were swollen a bit, she cried a lot just before coming here. Teodor, Michael and Gregory were walking immediately behind. Once or twice Irena glanced back to see who was there but she could not recognize anyone and she did not want to stare too long. The number of people seemed smaller than she thought it would be but it did not disappoint her, it was merely an observation. They all walked in silence although people at the back were talking a bit, they could get away with it. Some twenty minutes later they arrived at the gravesite where the gravediggers already did they work and were now standing a respectable distance away smoking cigarettes.

The priest began the final prayer after which the undertaker's crew lowered the coffin to the freshly dug hole in the ground and the priest said the final words: ashes to ashes, dust to dust. He then bent down, took a bit of soil, threw it on the coffin and stepped aside to allow all mourners do the same. He than left and the gravediggers began covering the coffin with the soil. One by one the guests left and by the time the gravediggers were finishing their work it was only Irena, Gabriela, Matilda, Teodor, Michael and Gregory standing there in silence. Each one of them had a different void to bear.

Irena's days became dull. She'd maintain her routine by getting up at the same time which was more or less the time Stan would get up to get ready to go to work. Her company now was the radio as Irena never ceased to listen to the Radio Free Europe which remained her window to the international as well as domestic affairs. The communism in Poland was still the same, still struggling with its hopeless inability to run economy which in turn made people upset. The regime was still spitting at and insulting the pre-war Poland and the Home Army. The greatest taboos like Katyń Massacre or names of General Władysław Anders and Józef Piłsudski were all in place, nothing has changed.

Poland was a signatory of the human rights Helsinki Declaration in 1975 but it did not make any difference to Joe Average on the street.

Irena's house was empty and that emptiness was staring straight into her eyes. Although she and Stan would sometimes argue over completely ridiculous and unimportant things, she was missing even those moments now. The time, which some say is a good doctor, was not exactly good to her because if anything she was seeing what she had not seen before – that Stan loved her unconditionally. Over the years of marriage, especially earlier ones, she had so many doubts. She agreed to marry him without much conviction and she struggled with intimacy for years. She got used to some aspects of it and hated some others. But now when it was all gone she was looking at it all from a different perspective, which she was never able to do before and it made her sad. Sometimes she'd wake up in the morning thinking it was all wrong and she felt guilty of not loving Stan enough or perhaps at all.

Her only living companion was a cat named Minnie, which Gabriela found somewhere and brought home. The cat was scruffy, thin and hungry. It was a white-red with patches of black here and there female of unknown age.

Animals were always an issue between Irena and Gabriela. Gabriela had something that attracted lost or misplaced animals – cats and dogs and over the years she'd bring them in to Irena's great dismay. She did like animals but at a distance. And those creatures adopted by Gabriela would do all of those things Irena did not like – taking over the beds and sleeping on them during the day and with Gabriela at night. They would sometimes have accidents indoors and every single time it happened would be when Gabriela was not around so it was Irena who had to clean up the mess. But in the end Irena would give in as this is what she and Stan always did to Gabriela's will. Irena eventually got used to a dog or a cat in her house and would feed them and within a reason take care of them. But with all of that she was not an expert and therefore she missed signs of imminent end to Minnie's pregnancy. She did not think much of the cat when it was looking for a quiet spot in the house when the nature told it the time was approaching. Gabriela was not always around as by now she had a tiny flat in Warsaw not far from her work and she was only returning home for week-ends, usually Friday evenings. She'd stay with Irena Saturday and Sunday and leave for work Monday morning. During the week Irena was alone. She kept herself busy with usual household chores, typical shopping, chatting with neighbors and going to church. She was not devoted like sometimes older women can be, she had just her faith in place. Her only break was Thursday as she would travel to Warsaw to meet with her friend Janina, visit the Krucza Street number nine and the chestnut tree, her only living link to her past. She visited the tree for so many years now and she loved doing so. The visits were possibly the only moments when she felt truly herself, free of the attachments brought upon her by life. For those few precious minutes it was just her, the girl from so many years ago, the beautiful tree and she could almost smell the pre-war Warsaw in the air. But then she had to walk back to the train station and take the one hour long train ride to Józefów, once merely a temporary stopover which turned permanent. And by a twist of fate Irena was stuck there alone now, while Gabriela lived in Warsaw now and was coming to her for week-ends only. Matilda and her family lived in Warsaw too, at the far end of it.

One night at about three in the morning Irena was awaken by odd noises. She didn't know what it was. She wasn't scared as she was not the type, she just listened for a moment. When the commotion was audible again she determined it was coming from Gabriela's room so she got up from bed, switched the light on and went to see what the source of the odd sounds was. As soon as she flipped the light switch she found the cat on Gabriela's bed giving birth to a litter of kittens.

Irena was standing frozen as she had never seen this before in her life and had no clue as to whether or not she should be doing something. As she was standing there it occurred to her that she was going to have not one but six cats in her house. Finding homes for kittens was not an attractive prospect as it was usually only kids that would found or get kittens from friends and bring them home and then argue with parents to keep them. Irena was definitely not going to go through the hassle of placing kittens in new homes. There were plenty of cats everywhere anyway. She also figured Gabriela would want to keep them, promise to find homes for them but this would be the end. No doubt to Irena, Gabriela would have hard time finding new homes good enough according to her.

Irena also knew what a common knowledge among people was as to the quickest solution when it came to the unwanted litters of kittens. It was repulsive and she did not like it at all but standing there in darkness all alone she felt she had no choice. How many times had she accepted what life had brought upon her? Not this time though. She went to the kitchen and opened the cupboard where she kept cleaning supplies and reached for rubber gloves and put them on. She then collected the tiny creatures, went to the bathroom and flushed them down the toilet. She stood there for a moment breathing heavily and suddenly threw up.

It took her about an hour to clean everything and wash herself and only then she finally returned to her bed. She laid on her back in complete darkness which seemed to be getting colder and colder with every passing minute. The dawn was still perhaps a half an hour away and there were no sounds at all.

Suddenly the cat in Gabriela's room began meowing and there was such desperation in its voice that Irena shivered and trying to escape it put a pillow over her head to muffle the sound. Before too long she was crying. It was just tears in her eyes at first but then she could not stop their flow. The arrow of sorrow penetrated her mind with a sudden and unexpected shot and she was sobbing uncontrollably until exhausted, she fell asleep.

She got up late, had breakfast about noon and only then realized it was Friday which meant that Gabriela was coming home for week-end. They were going to have dinner together which Irena was to make. As she was finishing her breakfast she thought she had not had all supplies for dinner so she ventured out, returned some hour and a half later and set to work. There was not much time left so she decided to skip dusting and vacuuming, the flat was clean anyway as she cleaned it the day before.

She decided to make pork chops in mushroom sauce, potatoes and chicory salad. She liked it and Gabriela liked it too.

Parents are always longing for their children even if the "children" are adults and Irena was no different. Deep down she was missing them both - Gabriela and Matilda but she knew she could not have them as often as she wished. Gabriela was coming home regularly, Matilda less so as she lived considerable distance away on the other side of Warsaw and she was running her household. Sometimes during her Thursday trips to Warsaw Irena would visit Matilda but it was a hassle as she needed at least extra two hours so she'd have to plan such Thursday in a different way and set off early. Matilda was trying to visit her Mum as often as she could and on many occasions while Teodor would go to visit his mother who also lived in Józefów, Matilda was coming to Irena. Sometimes Teodor and Matilda would make such visits unannounced during the week and it was always a nice surprise for Irena. She preferred to see her daughters separately as it was way better to talk one on one. Irena felt she could say a bit more to Matilda and be at ease with her more than with Gabriela. Matilda would make her at ease, she always listened and then tried to help or offer an advice.

Gabriela was wrapping up her day at the office and she was fuming.

Her boss, a woman named Cecilia decided to reorganize the department after one of their colleagues retired. Everybody expected the vacancy to be filled with somebody new which would hopefully be a breath of fresh air into the seasoned team. But instead of hiring somebody Cecilia decided to remove the vacant position while dividing the workload by the number of remaining employees and adding more work to everyone. The management was apparently pleased because there was an obvious savings for the company and Cecilia was praised for her initiative. To be fair while not universally liked she managed people well and was always ready to assist or advice in problem solving. She'd also defended her team if there was a need to do so. But getting more work for the same pay was not something Gabriela and others were not thrilled about. They tried to talk to her and used all sensible arguments but she was like an unmovable rock. The only concession she made was a vague promise that if it ends up being too much indeed she'd take it up with the management and reinstate the eliminated position. For now however they had to handle increased amount of work and that was it. Thus this particular Friday ended not on a happy note. Exactly at five o'clock Gabriela barked "good-bye" and stormed out of her office. Once on the street she did what she was not doing often – she reached for a cigarette and lit it. Smoking was relaxing her in times of crisis. A drink would be even better but she was not going to go to some café just to sit down alone and have a drink as it would be ridiculous. She marched half an hour to the station to take the train to Józefów. Alas – it was not going to be that easy. Public transport in the Communist Poland had a lot to be desired. There were days when it worked with its usual momentum. Never quite enough buses or trams or trains but they were more or less on schedule. But there were also days when for no apparent reason a train would be late. Passengers would find out about it the hard way – they would be waiting on the platform and it just wouldn't appear. A half an hour later it would be announced it was going to be delayed – for example – by fifty minutes. Sometimes a later train would come first and few minutes later the delayed one. But people would flock to the first one and travel packed like sardines in a can while the delayed train would follow half empty. Some other times all trains would be delayed by the same amount. But the passengers were always on time aiming for their trains so in the end higher number of passengers would be squeezing to coaches.

Gabriela hated such delays and hated travelling in crowded coaches as it sometimes meant she'd had to stand the entire journey which took about fifty five minutes. She was upset when she arrived at the station as she could see the platform filled to capacity. She was then even more upset waiting forty five minutes and by the time she was squeezed by her fellow commuters she was in really bad mood. She was overheating, her cloth was damp and if she had to ride few more stations she'd be swimming in her sweat. She was happy to finally disembark in Józefów but her mood was foul. The fact that some creep patted her on her behind in the crowded coach made things even worse. People were packed so tightly she could not even turn around to see which of the few men around her did it so she could not even let the culprit have piece of her mind.

If Józefów was good for anything it was its fresh air which welcomed her as soon as the automatic door opened. The scent of pine trees was in the air and it was so pleasant.

When Gabriela walked into the flat Irena was in the kitchen listening to the Radio Free Europe. Hearing commotion at the door Irena emerged from the kitchen.

"Oh, why are you so late?" she asked.

"The stupid train was nearly an hour delayed!"

"I was waiting with dinner for you."

"Give me a moment," Gabriela went to the bathroom to wash her hands and freshen up.

Irena returned to the kitchen to get their dinner. The plates and flatware was already on the table.

Gabriela sat at the table.

"The shelf under the mirror is dusty," she said.

"I didn't have time to clean the house today."

"Why not?"

"I got up late and had to go shopping."

"That's your excuse?"

"No, I'm just saying I had less time."

Gabriela gave her a look.

"I work from nine to five every day and keep my flat clean at all times and I'll continue to do so even though they've increased my work load."

"Oh, I see."

"No, it's not "I see". You don't go to work so you have time on your hands. Your flat should be spotless. Perhaps you should keep yourself busy instead of staring out the window and listening to the radio."

"I don't."

"You do. Dust is everywhere – look at the floor, window sills and the furniture."

"I do what I always did. Dad never complained."

"You are cutting corners. I'm coming back tired and the place is a dump."

"No it isn't. I told you I had less time today."

For a while they were eating in silence.

"Where is Minnie? She is due any time now I think."

"In your room," Irena felt suddenly uncomfortable noticing Gabriela was aware Minnie was pregnant.

"What's wrong?" asked Gabriela.

"Nothing."

"The cutlets are almost burned."

"I was waiting with dinner, I thought you'd be earlier."

"I told you the bloody train was late!"

"I didn't know that ahead of time, did I?"

They finished dinner and Irena cleaned the table while Gabriela went to have a bath. Irena washed the dishes and put them away, then made herself a cup of tea, sat down by the kitchen window and continued listening to the radio. She heard Gabriela opening the bathroom door and walking to her room.

"Good night Mum," she said to Irena.

"Good night, Gabriela," Irena responded.

Wish you'd at least walked in and look at me - she thought.

She heard Gabriela talking sweetly to Minnie.

"Oh, my Minnie where are you sweetheart? Come here, come to me."

It was quiet for a moment and then Irena heard quick steps as Gabriela was approaching the kitchen. She stopped in the door.

"Where are her kittens?!" she demanded.

Irena turned to face her. There was no point in denying.

"What do you think? They are gone."

"They are what?!" Gabriela was already agitated.

"What have you done with them?"

"I won't be taking care of cats. One is enough."

"Where are they?"

Irena was silent.

Gabriela moved closer to her.

"Where are they?!" she repeated.

Irena looked at her and Gabriela saw Irena's eyes had an odd gaze, perhaps fear, perhaps something else. They were eyes of a cornered animal. For a fraction of a second Gabriela thought she had not recognized her in that look or perhaps her mother was just not there but her anger did not allow her to consider this observation longer.

"What have you done with them?!" she demanded.

Irena's eyes returned to normal and face became determined and stoic.

"I flushed them down the toilet," she said without emotion, "you know it had to be done."

"Murderer!" Gabriela flew into a rage, "that's what you are! I should've known, I should've expected! How could you??? You know how I love animals!"

"Yes, I know. And you were going to keep them all here. It would be me living with them, not you!"

"I would take care of them!"

"How? - You come her only on week-ends."

"I'd find homes for them myself. And besides – you do nothing all day long. I keep coming here and I see the flat dirty, food burnt and you don't talk to me, just listen to the radio."

"No – it's you that come here as if to a restaurant, then go to your bed and go to sleep. It's you not talking to me, I feel left alone day in day out. Oh, if Matilda was here…" Irena began to cry.

"That's it – isn't it? Always Matilda! The better daughter. The sweet little idiot."

"How dare you calling your sister an idiot? I've always treated you equally."

"No! You haven't and same goes for dad, I know it. I saw it for years. And yet she'd suck your blood out without living teeth marks on your neck!"

"You are horrible! – how can you even think of something like this to say?"

"It's not me as a matter of fact, dad said that!"

"He'd never…"

"Oh yes he did and yet you were oblivious to that! Well it doesn't matter anyway. I'm leaving!" she stormed out of the kitchen and went back to her room.

Irena, hearing her shuffling things in her room walked there and found Gabriela getting dressed.

"What are you doing?"

"I won't stay here!"

"Where are you going?"

"Anywhere – back to my flat or to friends but I will not stay here!"

"Please don't go, I don't want to be alone," Irena pleaded through her tears, "I'm alone all the time and I hate it."

"Call your Matilda to stay with you," snapped Gabriela, "that's what you'd prefer anyway!"

"No, it's just came out like that…" Irena was sobbing.

But Gabriela was already dressed. She grabbed her coat from the rack, slipped her shoes on, opened the door and walked outside without saying a word and slammed the door shut.

Irena was sobbing uncontrollably standing motionless in the middle of the kitchen. Minnie emerged from Gabriela's room and slowly approached the door. She looked up at Irena and made a single meow. Irena mechanically opened the door and let the cat out. She then returned to the kitchen, sat on her stool by the window and stared into the darkness of the night. She remained sitting like this for the next few hours until she was so sleepy she nearly fell from the chair so she walked to the bedroom and without changing into her nightgown just collapsed on her bed, pulled a blanket over her head and fell asleep.

*

The sound of a meow woke her up. She opened her eyes and looked at the ceiling which seemed to by sky high, she could hardly see the features of the elaborated light fixture hanging in the center. She rubbed her eyes and the ceiling glided down to its normal position. Feeling somewhat uncomfortable she touched her chest and realized she was lying on her bed being fully dressed. Another meow outside her door made her get up. *Oh, its Minnie* - she thought and walked to open the door to let her in. The cat made one step forward but then stopped, looked at her, arched its back, bared its teeth and hissed at her. As it did so, Irena thought it was rapidly growing in size and its eyes took a red glow, so she quickly stepped back and the cat walked in. She went to the bathroom to brush her teeth. Looking at herself in the mirror she saw untidy hair, wrinkled blouse and skirt and somewhat swollen eyes. Only now she recalled the fight with Gabriela and sighted.

Feeling not fresh she undressed and stepped into the bathtub to have a quick shower. Warm water was pleasant and soothing and she was standing there for a long while holding the showerhead directly above her head. When she was done she stepped out of the bathtub and looked at herself in the mirror again. She looked better now. *I should have a perm done* she thought. Naked, she walked to her room and stopped by the window to look outside. The street was empty. To see better she pushed the curtain out of her way but with a delay she realized she was standing naked in front of her window so she pulled back. She now looked at her image in a large mirror standing in the corner of the room. As she was looking at herself the image fluttered a little as if it was a liquid rather than a mirror and a slight wave came across the surface momentarily distorting her face and figure. She turned away from it and went on to get dressed.

11. SPIRAL

"We must get her to see a shrink," Gabriela was sitting with Matilda in her flat.

"Do you realize what are you saying?" Matilda did not like it.

"Of course I do, I'm her daughter too. Besides, I've spoken to her doctor and this is what he recommends. She is not behaving normally."

"She does with me."

"Maybe she pulls up when you are there but you are there so much less frequently than me and you don't see what I see. It's not just being absent minded. She is sometimes just not there. She can sit with a vacant look at her face for hours, completely withdrawn."

"She is alone and no doubt lonely."

"It's not that. She does it even when I'm with her. Not all the time but frequently enough. She is also disinterested in whatever I say. Just listens to the radio but I suspect she is doing it merely by default, she is possibly not really comprehending what is in the radio."

"I'll take her to us for a while."

"And Teodor?"

"She's not well, he'll understand and besides I take his mother whenever it is needed."

"Well, you can take her all right but I insist she needs to be checked by a specialist. I've made an appointment for her in four weeks anyway."

"So how about I take her home as soon as Teodor can drive me to her and we bring her with us. She'll go for the appointment straight from here."

"If this is what you want," agreed Gabriela.

"Yes."

"I've also read a lot about this."

"Where?"

"What difference does it make? The point is she has an onset of something."

"You're not a doctor," Matilda did not like it at all.

"And that's why I made the appointment for her."

"Fine," agreed Matilda.

"You just need to understand and prepare her."

"What do you mean?"

"She is going for observation and assessment."

"Where to?"

"You know where it is."

"Pruszków?" Matilda was not ready for that.

Nearly all Varsovians knew that this town not far from Warsaw was known for its psychiatric clinic.

Gabriela nodded.

"I don't like how you are talking to me about this!" Matilda looked at her.

"What's your problem now?"

"First you said we must get her to see a shrink and it turns out you already made an appointment for mum to go for observation to the damn Pruszkow. How do you think she'll feel when you tell her?"

"I'm not," Gabriela looked at her hard, "I want you to do it!"

"Oh, yeah? So you sent her there but want me to tell her the bad news?"

Situation could escalate out of hand and Gabriela quickly scaled down because she really wanted Matilda to do so and arguing could go bad.

"Look, Matilda – we both know how different we are. You have..." she considered for a moment, "a softer touch. She will take it from you much easier. And in the end she does need an assessment because I really worry about her."

"You think I don't?" Matilda was upset.

"We must have doctor's opinion," insisted Gabriela and Matilda, while hating having to sent mum to Pruszkow, understood that even if half of Gabriela was saying was true perhaps mum had an onset of something indeed.

*

Nurse in the admission office smiled.

"All right, all documents are in place and everything is in order. If you are ready, Irena, I will take you to your room now."

Irena was sitting motionless between Gabriela and Matilda and did not move.

Gabriela and Matilda stood up from their chairs. Matilda had tears in her eyes but was fighting with herself to prevent them from running down her cheeks.

"We are going then mum," Gabriela said.

"I will visit you the day after tomorrow," added Matilda.

"I don't want to stay here," Irena said quietly.

"Mum, these are the doctor's orders," Matilda repeated one more time what they had discussed endlessly for the past week or so.

"They just need to run some tests so that they can help you better."

"This is a psychiatric institution. You are leaving me among the crazy people."

"We do not use words like that here," interjected the nurse with a professional smile on her face.

"We are a medical center and we have patients like any other hospital. We also have a chapel on the premises and you can go there any time you want."

"Bye Mum," Gabriela hugged and kissed Irena.

Irena did not respond at all.

"See you soon!" Matilda kissed her on both cheeks and as she was hugging her she noticed a single tear formed in Irena's eye and slowly rolled down her face.

Gabriela jabbed Matilda in the back.

"Knock off being mushy," she whispered.

Matilda just gave her unpleasant look in return.

"All right Irena, let's go," the nurse turned to Irena, "don't forget your suitcase."

Matilda and Gabriela walked out from the room and turned right to the exit while Irena with the nurse turned left and then climbed the stairs to the first floor.

They reached room bearing number 21, the nurse knocked and opened the door without waiting for a response from the single occupant.

"Hello Wanda," said the nurse "this is your new roommate, Irena. She will stay with you for a few days."

Zofia was a bit unkempt and she seemed older than Irena. She had alerted eyes but her face showed no emotions.

"Do you smoke?" she asked.

"No I don't" replied Irena.

"Are you a lesbian?"

"No."

"Good! The last time they brought a lesbian here and I spent all night fighting her off."

"It's all right, Wanda," said the nurse "you and I discussed it many times and you told me yourself it was just a dream."

"I'm not sure."

"Irena," nurse turned to her "breakfasts are at eight, we have a snack time between one and two and dinners are at six. Bathroom is down the hallway on the right side. Will you remember that or would you like me to write it down for you?"

Only now Irena noticed the window had bars installed.

"What's with the window?" she asked.

"It's a security measure," explained the nurse "this level is close to the ground and we don't want anyone sneaking in."

"Or out," Wanda pitched in and the nurse gave her a stern look.

"Just like a prison," Irena said half to herself half to the nurse.

"Have you ever been locked up?" asked Wanda, "I don't want to be stuck here with a criminal!"

"She's not a criminal Wanda," explained the nurse, "Irena has never been arrested and has never spent time in jail or a prison."

"Why are you here?" Wanda turned to Irena.

"I'm not well," Irena explained.

"Phew!" Wanda made an unspecific sound "nobody is well here, including the staff."

"We are a hospital Wanda, you know that," said the nurse "so the patients, when they first come in here are not well. The staff is well, of course. It was a joke on your part – wasn't it?"

Wanda had not responded.

She turned to Irena.

"Settle in then, or she will never leave!"

"The button on the table next to your bed is for calling for assistance if you need it," the nurse pointed the gadget to Irena.

"Don't forget the meals schedule. I'll see you later."

And she walked from the room.

Irena placed her suitcase on a chair, opened it and began unpacking her belongings.

"How long are you here for?" asked Wanda.

"Two weeks or so," Irena replied.

"I'm here for a month. I hate being stuck here."

"I don't like being here too."

"Food is not bad though and they prepare it for us."

Irena said nothing. She walked towards the window and looked outside through the crate. There was a courtyard belonging to the clinic and in the middle of it there was a large and pretty chestnut tree.

"Just like at the number nine," whispered Irena and kept looking at it.

"What are you mumbling under your nose?" inquired Wanda.

But Irena did not respond.

The tree made her think of her chestnut tree at the Krucza Street number nine and memories began to play in her mind like a film. She saw herself going there for the first time ever, then going to the flat after her wedding when Stan carried her up the stairs to their door and then across the threshold. She then remembered how they made love right there in the room full of white roses. Then there she was looking at the tree from her window feeling queasy and finding out she was pregnant for the first time. She recalled the day the war began and long years of living under German occupation. She heard bombs and explosions near and far. The worst was the sound of sirens which Stuka dive bombers had installed and pilots turned them on at the beginning of bombing runs. The screeching sound was terrifying and Irena's body shivered. It seemed the bombers were getting closer and closer.

Time was passing by and Irena was standing there looking at the tree outside but not really seeing it, for part of her mind drifted away from her body. Such moments were happening to her for a long while now. Sometimes in such state she would do things she was unaware of and only later she would snap back to reality, finding herself somewhere else in another room or in the kitchen preparing dinner. Once or twice she found herself with a bleeding finger as without knowing it she hurt herself with a kitchen knife when such odd state caught her preparing food in the kitchen. Few times she found herself in church and once in the cemetery where her mother's grave was. Her daughters were aware of her snapping in or out of reality but they did not know of the full extend of it as Irena was doing her best to hide it. All her life she could be shrewd and practical if she wanted to and now the old instincts were kicking in when necessary in the name of self preservation which in this case meant hiding certain things from her daughters.

There were days when she was sharp as ever and she thought there was something wrong with her mind, it was being rouge and out of control and Irena knew that the only medical help applicable was that of psychiatrist but that was something she always wanted to avoid. Psychiatrists were professionally trained doctors with diplomas but the patients had a stigma attached to them forever and there was no way back. Neighbors and entire neighborhoods would know there was a crazy person around. It was like being a leper and life could easily turn into living hell. It would not take long to be maltreated by crude adults and tormented by kids. And kids can be very cruel.

Irena knew of one woman deemed by the local populace as crazy whose life was a misery and she was not going to live such life. That woman was usually just aloof, but sometimes she'd slip into either another personality or would just behave very odd which quickly made her known as crazy. Sometimes she'd wander about the neighborhood in her nightgown with a candle in her hand, knock at neighbor's door and talk absolute nonsense. But what the populace didn't know was that she was repeatedly gang raped in 1939 by German soldiers. She was merely sixteen at the time. She was kidnapped and kept for their amusement for a while until somebody decided to send her to a concentration camp. Miraculously she survived the war but she was permanently damaged. She had no family – her parents died in the war and their house was burned to the ground and she was incapable of remembering where her home was. She supported herself by being a seamstress and despite her difficulties she was a very good one. She functioned relatively normally but every now and then something would trip her mind to go into the unstable condition for a day or two.

Irena's problems came from unknown reasons but it did not matter much; she was aware her mind was malfunctioning and the fear of the future was paralyzing at times. Talking to Gabriela was pointless because Gabriela seemed to have her mind made up. She thought Irena's brain was deteriorating and she tried to correct her by giving her tasks to keep her busy and focused but was quick to be irritated when Irena was not performing them to her liking. But the doctor after hearing what was it about suggested psychologist or psychiatrist and Irena was trapped. She could only hope for some support from Matilda, but Matilda lived considerable distance away and she was working and running her household. Irena knew and understood Matilda was very busy and worked harder than Gabriela although she did not have some fancy job. She visited Irena as frequently as she could manage but whenever she did Irena was so happy to see her and the adrenaline rush always lifted her up so she was always her normal self Matilda knew. In such circumstance Irena was simply enjoying every second spent with her daughter. Thus Matilda was not exactly aware of how her mum was except of what Gabriela was telling her. But then Matilda had doubts over what Gabriela was saying or to put it bluntly she did not quite believe her. The sisters had somewhat odd relationship for years. Gabriela was smarter and more eloquent and she had tendency to push her younger sister around. Matilda was weaker but she knew Gabriela could be manipulative and selfish therefore she never trusted her completely..

"Dinner time," Wanda got up from her bed.

Irena had not moved and had not responded.

"Dinner time!"

Wanda repeated louder with some impatience in her voice but it did not make Irena react either.

She approached Irena and nudged her with her hand.

"What's the matter?" asked Irena as if she had been awakening from a dream.

"Are you going deaf? I said it was dinner time. You were standing by this window for the past three hours!"

"Let's go then," said Irena and walked towards the door.

*

Gabriela was sitting with Matilda in her studio in Warsaw.

"I don't know what's going to happen to her," Gabriela said, "the medications she was getting worked for a while but then it was back to how it was before."

"Have you consulted the doctor?"

"He says he doesn't see anything. He can either double the prescription or refer her again to the clinic for even longer observation and tests."

"I have doubts over medicines for the mind," said Matilda.

"So what do you think we should do?"

"Let's find somebody to live with her. It's not easy to find somebody like that but it's possible."

"What do you mean by live with her?"

"In the flat so she won't be alone."

"You want to let a stranger in? What about me?"

"You have your flat in Warsaw and you're going to mum's only on Fridays and not necessarily every week if I'm not mistaken."

"It's not like you are there every week!"

"I have a husband and two sons. I go to mum whenever I can spare a moment."

"I've got my life too and I can't live with her permanently. I'm tired after work and need to rest. Those trips on Fridays and then return to work on Mondays are exhausting, you know."

"I'm raising two sons and until recently we lived in a flat without running water which was heated by coal. I never said I was tired!"

Gabriela, in Matilda's opinion was looking at her own convenience first and foremost. Being single and unattached she certainly did not have many chores.

"I need my rest!" insisted Gabriela, her tone annoyed, "my work poses certain stress and problems which you can't imagine!"

"Running a household and shopping which as you know is difficult due to shortages is also exhausting and very time consuming," Matilda was not giving an inch.

"You have it easier," retorted Gabriela as if it was obvious.

"You're forgetting that I'm working now as well, three times a week and I commute to the Old Town 45 minutes one way which is almost the same as going to mum's for you and still I never say I'm so tired!"

Gabriela was not used to see Matilda being that firm and she backed off.

"When I arrive on Fridays I find her sitting on a stool in the kitchen. The flat is neglected and dishes never look clean. And more and more often she only says yes or no to any question I ask."

"When I visit her I don't see anything like it."

"And you continue being stubborn!"

Gabriela was upset.

"Perhaps she puts up an act when she knows you are coming."

"I arrive without telling her in advance so how do you think it's possible?"

"And I'm telling you what I see. If you don't it doesn't mean it is not taking place."

"This conversation is going to nowhere," Matilda cut her off, "let's find somebody to live with her."

"No! I don't agree! Such person would need separate room so obviously it would have to be mine and where I'd sleep when I go there on Fridays?"

"In the room with mum," replied Matilda.

"I can't. I need some minimum space and privacy!"

"If you are unable to handle that we have to find a state home for her then."

"And live her with total strangers? I disagree!"

Matilda was beginning to boil.

"Look Gabriela, whatever I propose you reject. Do you have a better solution?"

"She needs to go to the clinic!"

"It's worse than going to a prison for her, don't you get it??? I talked to her for hours after the first time and she was begging me not to leave her there again."

"We both have to be firm and explain to her this is absolutely necessary for her own good. We have to have a common front so that she would not exploit differences between us!"

"We are talking about our mum, not about some business negotiations!" Matilda was annoyed again.

"Got a better idea?"

"I told you – it would be way easier to have somebody living with her."

"No! I'm talking about specific solutions based on medical opinion, while you are suggesting just patching things up with half measures! What will you suggest when things get worse?"

Matilda was silent. She was trying to sort out if it was better to use one's head or heart.

"Before and after the clinic I'll take her to stay with us for a while," she said.

"Oh, yeah? What about Teodor?"

"What about him?"

"He never liked her when she was younger and healthy. You think it will be better now?"

"She stayed with us every now and then and we had no problems."

"I have my doubts. I told you countless times you let him walk all over you."

"Keep such opinions to yourself, it has nothing to do with mum!"

"I know what I'm talking about, I care for mum and I don't agree with her staying with you for a long time."

"You don't agree with anything I say!" Matilda was fed up, "it is also my mum and she will stay with us as long as I want until I see she is fit to return home whether you like it or not!"

*

Matilda, Teodor and Gregory were sitting at dinner.

"I'd like to take mum for a few days before and after she goes to the clinic."

"Fine, I told you before," said Teodor "how is she?"

"They need to run some more tests and observe her behavior patterns."

"Is it a big problem?"

"Gabriela says she snaps into those dark moods as if she was absent, she doesn't clean the flat and seems withdrawn."

"Or she is not slaving for Gabriela as she would like her to."

"Don't start please."

"I only doubt in what your sister is saying. I made my observations over the years."

"Even if I agree with you the fact is something appears to be brewing and we need to help her."

"All right. Keep her here as long as you want."

"But…."

"I know what you are thinking but it's different. She is a human, she needs help and she is your mother. You do what you need to do. Why don't you find somebody to live with her, by the way? Remember Mary who lived with my mother after my dad died?"

"I do but Gabriella doesn't agree."

"Ah – of course!" he could not help sarcastic remark.

Matilda was silent.

"Do whatever you need and want to do," said Teodor, "it will be fine."

"Thank you, Teo."

He looked at her.

"Don't thank me," he said softly, "it's your mum."

*

Irena was sitting with Matilda in a small cafeteria in the clinic sipping tea.

"How are you mum?" smiled Matilda.

"Can you take me away from here?"

"You know I can't, mum. Nine more days and I'll come to get you."

"Do you know what kind of people are here? I am stuck with the real basket cases. The woman I share room with thinks she is the daughter of Józef Piłsudski and the secret service is out there to kill her so she is hiding as a patient in this clinic. Another woman screams every single night unless they give her strong slipping pills or some injection. Yet another one attacked the nurse shouting "what have you done with my baby? And the tests they put me through – the nurses are patronizing as if they was talking to an eight year old. Everything is fine and beautiful."

"Mum, I know it is not easy for you. But you do have an onset of something and we don't know what it is. The sooner we find out the better for you. This is all to help you, not to trouble you."

"I know sweetheart. Deep down I know, I just feel so out of place among these people here. And I fear the future."

"Gabriela and I are doing what we can to help you, we do it all for you."

"She screams at me."

"The nurse?"

"No, Gabriela."

"What do you mean?"

"When you are not around. When she comes on Fridays."

"What does she scream about?"

"Oh, she says I do nothing all day and calls me a slob. She complains the flat is dusty and dirty and that I'm lazy. But I do all chores like I always did."

"I'll have a word with her."

"Please don't! She'll know I told you."

"I'll tell her the neighbors told me they heard her screaming at you. For how long this has been going on?"

"Oh, I don't remember. Quite a while."

"I…" Irena hesitated, "I was afraid. It's good to talk to you, Matilda. You make me calm and I do not have thoughts."

"What thoughts?"

"You know… the odd ones."

"No I don't. Tell me. You never mentioned it before."

"I… I…" Irena struggled and her face suddenly turned visibly sad.

"What is it mum?" Matilda noticed the change.

"Sometimes I think I achieved nothing at all. I was like a butterfly flapping my wings and hopping from one flower to another. I was bad wife and bad mother. I was waiting for something that never arrived because I didn't even know what it was supposed to be. All I really wanted to do was to dance."

"Oh, mum, don't talk like that. You went through so much – the war, the Uprising, the communists. You had to leave Warsaw, the city you loved, you saw it destroyed. You raised two daughters, you have two grandsons. That's a lot."

"But it was all wrong… it should've been done differently. I see it now so clearly… so clearly."

"No, mum, no. It's all right. You did all and more in circumstances that you couldn't even dream of changing. You had to react to what it was, there were no options!"

"I'm sorry Tilly, but this is how I look at it and it worries me so much. It bothers me day after day, night after night week after week. I then wait for Gabriela to arrive but I don't think she is happy to be with me. She is tired and she can be unpleasant. So in the end she is in her room and I am alone."

A nurse came in.

"It's time for your session, Irena."

"I will come again tomorrow," promised Matilda.

Irena smiled.

"Would be nice but it doesn't have to be tomorrow. Make it the day after if you can."

"Okay," Matilda gave her a hug and kiss on both cheeks, "see you soon, mum."

*

About a week later Matilda took Irena to stay with her and her family and for the next several days and watched her carefully but could not see anything odd about her behavior. Irena was consistent day after day and she was in calm and normal mood.

They were going for walks to have some exercise and Irena helped her with chores. When Matilda was going to work Irena would stay alone. The first time Matilda was a bit nervous about it but she knew Gregory would be back from school soon so in the end Irena was left by herself for just three hours accompanied only by the dog. In the evenings Irena was eager to help with dinner and she was making the red cabbage salads for Teodor which he always loved.

After some two or three weeks Irena asked Matilda if she could go to the centre of Warsaw by herself. She wanted to do it on Thursday and visit Krucza Street as she did for so many years. Matilda was unsure of what to say to her. She was afraid Irena could easily get lost by taking a wrong bus. She no doubt knew her way from Józefów but not from Matilda's home. That is if she could be sure her mum was hundred percent well it would be easy but as it was Matilda just worried. Like many times in her life Matilda used her heart rather than her head and agreed but insisted that Irena carries written information on her. Not just about buses and stop. She also wrote basic information with Irena's name and Matilda's address and phone number to her neighbors. Matilda had no doubts Gabriela would oppose this. Next morning still uneasy but optimistic Matilda walked Irena to the bus stop and watched Irena getting in. For a moment she though of taking the next bus and then discretely follow her mum at a distance but she discarded this idea, turned around and went home.

Irena walked along the Krucza Street looking with dismay at the buildings on both sides of the busy street. Before the war Krucza was full of beautiful typical city buildings with lovely facades and balconies. Every gate had a concierge who was responsible for the courtyard, staircase and the sidewalk along the front of the building. Consequently everything was always clean, plants always watered and taken care of. All of that was destroyed after the Uprising when Germans at the specific order of Hitler himself, dynamited whatever survived and set it on fire. After the war the rubble was removed and Krucza was rebuilt but in the ugly and obnoxious socialist realism style. The street was now filed with poured concrete rectangular blocks adorned with reliefs portraying workers holding tools of their trade – hammers and wrenches or peasants holding sickles. It was cold, foreign and impersonal. It was also disproportionally oversized and people were dwarfed by the overwhelming structures. After ten minutes or so Irena arrived at the number nine and there was her beloved tree, her only living connection to her past. She came closer, touched the trunk and she patted it with the palm of her hand just like a dog owner pats his dog. With the other hand she touched one of the leaves.

"You came again," she could hear a whisper.

She looked around but there was nobody there. She looked up to see if perhaps there was somebody hiding up on the tree but there wasn't anyone there either.

"Don't be afraid, it's me, your tree."

Irena looked around again just to make sure.

"You can talk?"

"To you I can. I know why you are coming to me for all of those years. I know you love me."

Irena's eyes instantly filled with tears.

"Oh, yes - I do, I always did."

"I know."

"I came to say good-bye, I have to go and I won't be able to visit you anymore."

"I know that too."

"How it is possible?"

"You wouldn't understand. Take one of my leaves with you."

Irena looked down to search for a leaf.

"No, not a fallen one. Pick a fresh one from the branch, one that is green and pretty."

"It's not going to hurt if I do so?"

"Not if you do it."

"I will miss you just like I miss everything I lost."

"I will too. All of the happiness that once was around here. It was so different, so beautiful. Those were such happy days."

Tears were running down Irena's cheeks.

"I will never forget you."

"Neither will I. But don't be sad. We will be together some day."

"Good-bye," Irena could not speak anymore as she was choking with tears.

She walked away to the bus stop and returned to Matilda's home.

A week later the three of them – Matilda, Teodor and Irena drove to Józefów to bring her home.

"Tomorrow is Friday and Gabriela is coming," Matilda said before leaving, "and I will come on Tuesday, maybe I even stay overnight, yes?"

"That would be lovely. You can stay too Teodor if you like," Irena turned to her son in law.

"I will need to go back to see to Gregory and make sure he goes to school Wednesday morning," said Teodor, "but perhaps next time we both stay over."

"You are always welcome, Teodor. I don't want you to think it's just Matilda."

Irena watched Matilda and Teodor driving away and when they disappeared from view she sighted and went to the kitchen. She checked her supplies and decided she needed to go out and buy few necessities.

Teodor and Matilda were riding in silence for a while and then Teodor said:

"Your mother never spoke to me like that. Her entire time with us was so different."

"She upset you?" worried Matilda thinking it was probably wrong question but she was tense as she kept thinking of her Mum.

"No, not at all. There was something unusual about her, I thought, that's all. I'm sorry I was not pleasant to her so many times in the past."

*

Gabriela was sitting on the bench squished between two other passengers in the overcrowded train. Hardly any windows were opened and the air inside was foul. Stuck like sardines in a can passengers filled the space to maximum capacity. It was stuffy and the smell of human sweat was strong. Gabriela hated being stuck like this but at the same time she did not want to let the train go by and wait for the next one. It would take another hour or so. With some difficulty, pushing and shoving passengers along the way she reached the door almost one station earlier just to be sure she'd manage to exit the train in Józefów. When she finally stepped on the platform she breathed with joy. *Why theses people don't wash every day?* - she wondered. They were clearly lacking the elementary hygiene.

She crossed the street running parallel to the train tracks and turned into the Polna Street.

She stopped at the local shop, glanced at what they had and decided to buy a loaf of bread as it has just been delivered. A round, almost to hot to handle, 800 gram loaf with thick golden brown crust. She then continued on the Polna Street until it intersected with the Church Street.

She walked half way around the house to the back door and entered the staircase. After three steps she was in front of Irena's door. She could hear the radio. She pressed the door handle and walked in.

"It's me, Mum!" she announced but there was no response.

She hanged her coat and her purse and walked into the kitchen.

The radio was set on the RFE (Radio Free Europe) and Irena was busy at the countertop.

"Hi Mum!"

Only now Irena heard her and quickly turned around. She gave Gabriela a broad smile.

"Oh, hi Gabriela. How are you?"

"All right. I was on the really crowded train so it was not a pleasant journey."

"Sit down and rest or take a shower and change if you like, the dinner is almost ready."

"I do just that," said Gabriela and went to the bathroom. She noticed it was very clean and the floor was freshly wiped with some scented cleaner. The flat was otherwise clean too so was her room. It was like in the old days.

"Do you want to eat in the dining room or squeeze here?" asked Irena, "I usually eat here when I'm by myself but there is enough room for two."

"Let's go to the dining room, mum" replied Gabriela.

"We can carry it all in one trip."

They haven't had a meal in the dining room for a long time, Gabriela could not remember exactly. When the problems with Irena began and in the turmoil of sometimes unpleasant encounters they haven't used dining room at all and on many occasions had not even eaten together. But today it was all so different and Gabriela was wondering that perhaps those two weeks in the clinic made a big change in Irena.

"How are you, mum?" she asked.

"I'm good, Gabriela, really good. I feel like in the old days."

"That's great, mum. You will need to go for the follow up check-up with your doctor. I made an appointment for you for Wednesday."

"That's okay but I know I'm all right."

"Yes, mum, I'm very glad to hear that but still you need to go to see your doctor."

"All right, I'll go on Wednesday. I always go to those appointments. I just hated being locked up in that crazy house."

"The clinic, Mum."

"Whatever they call it. All I know is I was stuck with crazy people."

"Let's not argue about it," Gabriela was making sure she was not going to escalate.

"I've got a letter from Michael today," Irena said, "I think he made good decision."

"Immigration is not for everyone," Gabriela was skeptical a bit, "and I never thought he'd do that but since he did I hope he knows what he's doing and understands the consequences."

"He is a very good boy. I just miss him and I don't think I will ever see him again so I just pray for him. I had two grandsons and it feels like I have only one now."

"It may take some number of years before he can come for a visit."

"Yes, I know. If he comes now the bastards would lock him up."

"Or just not let him go back."

Gabriela was watching her mother carefully and was surprised how back to normal she was. Even her eyes which were showing that layer of sadness or lack of emotions for months on end looked alerted and bright today. Gabriela had not seen her mother like this in a long time.

Matilda will be pleased she thought.

"I'll clean up after dinner," offered Gabriela.

"Oh, that would be great as I wanted to go for the evening Mass," Irena went to the hallway and put a light coat on.

"It's less than an hour," she added, "so I will be back soon."

"Okay, Mum." Gabriela loaded a tray with dirty dishes and walked to the kitchen as Irena was leaving. She then returned to the dining room to clear the rest and went back to the kitchen to wash and dry all dishes, pots and utensils they used.

Irena came back about nine in the evening.

"It's me!" she announced.

"I'm already in bed, Mum. I had a long day today so I turned in early if that's all right. I'll just read a book and going to sleep unless you want me to do anything?"

"Oh, no – that's fine. You go to sleep. I'll take a bath, make sure all doors are locked and I'm going to sleep too. Good night!"

"Good night, Mum!" shouted Gabriela.

Irena checked the kitchen to see if everything was tidy, then checked the terrace door and the back door to make sure they were both locked. She then went to the bathroom and opened the faucet to fill the bathtub. In few minutes the tub was nearly full. She kept the water running but now she opened the valve to let it drain to avoid overflow.

EPILOGUE

The girl in the bathtub glanced at a small shelf above. She reached between the two neatly folded towels and pulled out an old kitchen knife. It was one of her few wedding gifts that survived all of those years until today. The handle was worn but still solid; the blade was very thin and while the cutting edge was no longer even it remained sharp. She looked at it carefully, took the handle in her left hand, placed the blade across the right wrist and without pressing hard she drove it across three times. It did not hurt as much as she thought it would. Blood appeared instantly after the first cut but after the third the flow was steady. She then switched hands and did the same to her left wrist. She then dropped the knife. She placed both hands in the water and watched how the blood was forming swirling patterns before dissolving and seemingly disappearing. Soon, the water was no longer clear, it had a pink tint to it but was getting darker and darker. The warmth made her sleepy and she was wondering about the pain. She didn't feel it much, merely as if her wrists were scraped. She no longer worried about anything.

She thought of her two grandsons, one somewhere far away on another continent and the other one, nearly a young man living in Warsaw with his parents. She then thought of her daughters – the sweet and cheerful, always eager to help Matilda and the older, more intelligent and outspoken but moody and snappy if not outright unpleasant at times Gabriela. It was all not how being young she thought it would be – not at all. She felt cheated by life and betrayed by decisions she had made.

The control over her existence that she thought she had up till that day in May 1935 was now back after all of those years, but so many things did not matter anymore.

She repositioned herself to be more comfortable supporting her head on the bathtub's edge as if on a pillow. She was feeling sleepy and relaxed.

Somewhere in a distance somebody was playing piano and she recognized Coppélia. She opened her eyes and found herself in the Lidia Jastrzębska Dancing School but then the light was getting brighter and brighter and she realized she was not in the studio at all.

She was on the stage and the bright lights were focused on her so she could not see the audience, she could only hear the distinctive sound of countless clapping hands in a thunderous applause. As she gracefully curtsied for the third time the curtain slowly dropped down, the lights were switched off and everything went black.

The End